# OF THE PRESENCE OF THE BODY

# OF THE PRESENCE
# OF THE BODY

## Essays on Dance and
## Performance Theory

Edited by André Lepecki

Wesleyan University Press
Middletown, Connecticut

Published by Wesleyan University Press,
Middletown, CT 06459
www.wesleyan.edu/wespress

Wesleyan University Press is a member of the Green Press Initiative. The
paper used in this book meets their minimum requirement for recycled paper.

Printed in the United States of America   5
ISBN-13: 978-0-8195-6612-6


Library of Congress Cataloging-in-Publication Data

Of the presence of the body : essays on dance and performance theory /
edited by André Lepecki.
    p.   cm.
Includes bibliographical references (p.    ) and index.
ISBN 0-8195-6611-x (cloth : alk. paper)—ISBN 0-8195-6612-8 (pbk. : alk. paper)
1. Dance—Sociological aspects. 2. Body, Human—Symbolic aspects. 3. Movement,
Aesthetics of. 4. Human locomotion. I. Title: Essays on dance and performance theory.
II. Lepecki, André.
GV1588.6.O4 2004
306.4'84—dc22                                                    2003023913

# Contents

*Acknowledgments*  vii

Introduction: Presence and Body in Dance and Performance Theory  1
ANDRÉ LEPECKI

## I. Genealogies of Presence

1. Trisha Brown's *Orfeo:* Two Takes on Double Endings  13
PEGGY PHELAN

2. Genealogy and Dance History: Foucault, Rainer, Bausch, and de Keersmaeker  29
RAMSAY BURT

## II. Dancing Othering

3. Dance and Its Others: Theory, State, Nation, and Socialism  47
RANDY MARTIN

4. The Black Beat Made Visible: Hip Hop Dance and Body Power  64
THOMAS F. DEFRANTZ

5. Danced Spirituals  82
SUSAN MANNING

6. Breast Milk Is Sweet and Salty (A Choreography of Healing)  97
BARBARA BROWNING

## III. Ontology's Events

7. Given Movement: Dance and the Event  113
MARK FRANKO

8. Inscribing Dance  124
ANDRÉ LEPECKI

9. Embodying Transgression  140
KARMEN MACKENDRICK

*Notes*  157
*Contributors*  177
*Index*  179

# Acknowledgments

This short volume has a long history. It originated around a panel on "Moving Ideologies" I organized for the second Performance Studies Conference at Northwestern University, in 1996. It was from the original contributions for that panel (by Barbara Browning, Mark Franko, Richard Green, and myself), as well as from the many comments and suggestions made by the audience (in particular, those by Susan Manning, Joseph Roach, and Tommy de Frantz) that the idea to compile a volume on new critical dance theory and performance studies first emerged. Expanded to its current format, this anthology would have never materialized were it not for the continuous support, critical thinking, and enormous patience of its dedicated contributors. To all of them I extend my sincerest and warmest thanks.

Suzanna Tamminen, editor-in-chief at Wesleyan University Press was, from the start, the most encouraging collaborator. I cannot thank her enough for her guidance and her incredible dedication and professionalism. I also extend my gratitude to the staff at Wesleyan University Press. In addition, I thank Hyun Joo Lee, my graduate assistant, who helped me in the final steps of the editing process, and Alice Reagan, who compiled the book's index.

I also must thank the intellectual and personal support that my colleagues at the Department of Performance Studies at New York University have given me in the past two years. Diana Taylor, Barbara Browning, Richard Schechner, Barbara Kirshemblatt-Gimblett, Peggy Phelan, Fred Moten, Allen Weiss, and José Muñoz have not only been mentors, but have taken to a higher level the meaning of academic colleagueship. Thank you, finally, to Anna Bean for her support.

The history of this book was also entangled with many personal joys and sadnesses. The sadness is for the heart to bear. But to the joy of having Elsa and Tobias joining this world I dedicate this book.

ANDRÉ LEPECKI

# Introduction

## Presence and Body in Dance and Performance Theory[1]

This anthology gathers nine original essays crossing the fields of dance studies, critical theory, and performance studies. Collectively, the essays investigate how dance critically reconstitutes social practices while at the same time proposing ever renewed theories of body and presence. This transdisciplinary approach to the cultural materiality of dances delineates epistemologies that consider and articulate how the presence of the body leaves its mark on critical theories and performance practices. Each contribution to this volume (by Barbara Browning, Ramsey Burt, Thomas F. DeFrantz, Mark Franko, Karmen MacKendrick, Susan Manning, Randy Martin, Peggy Phelan, and myself) explores the threshold of dance studies, performance studies, and critical theory. The anthology thus provides the reader with a sample of the diversity of current methodologies and new theoretical perspectives in the field of dance studies.

Acknowledging previous and noteworthy critical anthologies in the field,[2] the present volume contributes to the increasingly more sophisticated and open debate between dance studies, performance studies, and critical and cultural theory at three levels. First, this anthology offers both an updated extension and an updated critique of debates initially articulated in those volumes of the past decade. *Of the Presence of the Body* focuses particularly on the tensions and complicities between dance and writing, on the questions of subjectivity and incorporation, on the materiality of dancing bodies and their assessment by critical and cultural theories. Second, by focusing exclusively on twentieth-century dance practices, this anthology consolidates and systematizes its methodological scope as explicitly within a scholarship that critically assesses and simultaneously politically intervenes in its field. Lastly, each of the essays compiled here was commissioned and edited to foreground one of the most significant theoretical challenges currently traversing the disciplinary fields of dance studies, critical and cultural theories, and performance studies: the intertwining and conflicting discourses informing and challenging the notions of "presence," and "body." Indeed, both "presence" and "body" recur again and again in the essays, as complicated sites where subjectivity challenges subjection, where resistance initiates its moves. It is the diversity in analytical evaluations of these two central concepts for current dance, performance, and critical studies that unifies, updates, and distinguishes the current volume. These analyses allow the reader to encounter, in a variety of choreographic models, considerable social, theoretical, and political countermoves.

"Presence" and "body" bring epistemological cohesiveness to the anthology by bridging disciplinary specificities and connecting choreographic differences. At the same time, neither concept is ever taken for granted, as a stable entity. Rather, they are presented and critiqued in each essay as contested notions. Throughout the anthology, the reader will find that their use is never peaceful, and that each author proposes different ways of thinking on how, and with what political and aesthetic effect, dancing rethinks both itself and the social order, as bodies step into presence. Hence, "presence" and "body" trigger additional disturbances in the critical and artistic fields: incrementing agitation, instability, and divergence. The phenomenological intertwining of presence and body that dance brings about as it moves (even in its most microscopic gestures) forces the recasting of our understanding of performativity, and brings about the current turn in dance studies toward the fields of performance studies and of critical theory. This turn is not at all smooth. It generates a space of dizziness—that space Gaston Bachelard once saw as the generative space of thought. The willingness of all contributors of this volume to put (dance) theory into instability creates a general (and, it is hoped, generative) epistemological and methodological tension throughout the anthology. This tension is nothing more than this book's way of moving into its own dancing. For isn't tension precisely that quality Lincoln Kirstein once defined as being dance's "phenomenal name-essence"?[3] Epistemological and choreographic tension revives the force of dances and bodies discussed in each essay, allowing them to initiate, once again, their resistant motions as they reconfigure the limits and potentials of presence.

Historically, neither "presence" nor "body" have been central to Western choreographic imagination. Mark Franko notes how in Renaissance dance manuals "the body is suspiciously absent."[4] How is it then that both notions emerge so strongly in dance studies and dance making, and in discursive and ontological positions through which dance has defined itself as autonomous art?[5] With the uncanny quietness by which certain images reveal (or announce) yet-to-be unleashed tensions within a certain historical condition, presence and body emerge in their full force as intrinsic to dance in Feuillet's *Chorégraphie ou l'Art de Décrire la Danse, par Caractères, Figures et Signes Démonstratifs* (Choreography, or the art of describing dance with demonstrative characters, figures and signs [1699]). In this pivotal text in the history of Western choreography, a foundational, tensional, and only quite recently problematized disturbance in Western dance's own self-definition can be identified. In the opening page of *Chorégraphie,* we see a figure of a schematized theatrical space and a figure of a schematized body. The schematized theater is represented by an empty square. The schematized body is represented by a conglomerate of traces, in what appears to be a new calligraphy—unknown letters composing an abstract figure. This representational body that distances itself from its anthropomorphic source is nothing more than a body detaching itself from the certainty of its presence. Indeed, this calligraphic body is accompanied by an intriguing caption: "De la presence du corps" (of the presence of the body). Neither just presence (of the body) nor just (the presence of) body, dance announces itself as an interstitial imbrication of one into the other by the means of a dialectics of difference taking place in an empty space. Why this division of body and presence, announced as distinct entities in the opening pages of what is arguably one of the first modern choreographic manuals? Why write "Of the presence of the body" when one will definitively leave the body absent? Why not just write instead, "Presence" or, alternatively, just, "The body"? Why the poetic reiteration ("of the presence" / "of the body")? I suggest that what we may be witnessing here is the visual-grammatical form(ul)ation of the gap between body and presence in the history of modern Western subjectivity and of modern Western dance. It is nothing else than the positing of an interval between one and the other that allows choreography to announce and enforce its project of regimentation and inscription of bodily movements. Presence and body are no longer necessarily isomorphic; one does not necessarily imply the other. Moreover, what Feuillet's opening page seems to suggest is that the presence of the body is always preceded, always prefaced by, always grounded on, an open field of absence.

Thus the split between presence and body opens up complicated theoretical and choreographic problems. And these problems carry with them profound political implications for twentieth-century dance practices and dance theories. One may say that dance emerges as critical theory precisely from its uncanny foregrounding of the split between body and presence. One may even add that dance as critical praxis may draw its force precisely by a creative, if not altogether subversive, occupation of this gap. In this scenario, the pressing questions that have marked some recent scholarship in critical theory and dance studies (How is it that bodies come to be disciplined? How is it that bodies are invented, produced, re-produced and re-presented within a given social context?) can be read as questions deeply predicated (albeit most of the times unconsciously) on Feuillet's foundational presentation of the dancing body as bridge between presence and embodiment.

In her book *Choreography and Narrative,* Susan Leigh Foster reconsiders the question of dance by positing dance practices as "uniquely adept at configuring relations between body, self, and society through its choreographic decisions."[6] This reconfiguring of dance—as a field of knowledge in which what becomes known through "choreographic decisions" is the potential for the dancing body to transcend a narrowing aestheticization of its moving figure, and thus claim status as political agent—was explored by Randy Martin in *Critical Moves.* For Martin, a modernist narrative "continue[s] to exert [its] influence on contemporary discussions of the philosophical status of dance,"[7] most notably by perpetuating "the modernist conventions of an autonomous aesthetic domain distinct from other aspects of social life."[8] He notes how one of the most negative effects of this lingering modernist ideology in dance criticism and in dance studies is the perpetuation of the belief "that looking at dance politically might somehow interfere with its efficacy."[9] This anthology follows Martin's critique and proposes nine different views of looking at dance politically; that is to say, of looking at dance as critical theory and as critical action.

It is one of dance studies' major premises to define dance as that which continuously plunges into pastness—even as the dance presents itself to visibility. Mark Franko and Annette Richards have recently argued that this evanescence constitutes dance as essentially historic.[10] In capturing this evanescent dance, the scholar, the critic, the dance audience, even the dancer relies on a complex integration of sense-memories, associations, displacements, kinesthetic memories. Such is the inscription of the mnemonic traces of dance onto the body and the unconscious. But there is also an inscription of the dance onto the mnemonic mechanisms of technology, either through photography, film, the writing of the critic, or movement notation. Between one kind of memory and the other, the question of the presence of the dancing body becomes a matter of delicate excavation, as dancing body releases layers of memory-affects, photographic contact, digital depth, and choreo/graphing. As issues of memory, history, and visibility are brought to the fore, the notion of mnemonic trace emerges as a concept in crisis—a concept brought to crisis by the means of the dance. This is a crisis of the visible, of how to approach the visible body as its dancing presence plunges it into the past, into history, into a representational field that is perhaps too excessive to be regimented, contained, tamed. This is the epistemological crisis of writing in motion, writing as a body moving in the interstices of visibility, which is to say, writing in between the threads of the mnemonic/technological matrix. Such is the next challenge for thinking the presence of the body in performance and in dance.

Thus "presence" and "body" arrived at dance studies and performance studies with the double ballast of historical and theoretical overdetermination. The very formation of the disciplinary fields of performance studies and dance studies can be seen as a battle over the centrality, meaning, and relevance of those two concepts.[11] They were already insurmountable notions in post-Nietzschean and post-Freudian theories; indeed, it was only after the impact of Heidegger's notion of *Da-sein,* of Michel Foucault's critique of techniques of regimentation, and of Deleuze and Guatarri's Artaudian proposal of a "body without organs," that body and presence radically destabilized the epistemological grounding on which performance and dance practices are assessed. The challenges both concepts keep posing to scholars and practitioners of dance—as presence and body resist and elude any submission to theoretical elucidation—have come to fruition, in the past decade, bridging the fields of dance studies and performance studies.

Feuillet's uncanny presentation of the dancing body as perpetually in tension with inscription, presence, and absence lay dormant in the field of dance studies until quite recently. It was thanks to poststructuralism (and most notably to Jacques Derrida's critique of what he calls "metaphysics of presence") that the issue returned to the field. As Mark Franko argued elsewhere, under the Derridean notion of the trace, it is the very concept of "the body" that must be recast.[12] Thus, for Franko, through the trace, it is the entire field of dance scholarship that must reconfigure itself. (I discuss at length the consequences of these motions for dance studies under the sign of the Derridean trace in chapter 8). Franko revisited the notion of pastness and presence in performance to explore its ideological reverberations in the making of American modern dance.[13] Heidi Gilpin, through the notion of trauma also probed the question of displacement and disappearance in dance;[14] while Peggy Phelan explored the question of the ephemeral dancing body as historical problem within the field of desire and representation.[15] Peggy Phelan has also used this notion of the body's continuous self-erasure in time to define an "ontology of performance," in which presence resists reproduction by embracing the realm of absence. What this means for a theory of the "body" is that, at the limit, presence might very well impress its mark upon the social field as that which promises dis-embodiment. If, to follow Phelan, performance is a "maniacally charged present"[16] in which the body constantly (re)presents itself as always being at the verge of self-dissipation (this persistence of re/presentation being so many rehearsals for absence, for death), then critical theories of dancing practices must consider how is it that "presence" challenges the very stability of "the body." This challenge might be said to constitute dance's unique relation to temporality and to the manifestation of the body and of presence as interventions in temporality. This body, visceral matter as well as sociopolitical agent, discontinuous with itself, moving in the folds of time, dissident of time, manifests its agency through the many ways it eventually smuggles its materiality into a charged presence that defies subjection. Dance as critical theory and critical praxis proposes a body that is less an empty signifier (executing preordained steps as it obeys blindly to structures of command) than a material, socially inscribed agent, a non-univocal body, an open potentiality, a force-field constantly negotiating its position in the powerful struggle for its appropriation and control.

In the essay that opens this anthology, Peggy Phelan considers the emergence of Trisha Brown's dancing body in the context of the struggle between the force of law and the space of mourning. Phelan focuses on Trisha Brown's first experiment in opera, her production of Montiverdi's *Orfeo*. In "Trisha Brown's *Orfeo:* Two Takes on Double Endings," Phelan engages in a parallel reading of the libretto of the opera along with a close reading of the choreography of Brown's production as a site where traces of Brown's own historical materiality disturb the possibility of visioning her presence and of seeing choreography. Phelan proposes that a reading of Monteverdi's *Orfeo*, and of Trisha Brown's *Orfeo* necessitates a reading of its performance as falling into the blind spot of representation. Through the psychoanalytic notion of mourning, Phelan illuminates in which ways *Orfeo* not only reconstitutes Brown's choreographic concerns with presence and absence but how this reconstitution proposes new ways of configuring the absent-presence of both performance and love.

The question of absent-presence also appears in Ramsey Burt's essay, when he proposes in "Genealogy and Dance History: Foucault, Rainer, Bausch, and de Keersmaeker," the Foucauldian rearticulation of Nietzsche's notion of genealogy to consider the dancing body in the 1960s and 1990s. For Burt, genealogy allows dance studies to transcend normative framings of both body and presence. By bringing in feminist theory, gender studies, and a detailed comparative analysis of Yvonne Rainer's *Trio A*, Pina Bausch's *Café Muller*, and Anne Teresa de Keersmaeker's *Rosas*

*Danst Rosas,* Burt proposes how dance is presented as the very matter of historical inscription—transforming bodies and intensifying presence. Under this theoretical frame, the approximation between apparently distant choreographic practices Burt rehearses (European Tanztheatre and Judson), is particularly illuminating.

Randy Martin explores further how hegemonic narratives and practices impact on dance and dance theory in his essay "Dance and Its Others: Theory, State, Nation, and Socialism." Martin explores ways in which performance, and particularly dance, produces theoretical conditions for political reflection on the social realm. By invoking the notions of mimesis and simulacra Martin pursues a cogent reading of the many antagonisms and subtle partnering dance establishes with the nation-state. Martin's text proposes more than an analysis of dance within the nation-state; it offers a template for a theoretical engagement able to mobilize both thought and action into a choreography of resistance.

The two essays that follow probe central moments in American dance history: moments when dances radically proposed to intersect, dissect, and reform cultural memory by shaping social movements and identities, and by disturbing the very aesthetic domain to which they had been relegated. To invent bodies of resistance is to choreograph anew the body's potential for energetic social action, for engaging in discursive counterattacks under the form and force of movement. Thomas F. DeFrantz's essay "The Black Beat Made Visible: Hip Hop Dance and Body Power" analyzes how black social dance constantly reconstitutes narratives of identity and politics by choreographing the body's expressivity within the crevices of hegemonic racist systems. Here, presence assumes its nonmetaphysical aspect: it is synonymous with a will for power, and DeFrantz's essay rearranges the field of critical perception of the "power of the body in hip hop."

Susan Manning's "Danced Spirituals" investigates how black concert dance "developed a variety of strategies to contest the equation of high art and white art" from the postwar period until Alvin Ailey's *Revelations* (1960). Manning rehearses a close analysis of the interrelations between black and white choreographers in a crucial moment in the history of political dance in America. She reconfigures the history of American modern dance, by no longer seeing it as hermetically sealed within the constructs of authorship and race. Through her analysis of dances, Manning shows us how these categories are filled with subterranean influences, tensions, and canceled meanings.

Barbara Browning's essay portrays yet another powerfully dissenting body. In "Breast Milk is Sweet and Salty (a Choreography of Healing)"

Browning's treatment of the dancing body in Brazilian *candomblé* outlines new possibilities for bodily, spiritual, and social reinvention through dance as spiritual vehicle. Browning meditates on the "fluid body" of the mother, and considers how this motherly body gains materiality as breast milk; that is, as a substance that flows between the symbolic and the real, channeling energies to deliver either healing or death. Browning re/searches a body that dances what it cannot contain, a body projecting its agency throughout a rapidly shifting social context, a body fluidly complicating the relationships of race and gender stereotypes within the framework of its spiritual, dancing, power.

Mark Franko's essay, "Given Movement: Dance and the Event," directly confronts the question, What is the ethical ground on which we can propose an epistemology of the event? By asking a series of questions—How can we think of the event in dance and performance theory after September 11, 2001? How can we responsibly articulate an ontology of dance predicated on a falling into pastness, on an absence of the body, once one is confronted with the actual evaporation of living bodies?—Franko's essay excavates the ruins of the disastrous event as that which challenges our understanding of temporality, presence, ethics, and action. Franko invokes Derrida's notion of the gift, Blanchot's writings on the disaster, and J. L. Austin's model of the performative speech act, in order to challenge dance theory's most fundamental ontological grounding: the plunging into pastness of the dance, and dance's presence as the actualization of the impossibility of giving. Franko's proposals are both a challenge to philosophy through the project of dance and performance studies, and a challenge to dance and performance studies through the ethics of deconstruction before the facticity of destruction.

My own contribution, "Inscribing Dance," follows the intricate correlations that Western theatrical dance has always established between writing and a moving femininity. What does it mean to write with dance? What happens to the distinction of "body" and "text" once one critiques the putative distinctions between writing and dancing by the means of the feminine? By addressing Derrida's notion of the trace, and Derrida's own invocation of woman as siding with improvised dance, I show how certain ontological and linguistic homologies have shaped both the field of dancing and that of writing on dancing. These homologies propose an archaeology of dance's ontological and linguistic groundings on the notion of dance's ephemerality as siding with the Derridean trace.

Karmen MacKendrick's essay "Embodying Transgression" closes the volume, by addressing the philosophical implications of what could constitute a radically transgressive dance. For MacKendrick, dance's transgression can be found in "the artwork which is never the same and never within our grasp, as that which always seduces us precisely by exceeding us." While using literary theory and philosophy, particularly Maurice Blanchot and Nietzsche, MacKendrick argues for a notion of the dance in which what matters is less its ephemeral quality, its self-erasure, but its constant reappearance, its reiterative power of returning to embodiment and presence only to transgress. MacKendrick pays particular attention to stillness and intensification as two modes of embodying transgression and choreographing countermoves.

Countermoves; intensification; genealogy; blind spots; event as gift; dancing the trace; dance as healing, transgression, and the politics of philosophy—all these terms mobilize the pages of this anthology. All these words work to constitute an understanding of the dancing body within a theoretical and performative open field of exchanges, where presence remains as that which belabors the body as generative counterfeit.

# I ‖ GENEALOGIES OF PRESENCE

PEGGY PHELAN

# 1 || Trisha Brown's *Orfeo*
## Two Takes on Double Endings

*In memory of Julie Cameron*

The notion that Trisha Brown, a choreographer who honed her skills in the radically democratic venue of New York's Judson Dance Theater in the early 1960s, would find her most congenial partner in Claudio Monteverdi, a seventeenth-century Italian composer of opera, seemed a bit outlandish when I first heard it in Brussels in 1998. But after I witnessed the results of their collaboration (across the life/death divide), I thought it positively inspired. *Orfeo* is an opera rooted in complicated emotional and ethical challenges: How do we grieve? What do we owe the dead? Does art betray the love it seeks to honor? Does it exceed and overlook the beloved precisely in its aspiration to be worthy of the beloved? Monteverdi and Brown respond to the myth of Orfeo in ways that heighten and enhance their art; therefore these questions are more than a little bit personal. Any artist trying to contend with Orfeo's story must contend as well with her own relationship to the death of the beloved.

Brown began working with classical music fairly late in her career. In 1986, she choreographed and danced in Lina Wertmuller's production of Bizet's *Carmen.* In 1995, she choreographed *M.O.,* a dance set to Bach's *Musical Offering.* The following year, Brown choreographed *Twelve-Ton Rose* to Anton Webern's opp. 5 and 28. At first, I was hesitant about Brown's newfound dedication to classical music. Bizet, Bach, and Monteverdi hardly suffer from neglect; moreover, Brown's previous choreography interested me in part because she found wonderfully surprising ways to bring sound into her dances without resorting to classical music. Sally Banes notes that Brown used shouting to great effect in her duet with Dick Levine for her first contribution to Robert and Judith Dunn's workshops. Asked to create a duet of exactly three minutes, Levine cried for the full time while Brown, holding a stopwatch, was silent until the last seconds, and then shouted, "Stop it! Stop It! Cut it out!"[1] In her 1976 *Spanish Dance,* a chorus line of women goose-step to Bob Dylan's version of Gordon Lightfoot's "In the Early Morning Rain." This was choreography as inspired braiding, mixing cross-cultural associations with superbly measured dancing. A decade later, Brown was asked about her growing interest in classical music, an interest that became apparent in her choreography for *Carmen*. She replied, "I have started working with music [b]ecause I felt that the dancing was strong enough to be independent of the music and the two things could happen at the same time and the audience could relax."[2]

But as I try to remember Brussels in May 1998 and the premiere of *Orfeo* at the beautiful opera house, Théâtre de la Monnaie, I do not feel relaxed. The problem with remembering dance is that such memories seep into other recollections of embodiment. Memories often exceed their objects, but memories of dancing are especially tangled. When I remember Brown's dancers, I feel these memories in relation to my own body's movements, and the movements of other bodies I've looked at closely. In short, memories of dancing bodies have a kind of porousness around them, often making it difficult to distinguish between then and now, hers and mine. Walking through Brussels on my way to see Brown's production of *Orfeo* that May, I consciously conjured recollections of Brown's earlier work: on roofs in downtown New York, gesturing, a human semaphore sending coded messages across the city; in a harness walking up a building's exterior wall; floating on a raft in a lake, arm upraised; bowing at the Brooklyn Academy of Music. But suddenly a sharp doubt hit me. I could not discern which of my memories came from performances I'd seen and which memories were derived from photos, videos, descriptions in newspapers. I remembered, in *Glacial Decoy*, the way she made Robert Rauschenberg's costumes look like Italian ice, lemon-flavored but colored white; *Carmen* had been consolidated in my mind to an image of Brown's chin superimposed on Lina Wertmuller's. I began to suspect that my little stroll down the corridor marked "Brown, Trisha: Archive of Images," was impure reconstruction. Brown's work now appeared to me as a kind of dense film, projected at slow speed, half documentary and half Hollywood glamour pic.

Slowly I realized that my memories had been colored by Babbete Mangolte's 1978 black and white film, which beautifully captures the luxurious elegance of Brown's *Water Motor*. Mangolte's film slices through Yvonne Rainer's *The Man Who Envied Women* (1985), in the manner of a swimmer breaking the surface of a pool. Rainer set herself the task of creating a female protagonist who would not be seen on camera. Taking feminist theorists' elucidation of the oppressive power of the male gaze seriously, Rainer wanted to discover what kind of pleasure and frustration would result if a witty, intelligent, and emotionally complex protagonist narrated a film but never appeared on screen. Trisha Brown performed the role of Rainer's protagonist, who was also named Trisha. When Mangolte's film swims into focus in Rainer's frame, Brown's *Water Motor* takes on a quality of a dream or, more precisely, of a screen memory. Having listened to Brown's voice on the soundtrack for most of Rainer's film, seeing her suddenly moving there in *Water Motor*, visually accessible but silent, complicates a traditional assumption of narrative film: the protagonist's presence requires perfectly synchronized image and voice. Rainer's interruption of this assumption has the corollary effect of amplifying the silence of Brown's dancing. Within the narrative structure of Rainer's film, Trisha is without image; in Mangolte's documentary footage of Brown dancing, she is voiceless.

Brown's performance in *The Man Who Envied Women* was good preparation for her encounter with *Orfeo;* both works are concerned with injunctions against the gaze.[3] The prohibition of the gaze places more emphasis on the possibilities and limitations of identifications forged via sound. Opera is an especially rich theater in which to observe the layering central to aural-visual-psychic relations. Rainer's film is also relevant to a discussion of *Orfeo* because it reminds us of the tendency to overlook and ignore women's absence from the central myths of Western culture. In Monteverdi's opera, Eurydice functions as the instigator of Orfeo's extraordinary journey to the Underworld. Dead in the first act, she is more cipher than character, more object than subject. Feminists have noted that the repetitious structure of the quest narrative relies on the death or absence of women. Nonetheless, it is worth pausing to note the associative logic that underlines this structure: the absence of women in our persistent myths informs our response to the absence we call death, the signifier of absolute alterity. Repeatedly assigning women to this position of absence in our central narratives, we make an association between the dread of death and the dread of women that is still routine in contemporary life. Perhaps if we could begin to rethink our relationships to the death of women, we might begin to intervene in the intensely alluring, but psychically dangerous, myth of *Orfeo*. Brown's choreography, especially for Eurydice, helps bring the question of the presence and absence of women in this myth into focus.

## Interior Memories

To be haunted by the dead means to be beset with sound, smell, taste, image, memory, after the material body is gone. To attempt to write about dance after the performance is over is to submit to a similar haunting, but one that promises the possibility of a more orderly re-membering. There are documents to consult: reviews, photographs, scores, notes, sometimes even video. If one could place these artifacts delicately and precisely enough on an operating table one might reconstruct, if not completely resuscitate, the moving body. I wanted to bring back a dancer who moved me deeply, but I did not want to be Orfeo; I did not want my desire to overwhelm hers.

*I am remembering falling in love with a dancer named Julie. When she danced, she piled her hair on her head. I watched the strands loosen and fall away from their binds. She asked me to dance too, and I laughed and said I was much happier watching her. What I did not know when I fell in love with her was that her dancing and my watching would become the activity we had to repeat for a long time.*

*Looking back, I see how young we were. She was optimistic, eager, open to the world. I was cautious, a little bit afraid, holding back. But every Friday for two years, we went to a restaurant called The Oasis and ate cheesecake and drank two pots of coffee. We talked about feminism, the academy, the possibilities and impossibilities of love. She was getting her Ph.D. in Sociology. I was getting mine in English Literature. She wanted to be a professor. I wanted to write something worth reading. I liked the formal logic of sociology and she was attracted to the creativity of literature. She studied Tai Chi. I thought she was beautiful.*

*On the Wednesday before one of our Fridays, Julie called and said she had to get some tests done and would not make it for coffee and cheesecake. She said she had a terrible headache. Two days before her twenty-seventh birthday, Julie was told she had a brain tumor.*

*After the surgery, her eyes fluttered the way a doll's do, opening and closing as she was lifted and held. I stared into her eyes and saw a reflection of vacancy, an abyss of ocular absence, a gaze that was at once immense and utterly without focus.*

*Like Orfeo, I did not want to believe that my beloved had died. I wanted to bring her back to life. I stood next to her hospital bed, massaging her muscles, stretching her arms out of their awkward clenching. When I touched her skin I felt dizzy; each touch both confirmed her presence, her bodily nearness, and exposed the vast distance she had traveled from me. I was touching Julie's skin but I felt something enormous and amorphous between her skin and her. If this amorphous thing was death, it was unbearably alive in my hands.*

Is any memory of love not informed by mourning? Blessed with the capacity both to love and to express that love in exquisite music, Orfeo's dilemma exposes how love's hope—the sudden breath in the heart—responds to death—the end of all breath. In the pitch of his love for Eurydice, Orfeo remembers the melancholia he suffered before he met her, and in this memory, he seems to anticipate the grief he will soon suffer again. Composing his love songs for Eurydice from the same chords, the same lyre, the same heart he used to compose songs of earlier love, Orfeo understands that his melancholic history of love allows him to love Eurydice and to sing to her *as* Orfeo. The music of the opera conveys the alignment between music and love; the most heartrending music is reserved for the most sublime love.

## Brown's Memories of the Dead

Prior to her adventures with classical music, Brown had frequently joined dance with her own speaking voice. In *Accumulation With Talking* (1973), Brown said: "While I was making the dance my father died somewhere between these two movements."[4] The sentence stayed with me for a long time. I was amazed by the phrase "my father died somewhere." Death is an event of both temporal and spatial location. It occurs "somewhere" outside linguistic and kinesthetic reckoning. It can obliterate memory; it can spur memory. It often divides mourners' lives into *before* and *after.* The schism fuels the desire to map that "somewhere," for only rarely do events in the external biological world coincide with events in the internal psychic world. One day Brown's father died biologically; some other day she arrived at the fact and force of his death; on yet another day she announced it in her piece. In this sense, it might be more accurate to say: "my father died and he is going to die again in the ongoing recollection and accumulation that registers the work of mourning." The yawning space between these various temporalities is the "somewhere" that pulsates between the time death occurs and the time it takes (a) place—the time required for it to be experienced, witnessed, interpreted. One is not dead in a hospital until the death is pronounced; there is no death without an interpretation, a speech act, a declaration, a witness. In order to transform the act of dying into the fact of death, movement must occur. This is one of the reasons that variations on the Dance of the Dead have remained such a persistent cross-cultural form.

*Accumulation With Talking* might be seen as an attempt to calculate the mathematics of loss in both the physical body and linguistic utterance. Adding together that which is lost requires a double motion: one calculates the way in which subtraction, paradoxically, accumulates. "My father died somewhere between these two movements" indicates the physical, pedagogical, and conceptual space that distinguishes one movement phrase from the other. "My father died somewhere" references the world of movement beyond the dance, the ongoing melody of bodies poised between life and death that gives all human movement its measure. Crucially, death does not stop movement; it is not the cessation of transformation. After death, hair and nails still grow; the corpse withers, or perhaps becomes cinders and ash. Brown's verbal phrase signals the strange vitality of the dead, and the peculiar amnesias and memories of the living. Sometimes we forget the dead and sometimes we can do nothing but remember them. The subtle caesura that opens between the end of one movement phrase and the beginning of the next claims our attention because it seems both to promise and to threaten our restless longing to be still. Dance, like all living art forms, emerges from the oscillation of our desire to be animated, and our desire to cease to be.

Brown invites the spectator to consider the composition of her speech act with the same rigor she asks us to consider the composition of her choreography. To be in a body means that you will die; to be in language means that you know this. *Accumulation with Talking* moves through the accumulation of loss that fuels our desire to move "somewhere" between these two facts. As she stitches sound to movement Brown sews something soft but difficult to describe.

*Time dilated and became water, and still Julie stayed suspended in that bed. She was still beautiful to me, but her suffering, or what I took to be her suffering, was sometimes too much for me to watch. I felt helpless. There was little I could do. I cleaned the hole in her throat, put cream on her peeling skin, and massaged her feet when she would let me touch her. But mainly I stood next to her, stupid with my own useless worry, trying to keep my mind on her and not on my own grief. This effort was not terribly successful.*

*After a while, the doctors said she was in a "persistent vegetative state" and would probably never recover. These doctors, three crisp men, insisted on very precise distinctions and recitations of facts, but steadfastly withheld comment on the psychic and philosophical agony of what I took to be the central problem, a problem of being. I wanted to know if she was alive or dead, human or mechanical, Julie or not-Julie. They concentrated on infections, lack of brain stem function, response versus reflex. I wanted to know where and what she was, and by extension, where I was when I was with her? (And was it her I was with?) I could not tell if we were in some state of technological advance, a sort of future age just coming into being, or if we had slid back into some kind of waiting room for the not-alive and the not-dead. I kept trying to read, to interpret, to get my bearings, to find a way to make sense of things.*

*The doctors advised me not to be so determinedly intentional; her movements, they explained, were reflexive, not expressive. In this strange*

*theater after life and before death, I was asked to accept that there is*
*dancing, but no choreography. I had a terrible time believing this. I kept*
*thinking that the comatose of today were like the autistic children of the*
*1950s, expressing something we did not yet know how to read. I wanted*
*to know who knew how to decipher the code, the gurgle of the ventila-*
*tor, the contracture of her legs, the apparently random but persistent*
*flicker of her eyelids. I felt as if I were in a country whose language was*
*beyond me, but a country in which there definitely was a language, al-*
*though not one that I could properly call linguistic.*

*One night, feeling desperate and unable to escape my own desire to be*
*acknowledged by Julie, I asked the doctors what I could do to let her*
*know I was there. "Try singing," one said and curtly took his leave.*

*I assumed, in my blindly logical way, that he meant that her hearing*
*might still be working. I could not hear the other possibility in his remark,*
*that my voice might trigger some recognition or even comfort in her. I just*
*knew I was a terrible singer, so I played opera tapes for her. I thought that*
*maybe an aria would remind her how to breathe. But as the cassette bob-*
*bins wound round and the mechanical ventilator went up and down, I*
*tried to locate this space, this opening, after life and before death. Sus-*
*pended space. Coma, the medical name. Comma, the grammatical sym-*
*bol that marks the space that separates and joins thoughts. Suspended in*
*the tension of waiting, we were two commas in a long enigmatic sentence.*

*It was a long time before I realized that maybe she was asking me to*
*let her, to let us, hear silence. But in the first phase of my waiting, silence*
*sounded too disordered. I wanted all the notes arranged, all the machines*
*on cue. I wanted to orchestrate the hospital's whispers into a melody I*
*could hum. I wanted to find her in her eyes.*

Brown's sentence—"my father died somewhere between these two
movements"—partners our double desire to climb through the hills and
valleys of the body's mortality and to master the sharp horizontal lines of
cognitive prose, causality, and grammar that resist that mortality. Brown's
choreography climbs the walls, crawls the floors, and floats on water, but
it never for a moment forgets the duality of these two desires. In *Orfeo*,
Brown found a narrative situation large enough to respond to this duality.

## Monteverdi's Score

The libretto for Monteverdi's *Orfeo* was written by Alessandro Striggio
the Younger, a member of the Mantuan Accademia degli Invaghiti, to be
performed for the court during the Carnival season of 1607. The first performance on February 24 was immediately riveting, in part because few

present had previously heard the new recitative style forged by Striggio and Monteverdi, "let alone some two hours of continuous musical theatre."[5] As Cherubino Ferrari, a Mantuan court poet and theologian, noted at a repeat performance a few months later, "The poetry is lovely in conception, lovelier still in form, and loveliest of all in diction. The music, moreover, observing due propriety, serves the poetry so well that nothing more beautiful is to be heard anywhere."[6]

With praise like that for *Orfeo,* why add choreography to the opera? What does the "accumulation" of choreography do for the opera and what does the opera do for Brown's choreography? Monteverdi's score includes two sections for dance: a five-part ballet in act 1 in which the shepherds celebrate the love of Orfeo and Eurydice, and a concluding Morse dance. But Brown's production of the piece, rather than simply setting the score for the shepherds and updating the Morse dance, brilliantly interweaves the dancers from her company with the singers from the Collegium Vocale Gent.[7] Working with musical director Rene Jacobs and designer Roland Aeschilmann, Brown proposes an audacious solution to one of the most troubling aspects of *Orfeo:* the double ending. In what is generally considered Striggio's original version, the Bacchantes, incensed by Orfeo's scorn for them when his guilt over Eurydice's second death has destroyed his desire completely, prepare to stone him to death. In this version, *Orfeo* is a tragedy. But in the two versions Monteverdi published in 1609 and 1615, Apollo descends from the clouds in the final act and promises Orfeo immortality. Apollo assures Orfeo that he will be able to see Eurydice among the stars, and they both ascend, singing. The Chorus returns and celebrates Orfeo's release from his grief by performing a Morse dance, the traditional happy ending. Brown stages elements of both endings, and thereby creates a third interpretation.

The opera's prologue begins with La Musica's praise for the transformative power of music in general, and of Orfeo's lyre in particular. La Musica calls for silence so she can recount his story. In act 1, shepherds and nymphs celebrate the love of Eurydice and Orfeo. They pray for Hymen's blessing and begin to prepare for the wedding celebration. Orfeo addresses his father, Apollo, the sun who "holds our world in harness," and asks him if he has ever seen a happier lover than himself? He praises Eurydice for bringing him such happiness and she responds in kind. The chorus begins the ballet, asking for Hymen's blessing on Orfeo and Eurydice. Act 2 begins with Orfeo and the Shepherds celebrating the wedding and his love for Eurydice. At the height of his rapture, the Messenger comes on stage and announces Eurydice's death. (She was bitten by a snake.) Orfeo refuses to accept her death and resolves to go to the

Underworld to win her back, or, failing that, to spend eternity with her there. In act 3, Orfeo, guided by Hope, comes to the River Styx. Charon refuses to ferry him across because he is mortal and living. But Orfeo sings that his mourning is so overwhelming he is uncertain if he is alive or dead.

> Non vio'io, no, che poi di vita e priva
> Mia cara sposa, il cor non e peu meco
> E senza cor com'esser puo ch'io viva?
>
> No life have I, for since her life was taken,
> my dearest treasure, my heart has left my body.
> When heart is gone, how can it be that I am living?[8]

Charon, deaf to Orfeo's pleading, falls asleep. Taking this opportunity, Orfeo rows himself across the river and enters the Underworld. The Chorus of the Underworld praises Orfeo's passionate love. In act 4, Prosperina, deeply affected by Orfeo's grief, pleads with her husband Pluto to let Eurydice return to life. Pluto agrees, on the condition that Orfeo not look at Eurydice until they have left the Underworld. Just before they arrive in the world of light, Orfeo begins to doubt Pluto's promise. Orfeo hears a noise whose source he cannot place; thinking it is the Furies come to reclaim Eurydice, he turns back to look. She fades before his eyes. The Chorus sings that he has lost her forever. In act 5, a wretched Orfeo laments his loss, while Echo, rather than comforting him, repeats his cries. At this point, the extant libretti offer two divergent endings.

*Is it possible to love a human body with no "person" in it? Or was our idea of life so narrow that we could not accommodate the idea that, Julie, comatose, was still Julie, but in some other dimension of bodily and expressive being? Would we say that Julie had died when the fever burst her brain, when the chemicals to stop infection were overwhelmed by the chemicals to stop pain? Or would we insist that she had two deaths: one during the surgery and one after the coma absorbed her?*

*Sometimes when I left the hospital and felt the sunlight, I became disoriented. Everyday life, in its generous and brutal indifference, continued. One day, whether I liked it not, it would call me back from my deathwatch.*

Monteverdi prefaces the prologue with a five-part toccata, to be played three times (generally before the curtain rises). Functioning as a standard call-to-attention, the main tone of the toccata is a somewhat muted trumpet flourish in C, while the prologue is structured around a five-part ritornello that begins in D. In Brown's production, there is no curtain. When the toccata sounds, yellow light pours across the stage as day dawns. The proscenium is overlaid with a wide circle, the central conceit of the visual design. The seen space emerges from this large O, an optical lens par excellence. In the course of the performance, the circle becomes an eye, a moon, a circus hoop. It begins as a sliver of magic.

Juanita Lascarro, whom Brown places on a trapeze, sings La Musica's prologue. She comes tumbling across the O as the instrumental ensemble fills the hall. A soft yellow light bathes her and begins the dance of light that is a unifying motif in Striggio's libretto. Suspended from the bar, La Musica dances and flies, implicitly suggesting musical notes spilling across the bars of Monteverdi's score. The viewer becomes newly aware of the limitation of sight lines as La Musica tumbles beyond the frame of the visual field. The viewer begins watching, knowing she is blind to the whole scene. Crossing the optical and the aural, La Musica softly insists that opera, despite all its gorgeous instruments, is nothing without voice. Nor is it anything without silence.

> Hor mentre I canti alterno, hor lietei, hor mesti
> Non si mova augellin fra queste piante,
> Ne s'oda in queste rive onda sonante
> Et ogni Auretta in suo cammin s'arrresti.
>
> Now as my songs alternate between happy and sad
> Let no bird move amongst these trees,
> Nor wave be heard on these shores
> And let every breeze halt in its passage.
>
> (Ridler trans., in John, *Operas*, 35)

La Musica is herself a breeze swinging across Monteverdi's score and Brown's stage. As she tumbles outside the frame of the O, the viewer immediately hopes for her return. The score indicates a notated silence after "ne s'oda" (nor let there be heard) and then a second silence after "s'arresti" (let it halt). Staring at the empty O, the visual space that signifies La Musica's aural silence, the spectator takes up Orfeo's position after Eurydice's death, longing to see and hear La Musica again. Lascarro's dual performance as La Musica and Eurydice strengthens the symmetry of their roles.

## Silence and the Other Music

Brown's long apprenticeship with the staging of silence frames the four notated silences that occur in Monteverdi's score. The two silences in the prologue are repeated in act 4 when Orfeo is leading Eurydice from the Underworld back to the world of light. These second two silences bracket the single stage direction in the extant libretti: "a noise is heard offstage." Orfeo's tragedy is precipitated by a sound whose source he cannot locate.

*One day when I went to visit Julie her fever climbed higher than I could reach. Her hands were flung out away from her torso as if her own touch would wound her. I stood there watching a gray pallor climb up her face and settle just below her eyes. I shuddered, inches from drowning in a gray, gray fog.*

*After months of worrying about her, about what would become of her, and of me, it was as if the gray I could see painting her skin was now coloring my own eyes, making them lose their dogged focus. I felt a strange loosening, not a simple "letting go," a much more intense turning from myself. It was at once both painful and consoling, a kind of dream and a kind of horrible tearing. I felt as if I were falling away from what I had always considered foundational, and falling toward something I cannot quite call ground, nor quite call groundlessness. Perhaps it might be most accurate to say it was like entering a space without geometry or physics, a space without subject or perceiver. And yet, nonetheless, the space conveyed definable color, scent, movement, and a peculiar sense of a groundless ground. I did not really arrive in the space, because part of what I fell away from was my own I. It was more as if a new space appeared on top of the space I had been in a moment before. I was then "in" this new space but I was no longer an "I" I could fully recognize.*

*But it is true that something of that space remains with me, even now, years after Julie died. I am not sure I "remember" this, since in some sense I was not quite there. But I feel it return and I feel it return as dance. We might call this the space between memory and event, or, the space between life and death. It is the space of the chiasma between then and now, between her and me.*

## The Place of Play

Thematically, *Orfeo* dramatizes what Jacques Lacan has called "the place of play between two deaths."[9] What is at issue in this opera is the sound of death. If what we hear in the silence between two notes is music (and here it is useful to recall Brown's shared history with John Cage in the New York avant-garde of the early 1960s),[10] then the plot of the opera becomes the "place of play" between those notes, both at the literal level of Monteverdi's score and at the figurative level of Brown's dance notations. These notations function as embodied accents, transforming music into something to see as well as hear. Suiting the word to the action, endorsed by Shakespeare, requires two kinds of work in the staging of opera, and the art of combining singing and acting was not accomplished instantly. Joseph Kerman has succinctly discussed the sound "between two movements" in musical history in which Monteverdi composed *Orfeo:*

In 1600, however, there was as yet no concept of the considered emotional experience that later composers were to elaborate in purely musical terms—Bach in the fugue, Beethoven in the symphony, Handel and Verdi in the aria. . . . [I]n the tradition that he [Monteverdi] knew, musical expressivity was directed only to the painting of moods and images in madrigals. Now there was a more specifically neoclassic ideal: music instead should imitate the accents of passionate speech as best represented by the grand, exaggerated rhetoric of a great actor. Music should follow the cadence and thus the moving implication of the individual word, with little heed to the phrase, the sentence or even the total feeling. The result was recitative, tumbling emotion, a continuing heart-cry, undistanced, "the naked human voice" behind the measured voice of the poet.[11]

In short, Monteverdi's opera traverses the musical space represented by the madrigal and the aria. In the place of play between these two forms Monteverdi discovered the recitative of *Orfeo.* Thus the place of play between Eurydice's two deaths is also a place of play in the history of musical performance. In moving from the stylized passion of "the grand, exaggerated rhetoric of the great actor," characteristic of the neoclassical ideal, to the simplicity of the underlying bass line of Orfeo's recitative, Monteverdi emphasizes the journey one must undertake to move from the position of having "heard" death to becoming one who can pronounce it. In this pedagogy, Orfeo imitates the movement of the Messenger, who first pronounces Eurydice's death. This reversal of status—Orfeo the sublime artist learns what a female servant already knows—also sets in motion the associative logic between women and death central to the narrative.

The first truly shattering moment in the opera occurs in act 2 when the Messenger delivers the news of Eurydice's death to Orfeo. In Brown's production, the Messenger, sung by Graciela Oddone, wears light purple, almost mauve, and begins the elegiac note of mourning (the hypoaeolian mode, which signifies "tears, sadness, solicitude, calamities, and every kind of misery") that Monteverdi carries throughout the remainder of the act.[12] The Messenger tells Orfeo that Eurydice's final breath is spent pronouncing the O of Orfeo's last syllable—a sound that the Messenger, like the production's visual circle, echoes across the dramatic space. Reciting Eurydice's last words, the Messenger's mimetic act also anticipates her own death:

> Ch'ella i languido lumi alquanto aprendo,
> E te chiamando Orfeo
> Dopo un grave sospiro
> Spiro fra queste braccia, ed io rimasi
> Piena il cor di pietade e di spavento

> She but lifting a moment her closing eyes
> cried out your name Orfeo! Orfeo!
> Then sighed deeply and sadly
> and in my arms she died; and I was left there
> with my heart full of anguish, my soul in terror.
>
> (Ridler trans., in John, *Operas*, 42)

The Messenger then dies, tumbling into the orchestra pit. Her death, visible to Orfeo, only increases his desire to see the death he missed. Eurydice cannot be dead, he reasons, because he has only heard the news, and has not seen it. He refuses to believe the Messenger and addresses Eurydice as himself, his very own life: "Tu se morta mia vita ed io respiro?" (You are dead, my life, and I'm still breathing.) Not having witnessed her death with his own eyes, Orfeo resolves to find her in the Underworld.

Encountering the liminal space between the world of light and the world of shadows, Brown's production considers the relationship between memory and repetition, enactment and recitation. After Orfeo is abandoned by Hope to face the Underworld alone, Brown's own artistic history enters the opera more explicitly. As Orfeo begins to comprehend the immensity of the space he must traverse, he wonders if he will be suspended between two movements forever:

> Onde qual ombra errante
> D'insepolto cadavere e infelice
> Privo saro del cielo e de l'inferno?

> Am I to stray forever like a dead man
> all friendless and unburied
> Exiled from heaven, must Hell be barred against me?
>
> (Ridler trans., in John, *Operas*, 47)

Despairing of finding a narrative and musical "somewhere," Orfeo now sings exactly on the notes for the first time in the opera. His plea, expressed in the famous refrain "Rendetemi il mio ben, Tartarei Numi" (Give me back my love), only succeeds in putting Charon to sleep; what makes Hell hell for Orfeo is that his music does not inspire response. But taking Charon's indifferent silence as his opportunity, Orfeo rows across the river. This crossing also crosses with memories of Brown's previous work. Orfeo piloting Charon's boat recalls Brown's work with floating dancers on rafts (*Group Primary Accumulation* [1973]). The wall dividing the world of light from the Underworld recalls Brown's famous wall piece (*Planes* [1968]), now restaged for a grieving Orfeo. His encounter with the space of death prompts Brown to make a bridge between the history of her artwork and the mythic past of *Orfeo*. Brown's references to her earlier work, at the moment that the play dramatizes the space between the world of light and the Underworld, compose a chiasma between the Orfeo's mythical then and our still pressing now.

Orfeo does cross this suspended space. And once in the Underworld, another woman intercedes on his behalf. Prosperina, hearing Orfeo's lamentations, begs Pluto to allow Orfeo to return to the world of light with Eurydice. Pluto agrees, on the condition that Orfeo return without looking back at Eurydice. Like the instructions for Robert Dunn's workshop—make a three-minute duet—Pluto's instruction is more complicated than it first sounds. To return without turning is akin to repeating something that has no original.

Operatically, the myth's enigmatic question—why does Orfeo turn back to look?—must be resolved at the level of sound. Combining Virgil's and Ovid's version of the myth, Striggio also adds what we might call motivation and logical cause and effect, thus rendering some narrative coherence to Orfeo's turning back to look. Monteverdi resolves the crucial question of why Orfeo turns back to look by turning back to the two notated silences in the prologue sung by La Musica. As he travels toward the world of light, Orfeo asks, "Who can assure me that she is following?" and his question produces no response. In the next line, he asks: "Ah, who may be hiding from me the light of those beloved eyes?" Once more, he is answered with silence.

The silence unnerves Orfeo, for it suggests that he is no longer addressing Eurydice, the source of his desire to sing. Straining to hear a response from her, Orfeo hears instead an enigmatic sound. The two notated silences in Monteverdi's score are made even more dramatic by an offstage noise that Orfeo cannot place. If the first two silences are a kind of inward hell, the unlocatable sound reminds him that he is "somewhere" beyond light, beyond vision and orientation. Desperate to place a sound whose source he cannot discern, Orfeo tries to interpret it. His fear is so great that he forgets Pluto's prohibition and turns back, only to lose Eurydice in that act. In the "place of play" between the sound that comes from an unknown source and the act of turning back to look, Orfeo gets caught in the double cross of the chiasma, and Eurydice dies for the second time.

While Monteverdi uses silence and an offstage noise to render the myth musically coherent, Brown must find a resolution for Orfeo's actions in terms of movement. In her notations on Monteverdi's score, Brown has Orfeo moving in quarter turns stage left (that is, toward Eurydice) on each of the notated silences.[13] Eurydice walks behind Orfeo, leaving only her outline visible to the audience. As he turns back toward Eurydice, Orfeo slowly twists his hands together at shoulder height. Orfeo's jour-

ney away from the Underworld to the world of light, from musical ecstasy to fatal silence, is embodied choreographically by a corporeal crossing. Orfeo's own body turns in on itself as he turns back to look at Eurydice. As he turns fully around to face Eurydice, the catastrophic force of
that sighting registers as a turning from which there can be no returning.
Orfeo sings, "Indeed I behold you" and Eurydice slowly falls into a soft
roll. As she tumbles, the score shifts to G, and Orfeo sings, more darkly,
"But what eclipse obscures your light?" Eurydice, now standing upright,
responds with her final lines in the opera: "Ah, vision much too sweet and
much too bitter! / Like this, for too much love you lose me now?" and
then exits, stage right. Orfeo's fear causes her second death.


## To End Again

Brown's staging of the opera interweaves Striggio's original libretto with
Monteverdi's published versions. Insisting that death is a multiple and in-
deed a social act, Brown stages the happy ending and the tragic ending.
In both, it is the interpretation of death that completes the act of dying.
The pronouncement of death transforms and moves the act of dying into
the fact of death.

In the happy ending, Orfeo and his father Apollo ascend to the heav-
ens singing. Released from his misery, Orfeo will contemplate Eurydice's
form in the starlight. In the tragic version, however, Orfeo's single-minded
dedication to pronouncing Eurydice's death leads him to scorn the pleasures offered him by the Bacchantes. Refusing to love is a refusal to live;
Orfeo's excessive mourning might be seen as a plea for death, which the
Bacchantes answer. Brown's choreography transforms the traditional happy
Morse dance into a frenzied dance of death, thereby leaving Orfeo's death
a question of interpretation.

_Julie's mother said that Julie had died during the surgery. Her sister
thought she died during a fever months after the surgery. At the memorial service, some of her friends spoke of Julie as a child, some as an adult,
one as a teenager. It rained. Someone remembered Julie's dead father. Someone else found a way to laugh. As we began to leave, someone else turned
on the CD player. I heard Monteverdi's opening toccata before I left._

_Now mainly I remember her dancing at a party and I remember watch-
ing her hair come undone. I remember the hospital and the way her muscles
contracted, the way she looked beyond me, the shape of her head without hair. I remember the enormous distance between us, even when I massaged her legs._

*Julie showed me a space between two versions of her body, two ways of being at once alive and dead. The day I watched the gray climb up to her face haunts me even now. Arriving in the space of that groundless ground did not feel exactly loving, but it was so animate and vital that it is difficult for me to call it death. Although it is also true that the crisp doctors pronounced her dead later that evening. Perhaps we can call this chiasmatic space the place of play between two deaths, between two loves.*

This place of play insists that play is not easy. Brown is neither Eurydice nor Orfeo, but her choreography for Monteverdi's score honors the urge to think more carefully about the movement between Eurydice and Orfeo. Staging Eurydice's roll as a response to Orfeo's turning makes visible the causal logic of linking women and death. His vertical mastery of the visible world is purchased through her collapse back into the Underworld. His quest seems to require her death. If we are to revise this logic, we need ways to begin to think beyond the logic of causality, new ways to transform the chiasma from the X of his crossing to the Y of her dying. Brown's attention to the caesura between each movement phrase invites us to consider whether this pause holds breath, or death, or both. Death's breath danced across the suspended bridge between Monteverdi's opera and Brown's choreography. It reminded me of Julie's suspended journey between life and death. In the absence of Eurydice's story, I want to give you Julie's.

*I have no sense of what she sensed then, or how she handled that long suspension. I offer my not knowing to you, as a space in which we might begin to rethink the groundless ground of dancing's deepest crossings.*

# 2 || Genealogy and Dance History

## Foucault, Rainer, Bausch, and de Keersmaeker

This essay examines issues of body and presence in three ambitiously innovative dance pieces from the second half of the twentieth century: Yvonne Rainer's *Trio A* (1966), Pina Bausch's *Café Müller* (1978), and Anne Teresa de Keersmaeker's *Rosas Danst Rosas* (1983). Rainer's *Trio A* was the first part of her evening-length piece *The Mind is a Muscle*, first performed in April 1968. In a program note for this, Rainer stated first her aesthetic preference for minimalist movement, asserting that she loved "the body—its actual weight, mass, and unenhanced physicality"; she then, responding to current, turbulent social and political events, concluded that "my body remains the enduring reality."[1] To say that one's dancing body remains an enduring reality is to imply that, by enduring, it can resist normative social and aesthetic ideologies. In what ways, during the last forty years of the twentieth century were dancing bodies subject to normative ideologies, and how could radical, experimental performance practices transform these bodies into sites of resistance? What was the historical specificity of the tension between the physicality of the dancing body and notions of the subject and its presence? These questions, which arise from Rainer's 1968 program note, inform the particular historical trajectory that this essay investigates. This trajectory starts in New York with Rainer during the 1960s and, crossing the Atlantic, continues with Bausch and de Keersmaeker during the 1970s and 1980s, and, by way of the revival of interest in Judson Dance Theater during the 1990s, returns to New York with Rainer's *Trio A Pressured* in 1999. While provocative traditions of radical dance practices were thus crossing and recrossing the Atlantic, theoretical ideas about the body, metaphysics, and history (in the work of Michel Foucault and other poststructuralist theorists) were also provoking readers around the world. Indeed, the use in this essay of poststructuralist methodologies to investigate issues of body and presence is prompted by the coincidence of these philosophical and performative investigations of the body.

*Trio A, Café Müller,* and *Rosas Danst Rosas* are in danger of being reified by the discourse of dance history as it creates the canon of late twentieth-century postmodern dance. This process of reification is one in which the challenges to normative ideas about body and presence that have been made through the performance of these works become displaced by concerns about the stylistic identity of individual choreographers and their place within a narrative of formal and aesthetic innovation. While the formation of the canon does not necessarily entail an ahistorical detachment from the social and political contexts of the production of these works, too often dance analysis means the analysis of a disembodied ideal essence conventionally called "choreography"—rather than an analysis of the performance of that choreography by sometimes troubling and disturbingly material dancing bodies. Where the materiality of the body troubles and disturbs the idea of aesthetic truths that are timeless and thus ever present on a metaphysical plane, normative historiography can sometimes contribute to the process through which the potentially subversive physicality of the body is in effect erased. This is not to accuse dance historians of sometimes ignoring the body but to indicate problems within the underlying epistemologies on which dance historiography is predicated.

The same tension among ideologies of body, metaphysics, and history that haunts the process of canon formation in dance studies is the subject of Michel Foucault's essay "Nietzsche, Genealogy, History" (published 1971). Foucault proposed here a type of history that attempted to identify a "genealogy" of divergent traits through focusing on the corporeality of experience and the ways in which the embodiment of subjectivity is vulnerable to impositions of power. In exploring this idea of genealogy, Foucault drew on Nietzsche's arguments against Darwin's account of the origins and descent of species and against Hegel's evolutionary theory of historical progress. In so doing, Foucault (like Deleuze and Derrida and, in a different way, Althusser) was distancing himself from a particular Hegelianism within existentialist philosophy. In Foucault's account, the genealogist, through patient and documentary processes, resists history's promotion of the myth of the transcendental subject and of metaphysical presence: "If the genealogist refuses to extend his faith in metaphysics, if he listens to history, he finds that there is 'something altogether different' behind things: not a timeless and essential secret, but the secret that they have no essence or that their essence was fabricated in a piecemeal fashion from alien forms."[2] What particularly concerned Foucault is the fiction that there is an essence or timeless, metaphysical presence of the rational unitary subject within the body. Arguing that this is not the case, he proposed that the body is the inscribed surface of events (traced by language and dissolved by ideas), the locus of a dissociated Self (adopting the illusion of a substantial unity), and a volume in perpetual disintegration. Genealogy, as an analysis of descent, is thus situated within the articulation of the body and history. Its task is to expose a body totally impregnated by history and the process of history's destruction of the body.[3]

Unlike traditional history, genealogy[4] thus reveals a process of subjection in which humanity is forced to participate through the imposition of directions and through submission to an alien will that leads to destruction of the body.[5] Resistance to this process of normative subject formation, however, also runs the risk of "the destruction of the subject who seeks knowledge in the endless deployment of the will to knowledge."[6] Genealogy is thus the reappropriation of those archival records out of which the myths of traditional history have been created in order to find something altogether different.

Rainer and her fellow artists who presented work at Judson Memorial Church during the early 1960s engaged in an avant-garde attack on the traditions and conventions of theater dance (which has parallels with Foucault's genealogy). They too sought to reappropriate traditions and conventions in ways that revealed the conventions' essence to be an illusory fabrication of alien forms. Through fragmentation of these forms, they opened up the various levels on which theater dance operates as a signifying practice in such a way as to make it necessary for spectators to engage in creating their own readings of the performance text. When Foucault stated that the body is the site of a dissociated self that adopts the illusion of constituting a rational unitary subject, he was articulating a set of antihumanist ideas that have become associated with the notion of the death of the subject and of the particularly privileged subject known as the author. The idea of the "death of the author" is applicable to the situation I have just described at Judson Dance Theater in that works of art were no longer seen as meaningful only insofar as they exemplified the author's presence and were controlled by it. Foucault argued in his essay "What is an Author?" that what matters is not who is speaking within a particular discourse but "where does it come from, how is it circulated, who controls it?"[7] These questions were surely also implicit in the more radical work produced by the artists associated with Judson Dance Theater, work that explored a discourse of experimental dance practices asserting the finite materiality of embodied experience.

While there may be some common ground here between Foucault and Judson Dance Theater, it is surely significant that Rainer claimed her body remained the enduring reality on the eve of the events of 1968, while Foucault wrote about the process of history's destruction of the body in the aftermath of those events. Rainer's statement is essentially affirmative (despite her avant-garde rejection of artistic conventions and traditions), while Foucault's view of history is deeply pessimistic. In order to link Rainer's claim that the physicality of the dancing body can be a site of resistance to normative ideologies with Foucault's account of the process of genealogy, it is necessary to establish in what ways the dancing body can be considered subject to inscription. While Foucault was not thinking about theater when he developed his notion of inscription on the body, there are similarities between his formulation and the account given by Jacques Derrida, in an early essay, of Antonin Artaud's disgust with writing. In particular there is a similarity between Derrida's notion of the erasure of the body and Foucault's notion of the process of the destruction of the body. Derrida pointed out that whereas Plato, in the *Phaedrus,* was disgusted with writing because it interposed itself between the body and truth and was exterior to the inscription of truth in the soul, Artaud's disgust with writing was because he saw it "as the site of the inscription of truth, the other of the living body, writing as ideality, repetition. Plato criticizes writing as a body; Artaud criticizes it as the erasure of the body, of the living gesture which takes place only once."[8] In Derrida's view, Artaud attempted to disrupt a "dialogue between theology and humanism whose indistinguishable reoccurrence has never not been maintained by the metaphysics of western theater."[9] Crucially, Derrida proposed that writing as ideality and repetition produces a kind of theological, humanistic presence that erases the body. Theatrical representation, he argued, "is finite, and leaves behind it, behind its actual presence, no trace, no object to carry off."[10] To appreciate and fully experience the unique moment of live performance, theater must break its ties with the repetition and representation of the author's presence in the theatrical text, and with the presence within this of timeless truths. It is only when theater makes this break that it will create "a present whose plenitude would be older than it, absent from it, and rightfully capable of doing without it: the being-present-to-itself of the absolute Logos, the living present of God."[11]

If one accepts parallels between Artaud's project and that of Rainer, Bausch, and de Keersmaeker, what is therefore at stake is the extent to which radical, experimental performance practices refuse to represent this theological, humanist presence. In Derrida's terms, such practices reveal the ways in which the metaphysics of Western theater erases the body—or, in Foucault's terms, the process of history's destruction of the body. An avant-garde attack on this type of presence should not, however, be seen as negative, but as affirmative insofar as it has the potential to allow other, previously imperceptible kinds of presences to emerge, and new, more open ways of conceiving and experiencing theater dance.

Judith Butler's critique of Foucault's account of cultural inscription on the body helps clarify what is at stake in the tension between presence and repetition. Butler's concept of the performativity of gender has much in common with Foucault's notion of genealogy. Just as Foucault sees individuals as subject to impositions of power that have accumulated over time, Butler argues that individuals are forced to conform to preexisting cultural relations: "The act that one does, the act that one performs is, in a sense, an act that has been going on before one arrived on the scene. Hence gender is an act which has been rehearsed, much as a script survives the particular actors who make use of it, but which requires individual actors in order to be actualized and reproduced as reality, once again."[12] Where Foucault's genealogist reveals that the essence of the body is a fabrication that adopts the illusion of a substantial unity, Butler argues that gender attributes do not express an essential interiority but create the illusion of a preexisting interiority or essence through performative acts. One striking difference: whereas Foucault sees the body as a passive recipient of cultural inscription, Butler sees embodied subjects as agents, albeit restricted ones who enact interpretations "within the confines of already existing discourses."[13] Thus for Foucault, the body is the subject of inscriptions; for Butler, however, subjects as agents "dramatically and actively embody and, indeed, wear certain cultural significations."[14]

Nevertheless, Butler points out that, for Foucault, the body must exist first as a blank surface or page prior to the moment when it is inscribed with cultural meanings by the metaphorical figure or writing machine of history. Thus she argues that, for Foucault, the body is the medium "which must be destroyed and transfigured in order for 'culture' to emerge."[15] Butler points out that Foucault occasionally "subscribes to a prediscursive multiplicity of bodily forces [that] break through the surface of the body to disrupt the regulating practices of cultural coherence imposed upon that body by a power regime understood as a vicissitude of 'history.'"[16] If, however, these are prediscursive properties of the blank page or pure, unmarked body that existed prior to the process of cultural inscription, then the possible ways in which embodied subjects might disrupt or resist impositions of normative ideologies cannot be revealed by Foucault's genealogist. In order to conceive and identify a theoretical account of the ways in which embodied subjects might resist normative ideologies, it is necessary to understand that "the very contours of 'the body' are established through markings that seek to establish specific codes of cultural coherence."[17]

The individual's experience of the physicality of the body is inseparable from that body as it is constructed through discourse. To apply this
premise to dance history and theory, issues of body and presence arise because of the ways in which dancing bodies are produced through the inter-
section of codes of the social and the aesthetic. The radical, experimental
performance practices whose histories I discuss in this essay can only disrupt or resist impositions of normative ideologies by revealing the otherwise hidden strategies through which the fiction or illusion of an a priori
presence is performatively produced. I am therefore taking genealogy to
include both an uncovering of the process of history's destruction of the
body *and* the possibilities of agency and resistance within performative repetitions of discourses despite the all encompassing nature of the disciplinary effects of those discourses. A genealogy of recent dance will therefore primarily focus, not on the choreographic concerns of particular
ambitiously innovative dance makers, but on the ways in which performances of their choreography have had the potential to open up new
possibilities for agency within discourses of theater dance.

Given that Butler is concerned with performative speech acts while
dance scholarship deals with live performance, it is important to clarify
the relationship between these two different types of performativity. Butler and Foucault have been concerned with subject formation through
acknowledgment of social values by the repetition of socially mandated
discourses. Dance performance involves the circulation, within a particularly privileged context, of speech acts that are generally nonverbal. The
fact that Rainer, Bausch, and de Keersmaeker have all engaged in strategies that have troubled and called into question normative conceptions of
performance makes any provisional definition of it for the purposes of
this essay problematic. Nevertheless, whereas Butler is concerned with
interpellation and the political effects of performing repetitions of normative discourses, in live theatrical performances meanings are produced
through a collective and reflexive awareness, shared between performers
and an audience, of nuances of interpretation within intersections of a
number of overdetermined discourses. Having said that, when one considers Rainer's *Trio A*, it becomes apparent that this piece was conceived
and structured in such a way as to make this collective and reflexive awareness as difficult and problematic as possible. "Dance is hard to see," Rainer
wrote (in her essay "A Quasi Survey of Some 'Minimalist' Tendencies in
the Quantitatively Minimal Dance Activity amidst the Plethora, or an
Analysis of *Trio A*"). "It must either be made less fancy, or the fact of that
intrinsic difficulty must be emphasized to the point that it becomes almost

impossible to see."[18] The following brief description of the piece and its performance shows how it emphasized that intrinsic difficulty.

*Trio A* lasts about six and a half minutes and consists of one continual phrase of task-based movement performed in such a way as to minimize the effects of rhythm, phrasing, and dynamics in dance movement. This is achieved by hiding the transition between actions. No pose is ever struck, as Rainer later explained:

> No sooner had the body arrived at the desired position than it would go immediately into the next move, not through momentum but through a very prosaic going on. And there would be very different moves—getting down on the floor, getting up. There would be this pedestrian dynamic that would suffuse and connect the whole thing. So the whole thing, though it would be composed of these fragments of movement unrelated both kinetically and positionally or shapewise, would look as if it were one long phrase.[19]

The first move of Rainer's *Trio A* is for the dancers to look over their left shoulders at a spot on the floor about two paces diagonally behind them. The dancers then pat their stomachs and backs with alternating hands circling close to the trunk five times, then turn and take two steps in the direction of their gaze.[20] As Rainer observed in her "Quasi Survey": "The execution of each move conveys a sense of unhurried control. The body is weighty without being completely relaxed."[21] The demands placed on the body, she went on, are like those made by everyday tasks such as getting up out of a chair, reaching for a high shelf, or walking down stairs when one is not in a hurry. The dancing is pedestrian, not mimetic; Rainer liked "to think that in their manner of execution they have the factual quality of such actions."[22] Rainer's intention seems to have been to reduce dance movement to the simple, phenomenological experience of mundane physical activity.

In terms of temporality, every activity, Rainer observed, therefore took the actual time it took the actual weight of the body to go through the prescribed movement.[23] What descriptions of the piece often omit is the fact that *Trio A* was primarily performed as a trio. Thus although all three dancers began at the same time, one behind the other on the righthand side of the performance space, as each of the three dancers inevitably took a different time to go through each of the prescribed movements, they each came in and out of sync with each other. This can be clearly seen in Al Giese's photograph of the first performance at Judson Memorial Church in 1966. As a spectator in 1999 I found that although I could see that each dancer was dancing the same piece, the fact that they were each doing it at slightly different times made it even harder to watch. Giese's photograph also shows, in the far right corner of the performance space, a pile of slats of timber. Throughout the piece these were dropped with metronome-like regularity from the gallery to the floor of the sacristy. In the 1968 performance at the Anderson Theater of the evening-length version of *The Mind is a Muscle,* slats were dropped onto the stage from the top of a ladder hidden in the wings. Rainer noted that audience members complained after the 1966 performance "about the relentlessness of this 'music.' It may have been at this performance that a man in the front row picked up a slat, attached a large white handkerchief to it, and waved it over his head."[24]

Rainer was not only concerned with minimizing the space, time, and movement dynamics of her choreography; she also sought to deconstruct modes of performance and presence by disrupting the way the performer conventionally presented her- or himself to the audience. Through discussions with Steve Paxton, she had become aware of the narcissistic involvement of the performer and of her own narcissistic pleasure in performing. When she had first performed, as she later recalled:

[I]t was as good as orgasm. I knew that was where I lived, that was where I belonged, doing that work and presenting myself physically to an audience. And that, of course, was part of the charisma. That is the urgency, and that pleasure in exhibiting oneself is part of the seduction of an audience. The performer has to experience that in order for the audience to get a sense of this presence or to be taken in by it.[25]

In *Trio A* Rainer decided that she was not going to pander to the audience or seduce them with her presence in this way. As she wrote in the program note for the 1968 performance: "If my rage at the impoverishment of ideas, narcissism, and disguised sexual exhibitionism of most dancing can be considered puritan moralizing, it is also true that I love the body—its actual weight, mass, and unenhanced physicality."[26] The key word here is "puritan"; what Rainer was raging against are qualities that she herself had used in previous pieces and recognized that she enjoyed using. In performing *Trio A* dancers try to avert a quality of theatricalized self-presentation and exhibitionism through a careful avoidance of eye contact with the audience. Right from the first movement, turning the head to look over the shoulder, the dancer's gaze is carefully choreographed. Rainer said that "the 'problem' of performance was dealt with by never permitting the performers to confront the audience. Either the gaze was averted or the head was engaged in movement. The desired effect was a work-like rather than exhibition-like presentation."[27] In this way Rainer hoped to avert what she later called the "narcissistic-voyeuristic duality of doer and looker."[28]

In 1968, the year when Yvonne Rainer's *The Mind is a Muscle* was completed and received its first full performance, the public in developed countries was watching almost nightly television news of technologically sophisticated carnage from Vietnam. Rainer's piece was premiered in April a few days after the assassination of Martin Luther King Jr. and just before a long summer of mass political action by students and young people in many parts of the world: in Paris and Prague these provoked major political crises. If one looks for dance reviews, listings, and advertisements relating to Rainer and her contemporaries in the pages of the *Village Voice* newspaper during this period, they often appear near, and sometimes side by side with announcements of meetings to discuss civil rights issues, resistance to the war, help for draft dodgers, and other oppositional activities.

In the face of this chaos and anarchy, Rainer's statement accompanying the program for *The Mind is a Muscle* in April 1968 took up an austere, uncompromising aesthetic position. In this Rainer acknowledged current political events—"The world disintegrates around me. My connection to the world-in-crisis remains tenuous and remote"[29]—but only in order to deny that this has anything to do with *The Mind is a Muscle*. "Just as ideological issues have no bearing on the nature of the work, neither does the tenor of current political and social conditions have any bearing on its execution." She observed that despite her puritan critique of seductive dance movement, she loved the body "its actual weight, mass, and unenhanced physicality"; thus at the end of the program, after briefly discussing the Vietnam War and its appearance on television, she described her "state of mind that reacts with horror and disbelief upon seeing a Vietnamese shot dead on TV—not at the sight of death, however, but at the fact that the TV can be shut off afterwards as after a bad Western. *My body remains the enduring reality.*"[30]

I am arguing that *Trio A* attempted to forefront the actual weight, mass, and unenhanced physicality of the dancing body by eliminating the kind of presence that is produced when the audience senses the performers' pleasure in exhibiting themselves. Rainer apparently hoped that freedom from historical and political processes could be achieved through this radical deconstruction of normative modes of dance performance. In claiming her independence from ideological issues, Rainer was taking up a recognizably modernist position of artist-as-outsider. Modern dance artists, like modern writers and visual artists, were often seen as exemplary outsiders. As Zygmunt Bauman has observed, "a hate-love relationship [was inherent] between modern existence and modern consciousness"; artists were valued, but also feared and censured, for their ability to articulate a critical modern consciousness.[31] From their resulting position of "objectivity," Bauman observed, modernist work was implicitly critical, warning and alerting to problems and shortcomings in the project of modernity. The possibility of occupying such an outsider position was, in effect, largely problematized by the events of 1968. One of the slogans of the French student revolutionaries was "nous sommes tous indesirables" (we are all undesirable aliens, outsiders). The French Left however failed to mount a revolution, Russian tanks crushed the Prague Spring, and the peace and civil rights movements effectively foundered in the fall when the Republican candidate Richard Nixon was elected president in the United States, bringing with him, as secretary of state, Henry Kissinger who intensified U.S. involvement in Vietnam.

In trying to account for these failures, poststructuralist theorists shifted their focus onto the ways in which individuals are consciously and unconsciously inclined to accept conservative norms. Following Althusser's 1971 essay on ideology and ideological state apparatuses, some poststructuralist theorists have examined the ways in which individuals are interpellated within ideological discourses. Rather than all being undesirable aliens, individuals now seemed to be always already insiders, and their bodies, in Foucault's words, totally impregnated by history and the process of history's destruction of the body. Judith Butler has argued that it is only possible to take up a critical position through recognizing the extent to which one is always already implicated within the very power one might wish to oppose, so that political possibilities only emerge "when the limits to representation and representability are exposed."[32] Therefore, although in the aftermath of 1968 Rainer's claim that ideological issues had no bearing on the nature of her work appeared illusory, her exploration of performance practices that radically refused to rehearse conventional forms of presence exposed, in libertarian ways, the limits of dance representation and representability. This exposure, I argue, was continued by Pina Bausch's *Café Müller* and Anne Teresa de Keersmaeker's *Rosas Danst Rosas*.

*Café Müller*, first performed in 1978, is a dark piece full of missed encounters and failed acts of communication among a small ensemble of dancers including Pina Bausch herself. Its stage set represents a café full of tables and chairs that obstruct the dancing; a chair mover (originally the piece's scenographer Rolf Borzick) has to move these out of the way to save the seemingly blind or sleepwalking dancers from injuring themselves. In an oft-described scene, Jan Minarik intervenes in the way a couple—Dominic Mercy and Malou Airaudo in the original cast—are embracing, and make them learn to do it differently. It begins as Mercy and Airaudo fall into one another's arms in a tight embrace. Minarik walks up to them, wearing a suit but barefoot. Slowly, without any particular force, he shifts their arms around, makes Mercy kiss Airaudo on the lips while holding her awkwardly in midair in front of him, and then walks away as if about to leave the stage. The instability of the new embrace leads Mercy to drop Airaudo, who picks herself up off the ground and urgently hugs him again the way they had kissed before Minarik's intervention. Minarik pauses when he hears the fall, comes back, and rearranges the couple the way he had left them before, in an unhurried, matter-of-fact way. He leaves them again, the new embrace collapses, and the whole cycle is run through again. This continues a number of times, gradually becoming faster, as Airaudo and Mercy begin to tire and Minarik gets shorter and shorter distances from them before having to come back. There eventually comes a moment when Airaudo picks herself up off the floor and embraces Mercy directly but then the two of them go on to kiss in the way Minarik had directed them to do without his intervention, and Minarik leaves the stage. Airaudo and Mercy go through their now hectic cycle repeatedly until they are clearly out of breath and weary. It is as if they had internalized Minarik's role and no longer needed him there. In the end they prop one another up clasped in their original embrace, their bodies heaving with gradually subsiding pants of exhaustion.

This scene is shocking and deeply depressing, with characteristics that recur in many other moments in Bausch's work, especially from the 1970s. These include the seemingly endless repetition, the intimately violating nature of the tasks, and the way in which, like *Trio A*, actions are performed in real time without attempting either to hide or to exaggerate the real effort expended in them. Perhaps the most depressing yet at the same time most impressive aspect of the performance of this scene is the way that Airaudo and Mercy refuse to admit that what they are attempting is impossible, but try to execute it to the best of their abilities. In Foucault's terms, they are risking "the destruction of the subject who seeks knowledge in the endless deployment of the will to knowledge."[33] Because the performers won't give up, the audience witnesses their gradual and inevitable failure. At the start of the twenty-first century, Bausch is accepted as a major figure. Audiences come to performances by her company, Tanztheater Wüppertal, prepared to endure a harrowing experience and then give the dancers a standing ovation. Her new works are much lighter than the older ones but the latter are still regularly revived. In the early days at Wüppertal, while Bausch had some loyal supporters, many of her audience hated her work.[34] When the company first appeared in New York in the 1980s, people walked out and some critics dismissed what they called the senseless repetition and sadomasochistic scenarios in her work.[35] However, many of those on both sides of the Atlantic who responded positively to her work came from a generation for whom it was important to acknowledge that the personal is political, that we are all racist and sexist, and that what we most object to in others is often something we don't want to accept about ourselves. This was of course a generation for whom the events of 1968 were a key point of reference.

What this scene stages, I suggest, is the process of interpellation described by Althusser. In Althusser's well-known example, the policeman calls out to someone on the street "Hey, you!" and the person turns round to face him. A policeman's call, Althusser proposes, interpellates them into the discourse of the law, and their response to his call is an admission of their obligations as subject.[36] In *Discipline and Punish,* Foucault describes a similar situation in which penal instruments of power make a symbolic demand on the body of the prisoner, these having a performative capacity to constitute the subject whom it defines. Judith Butler has emphasized the importance of performative repetition within this process of subject formation. Individuals, she argues, are compelled to repeat acts that can neither be refused nor followed in strict obedience.[37] In the scene from *Café Müller,* Minarik's role resembles that of Althusser's policeman, and the café itself a prison. The gap between what Minarik demonstrates with their bodies and their failure to perform it points to the inadequacy of Western theater and dance forms to express contemporary Western experience. In Butler's terms it reveals the limits of representation and representability. What I, the spectator, found compelling about this scene was how the excessive repetition leaves the dancers dazed and confused, suggesting that, in the face of Minarik's violating demands, there is no possibility of agency.

Speech act theory states that performative acts always exceed their literal content—there is always a supplement.[38] Butler has proposed that, although the compulsion to repeat the interpellating call cannot be refused, it is equally impossible to perform the required response in strict obedience. It is quite clear in the scene from *Café Müller* what Airaudo and Mercy are called to do. What is supplementary to its enactment is the dancers' exhaustion, the messiness of bodies out of control, the visceral, intimate mixing of bodily fluids, and the apparent blurring of interpersonal boundaries of these dazed, confused performers. Rainer might almost have been thinking of their apparent experience when she wrote ten years earlier: "The world disintegrates around me. My connection to the world-in-crisis remains tenuous and remote."[39] Unlike Rainer's work in the 1960s, however, Bausch's dancers exemplify the recognition that we are all implicated in the power we might wish to oppose. Nevertheless, in the face of the process of history's destruction of their bodies, the supplement of Airaudo and Mercy's performance seems to affirm that their bodies still remain the enduring reality.

If the shift from Rainer's work to Bausch's is one in which there is less confidence about possibilities of resisting normative ideologies, the shift from Bausch to De Keersmaeker is marked by an increasing recognition of the fragmentary and conflictual nature of embodied subjectivity, exemplified on stage through a confusing play between reality and artifice. De Keersmaeker's *Rosas Danst Rosas* is characterized by serial repetition of gestural movement material largely performed in unison by four similarly dressed young women, first on the floor, then sitting on chairs, then standing, and finally walking.[40] These gestures consist of what appear to be trivial, everyday, feminine behavior: running a hand through her hair, or jerking the head upward to toss her hair out of her eyes, tugging the shoulder of her T-shirt so that its loose neck reveals and then hides again a bare shoulder, wedging clasped hands between tightly closed thighs. These movements seem to be very personal, private, idiosyncratic, habitual. De Keersmaeker choreographs subtle shifts between unison material performed by all four dancers, and unison by three with one performing slightly different gestures, and counterpoint between movement sequences performed by two pairs. The seemingly endless repetition (although there is actually an almost imperceptible development in the material) and the apparently shifting alliances or identifications between the dancers trouble the apparently intimate qualities of the gestural material. This is a play of surfaces rather than an expression of depth. The minimalist monotony of the repetition of mundane gestures suggests compulsion to conform to prescripted behavior. When performed by one dancer on her own they suggest a psychological interiority, an individual who is slightly self-conscious and uneasy. Nevertheless, although de Keersmaeker references this young, feminine self-consciousness in her choreography, that these gestures are repeated changes their import and troubles the notion of psychological interiority.

If the scene in *Café Müller* requires Minarik to represent a figure of authority in its staging of interpellation, De Keersmaeker and her dancers seem already to have learned the movement script of the normative discourses into which they are interpellated. Unlike Mercy and Airaudo, De Keersmaeker and her fellow dancers do not fail because, on one level, the uniformity and clarity of their performance fulfill their obligation. In the chair section, there are even choreographed moments for them to register their exhaustion, slumped over or sprawled back in their chairs in dejected poses for a specified number of beats of Thierry de Mey's machinelike, minimalist music. The latter sounds like Foucault's writing machine of history, inexorably inscribing its violating marks on their bodies. There are signs, however, that there may nevertheless be a gap between what is demanded of the dancers and their performance of these demands. Every now and then during the seated section there are little, complicitous looks exchanged between dancers, generally in pauses between the completion of one cycle of movement material and the initiation of a new cycle. In the standing section, there is a key sequence in which the women, one by one, step forward and each go through the same seemingly spontaneous, intimate gestures. Each starts by sweeping the hair back out of her eyes, looks directly at the audience then turns impulsively away (one shyly, one angrily, one nervously). Then she gently drags down the shoulder of her T-shirt to reveal a bare shoulder, and folds her arms. Then, a moment later she abruptly (one shyly, one angrily, one nervously)[41] covers it up again, turns away and rejoins the unison swaying and turning sequence that the other three have gone on performing behind her. When each soloist looks at the audience, she seems to be exhibiting herself to them and exploiting precisely the sort of seductive presence that Rainer had rejected in *Trio A*. However, their knowing looks at one another in the chair section and their coy, bold, or nervous glances toward the audience in the standing section each in different ways suggest that, although the dancers are conforming to their script, there may be some unfaithfulness in the way they are doing it. Their complicity with each other and with the audience suggests a shared awareness of an excess or supplement that troubles and disturbs the normative ideologies with which their performance seems otherwise to comply.

In 1985, a few days after I saw a performance of *Rosas Danst Rosas* in Montreal, I was briefly introduced to de Keersmaeker. I was struck at the time by the difference between the intense, serious choreographer and the seemingly younger and less thoughtful female persona she had presented on stage. Both *Rosas Danst Rosas* and *Café Müller* use a theatrical tradition within which fictional roles are performed even as they attempt to deconstruct the conventions and traditions through which such roles can be represented. Rainer seemed in the 1960s to believe she could free herself and her dancers from the normative ideologies that underpinned these conventions and traditions. With *Trio A* she tried to create a performance context in which dancers could be themselves and present the enduring reality of their bodies. The performance that she believes came closest to this was *Convalescent Dance* (1967) a solo version she performed at an antiwar event while recovering from a serious operation and thus least capable of projecting any seductive presence.

These radical attempts to deconstruct performative presence that developed from initial experiments within Judson Dance Theater were largely forgotten by subsequent generations of dance artists in the Unites States (Rainer herself abandoning choreography for filmmaking in the early 1970s). In the 1990s Quattuor Albrecht Knust performed what Christophe Wavelet insists were interpretations and not reconstructions of Rainer's *Continuous Process Altered Daily* (1970) and Steve Paxton's *Satisfyin' Lover* (1967). These productions involved many of the younger European dance artists who have begun to explore similar deconstructive choreographic and performative strategies. A discussion of this new work is beyond the scope of the present essay, so I shall merely note here the difference between the seriousness of Rainer's project in the 1960s (partly due to its relation to the antiwar movement and other radical political projects) and the more ironic playfulness of a piece like Jérôme Bel's *Xavier LeRoy*. Despite the choreographic credit, this piece was actually choreographed by LeRoy and consists of repetitions of sequences of task-based and pedestrian movement performed by a blonde-wigged figure—each sequence starting and finishing behind a movable screen midstage. The piece gently teases the audience about the quality of their attention when it reveals that there is not one but two quite different performers: a taller male and shorter female dancer both wearing identical coats and wigs. Such irony and play creates a knowing complicity between audience and performers, and it is this which also characterized Rainer's *Trio A Pressured*.

Rainer, Paxton, and David Gordon, who first performed *Trio A* at Judson Memorial Church in January 1966 each remember the concert as a most dispiriting occasion. The audience was highly unsympathetic and some even walked out—which, because of the way the seating was arranged, necessitated crossing the space in which the dancers were performing.[42] The audience who had crammed themselves into Judson Memorial Church on October 4, 1999, for the program *Trio A Pressured* were, of course, highly reverential about the occasion of Rainer's return to dance after more than twenty-five years as a film director and about the opportunity to see her most famous piece in the same venue in which it had first been performed.

The section that elicited the most positive response was a new duet version for Rainer and Colin Beatty. Rainer was a rather gaunt, bespectacled figure; a breast cancer survivor (she reveals her mastectomy scar in her

1996 film *MURDER and murder*), she had already danced *Trio A* twice that evening in different sections. Those who had been unfamiliar with the piece—either from previous performances or from video versions— were by now becoming familiar with her deliberately flattened presence on stage and with the piece's minimalist vocabulary and style. This new duet gave a twist to the way the dancer's gaze is choreographed so as to avoid making eye contact with the audience. Beatty was not a trained dancer but a filmmaker. His task was to move around Rainer so that he was always making eye contact with her wherever the twists and turns of *Trio A* directed her gaze. With a fine sense of comic timing he would lie down and look up with nerdish intensity from just the point that she was about to look down on. Then, picking himself up and circling rapidly round her in one direction while she herself turned in the other, he would again stop and once more meet her gaze. Even when she stared up at the ceiling, he was there, jumping up in front of her. His role thus put pressure on and drew the audience's attention toward her attempts to minimize her presence. By doing so, this duet created a knowing, complicitous relationship between audience and performer about the particular rules of this game.

Earlier in this essay I offered a provisional definition of live performance as a situation that enables a collective and reflexive awareness to develop between audience and performers. Rainer was one of the first to demonstrate that this relationship need not be based on the seductive presence created by the dancer's pleasure in exhibiting her- or himself but through a conceptual appreciation of the finite materiality of the dancing body. Bausch and de Keersmaeker showed that revealing the process of history's destruction of the body exposes the limits of representation and representability. As we watched Rainer discover Beatty again and again looking back at her from all the previously empty spaces toward which she directed her gaze, Beatty was like a hyphen connecting us in the audience with Rainer, the performer. It was as if we were acknowledging the extent to which we cannot escape being seduced by Rainer's presence, however much she tries to avoid seducing us. Dancers and audiences are always already implicated in the power they may seek to oppose. This complicitous understanding nevertheless opens up the discourse of theater dance and allows new kinds of presences to become perceptible, presences that exceed the literal meaning of the acts that performatively create them.

# II || DANCING OTHERING

# 3 || Dance and Its Others

## Theory, State, Nation, and Socialism

A formal performance event is supposed to hold a mirror up to life, its "double." The audience for a given performance, however, is not simply viewing some other experience, but using the occasion of the event to look at itself. Attending to the way in which life is represented is also the role of theory, which is, in this regard, the other double to live performance, the reflective activity that occurs offstage. As means of reflection, both performance and theory operate to produce certain self-understandings, or concepts of identity based upon a situation of seeing some other.

If performance not only produces images of life, but acts as the very mirror through which we reflect on life, then it is possible to study not only certain depictions of the world, but how the world is depicted. Hence, the shifting place of performance in the world can help us understand how the very conditions for theoretical reflection are produced. And yet, for many who take reflecting upon the world as their vocation, it is precisely the stability of the means for representing the world that has been called into question.

At the same time, it is increasingly common to hear that the world as we have known it has entered an epochal crisis, a dizzying turn of events that disorients all efforts at understanding, subverts critical reflection and oppositional intervention.[1] From this perspective it is far from clear whether the world, the means of representing it, or the relation between the two, is in crisis. Each proclamation of crisis seems to produce a certain amnesia as to all those that have come before, allowing the claim to appear fresh and compelling. While this crisis of the world and our place within it has been variously described, an understanding of what analytic means we use to produce that description is much more elusive. That understanding is what I pursue here. I shall employ performance in general and some recent U.S. dance examples in particular, as an analytic device that allows us to imagine the conditions for producing a crisis of identity; that is, a generalized doubt as to particular conditions of possibility. As the imperial presence of the moment, the United States is as prone to treat itself as a model of what state and nation should be as it is uneasy with self-ascribed crisis. The concrete particular bears a reflection of its own idealization. The most distant double to a United States in trouble is less the end of state and nation per se, than the appearance of its own impossible other: socialism. In what follows, I shall seek to construct this hall of mirrors in which objects are both elusive and closer than they appear.

Performance becomes live through the encounter of two immediate presences that depend upon each other. An idea is borne on stage through an elaborate series of preparations from which technical training and rehearsal of performers emerge. Equally elaborate are the processes that orient people so that they will come to the event, a mobilization of resources, the gathering of a public faculty with the express purpose of taking something in. This something is a determinate practice that unfolds live not only for but through that public act of attendance. Dance is arguably the most particularized version of this encounter of action and reflection. The dance as such is actualized through that encounter in a way that makes the codependence and copresence of both terms most evident. If the crisis of social thought results from the disaggregation of reflection and its object, dance performance models a situation where theory and practice are mutually insinuated in time and space. Dance is an artistic practice where time and space are expressly generated in the course of performance and not simply an activity that passes through an already given spatiotemporal medium. Dancing bodies reference a social kinesthetic, a sentient apprehension of movement and a sense of possibility as to where motion can lead us, that amounts to a material amalgamation of thinking and doing as world-making activity.

If part of what is considered crisis entails an ambiguity as to the attitude of representation to reference, for dance this instability of meaning and thing, of movement's significance and its animating motion, is a fundamental feature of dance's own specificity. Whereas theater can be scripted and music scored, lending some credence to a separation of sign and referent in these performance idioms, choreography is most commonly realized only in and as dance. If musical composition appears legible through a score, choreography achieves inscription through the activity of dancing. In this regard, representation and reference are made one, as are signifying narrative and non-narrative motional expression. Stories can be told about dances just as much as dances can tell stories. In either case, the agency of telling, what moves the tale itself, is palpably on display in dance performance. The capacity to move an idea in a particular direction through the acquired prowess of bodies in action, is what is meant by social kinesthetic. Without doubt, these abstract comparisons confine music and dance to examples where literacy is already separate from practice. There are many kinds of improvised or nonliterate instances of performance where the distinction made here would not arise, just as there are countless dances that do not take place through proscenium conventions.

It is also the case, however, that not all articulations of theory and practice suffer the kind of separation in concept that would make them seem to be in crisis. For this reason, examples of concert dance rather than popular idioms will be the focus here, insofar as the former share a certain formation with the traditions of theoretical reflection under such strain at present. Public funding for the arts in the United States was never particularly robust. Yet in the 1980s, defunding the arts was justified on the basis of aesthetic insufficiency just as cuts in social expenditure were attributed to the moral turpitude of the underprivileged—both signs of a decadent socialism in need of excision from the body politic. This same historical conjuncture confronts all who would recognize themselves through that more general loss with a sense of crisis. With a sober historical sense, it may be difficult to locate a moment when one could not hear cries of a world in crisis, or of the insufficiency of critical and creative responses to ameliorate the pain of a world that changes by tearing at itself. The sense of perpetual crisis is not inconsistent with a modernist optic in which the ceaseless passage of the "just now" (the root of the term *modern*), requires killing the present to make room for the future. Of late, however, certain strands of critical thought have proposed something quite different: that the most comprehensive means to represent a world transformed are no longer available to us. By blurring the boundary between life and its representation, which includes both theory and art, the ability of the latter to imagine the entirety of the life process has been compromised.

This formulation is used, most famously by Jean-François Lyotard in *The Postmodern Condition,* to postulate a break with modernity's incessant forward march, and the means of grasping this societal movement as a whole—what he refers to as the collapse of grand narratives.[2] While Lyotard's formulation has much to teach, one thing we cannot learn from the absoluteness of its pronouncement, is that so-called grand narratives are dead; his account of their fall assumes an outlook still grander, more universal in its sweep, than those it would presumably replace. Clearly his is not a *petit récit,* but a narrative of the relation among all conceivable narratives, in short, a metanarrative. That the critique of metanarratives also produces one, is a problem only if this result is elided, for then theory abdicates responsibility for the very grounds from which it springs. It fol-

lows, that the exclusions from present conditions for producing knowledge that Lyotard suggests, are less on epistemological grounds than political ones. In this case, both dance and socialism would be eclipsed by
other language games that allow no less for the play of identity and difference.

While it is possible to accept Lyotard's proposal that the very context
for producing our self-understanding has been reconfigured, I want to
problematize some of the more specific inferences that might be drawn
from his undeclared universalization of the newborn conditions of the
contemporary. In particular, I wish to counter the twinned claims that the
aesthetic impulse for live performance (here instanced as dance) is in crisis and the social base for socialism has disappeared. Live performance
and socialism can be paired as remnants of a past that we have now finally broken from. While such claims often circulate without benefit of
comprehensive evidence, the acceptance of a general malady can rest
upon recognition of a few symptoms. On the performance front, serious
drama has gone missing from Broadway stages. A poignant sign in dance
was the appearance of the Martha Graham Company in the Brooklyn
Academy of Music's self-proclaimed cutting-edge series The Next Wave.
The Graham Company premiered after the choreographer was deceased,
a rightful honor to a great figure that also showed up the absence of suit-
able successors. What had been proclaimed a dance boom in the 1970s
was, with equal confidence, said to have met its demise in the mid-eighties
(along with "declining standards of American literacy"). Dance was rendered a "respectable form of anti-intellectualism," a victim of its own
success or excess.[3] In politics, the death of socialism is typically pinned to
the demise of governments and to one interstate alliance, that of the So-
viet bloc. The representativity of these symptoms for the wholesale break
or elimination of possibility and actuality that they proclaim is taken as
self-evident. But the place from which this rupture has been declared has
itself eluded theorization. If we include the place from which we theorize
into our pronouncements about the world, what emerges is less an end to
history and its representations as they have been known, than a crisis of
the very terms of evaluation of our changing world. To put the problem
differently, how do we recognize what we desire when the very grounds
upon which we make our observations are themselves shifting? The temptation is to displace the crisis onto the object of our attentions, rather
than reflecting back upon what produces our own vision.

For the purposes of reimagining the grounds upon which socialism
continues to develop, I attach its fate to that of the particularized grounds
of dance performance, locating in the latter and its other, the means for

tracing the contours of society's own presence. Before moving to some dance examples, I make some general observations about the political significance of Augusto Boal's account of Aristotelian tragedy (in his *Theater of the Oppressed*).[4] This account will be contrasted to a different conception of identity formation, Jean Baudrillard's concept of simulacra.[5] I shall employ these contrasted types to retell the now familiar tale of modernity's breakup in a different key, which will then be redeployed in the service of thinking through the identity crisis of dance's aesthetic and socialism's politic.

## Mimesis and Simulacra

For Boal in his formulation of Aristotelian tragedy, attending the performance extracts a high price: obedience to the law of state, or death. It could be said that such coercive means lie at the very heart of the formation of the state and its principal accomplishment, the sovereign subject. Lacking any precise ethnological evidence, Greek tragedy can stand in the modern imagination as a myth of origins of the body politic gathered and held firm in the amphitheater where the self-before-the-law is forged against the threat of death. It is against this threat of death alone that the order of society and the authority of the state is secured. The sacrifice of the one stands in for the unity of the many.

The mimetic function of art is a corrective one. The identity produced in the amphitheater where art yields a better version of life, is to be imitative of the ideal and not the actuality. Flaws found in the nature (of humans) can be brought in line with the ideal, assuming that those ideals (of state) can be embodied in human form. This is the protagonistic function, that establishes the principal actor as a mirror in which the public sees itself. The attention to this ideal reflection of self allows the disparity with the ideal to be revealed, in the form of a change of fate that reveals the character's own internal flaw. The correction of the flaw is not accomplished by the character's own self-transformation, but by a change in the plot, which assumes that the same attention that was applied to the protagonist now adheres to the means of dramatic narrative itself.

What prompts this shift from the performance's action to its law, is the death of the protagonist, an occurrence meant to leave the public with a clear choice: identify with the state or with the object of its punishment, the outlawed other. Presumably, if this identity shift can occur once, it can occur again in a different direction, and therefore the state must be vigilant in the continuity of its performance offerings. Whatever challenges to their identity citizens may experience, they must return to the theater to experience the production of their own true self. This compulsion to gather the public body, which state theatrics insist upon, renders art less the means of transcendence than the occasion for the desire to transcend the errant corpse that thought the stage his own. Under these conditions, avoiding death becomes identical with the freedom the state grants its citizens. The theater represents the otherwise implicit state contract, based in coercive power, that constitutes citizenship.

Tragedy reaches its apotheosis in dance at a moment when the state is withdrawing from the kind of formal sponsorship of performance associated with the Greeks (at the same time the powers of state are becoming more diffuse in society). As Susan L. Foster astutely observes, the romantic story ballets of the mid-nineteenth century themselves constituted a transition from an eighteenth century ballet conception of classic Greek translation of language into physical gesture. The romantic ballets eschewed gestural steps for movement-driven narrative, to which they become enslaved.[6] Dancing becomes the agency of tragic narrative, which does the state's cathartic bidding.

Most renowned of these ballets are Filippo Taglioni's *La Sylphide* (1832), and *Giselle, ou les Wilis,* conceived by Théophile Gautier (1841). In *La Sylphide,* the groom's impossible desire for a phantasmic sylph interrupts his own wedding celebration and culminates in the death of what he longs for. Giselle makes use of the legendary figure of the wili, a woman who dies on the eve of a wedding and then forever seeks out men to woo them into a dance literally to the death. Giselle is caught in a love triangle: one man adores her but is spurned; the other she loves but considers herself unworthy because he is of noble rank. The revelation of this Duke's true identity leads Giselle to excessive dance and her own demise. Giselle is taken up by the wilis who command her to entrance the Duke. He is saved ultimately by the dawn's light, which removes the wilis' powers; crestfallen, he returns to his legally betrothed. These women have the power to draw on the weakness of men in a situation where dance itself is taken to be that power. But the power is unsustainable in its own terms and allows the men to return to the bonds that assure the marriage of property and propriety.

Dancerly mimesis produces on its own scenographic grounds an other who masks the very alterity between the state law and the sovereign people. While in the Greek tragic form, the protagonist must die, a male public can identify with a survivor subordinate to the dance but relieved to leave its pleasures and return to normalcy, an enactment of free will without apparent coercive state action. But not all of life is a stage; in this case, there is life beyond the scene that also acts as its double. If dance is the act of pure production, of art, then its other is that which imitates art without the latter's originating referent. Dance is the consummate version of sheer self-production, an originary body of movement that drives and dies within the space of performance. This is the now familiar modernist juxtaposition between art and popular culture, between the model that fails in its realization, and the modeling that succeeds only in replicating its own activity. Art must be repeated because it falls short of the ideal but nonetheless produces an origin, an apparent singularity as its source. Popular culture exists as sheer mediation, it comes into being already en masse, and can only replicate itself as such.

This incessant copying without reference to an orienting value or origin, Baudrillard termed the *simulacra*. The dizzying equalization that ensues when all images are offered up in seamless spectacle, affects a reverie of consumption. In contrast to the grip that performance holds on the body politic, this spectacular consumption has the effect of dispersing individuals, each isolated by the distance obtained toward what they gaze upon. This assumes that unlike the tragic identification with the protagonistic subject, replicative consumption only demands a visual fixity upon the object.

Within the amphitheater, the state makes its presence felt as patron, placing its own representatives in the front seats between the players and the public. On the other hand, with marketized consumption that state is nothing more than an absent presence, a shadow that one can never capture as one shifts glances toward a new horizon of consumables. With the death of the protagonist, one feels exposed for the prior misidentification that is, with the tragic ending, purged through catharsis. But in the mediated society of the spectacle, one watches anonymously but constantly for that image which might finally give place to identity. This process of watching life go by outside oneself, means that the virtual life of the spectacle looks back, casting judgment upon the onlooker as a negative reference to what he or she lacks. One looks in the mediated mirror to see oneself, but the image is constantly changing and the self is reflected back as other, less a determinant content than an approach to life where the gaze is turned back on the self.

The other to spectacle is autosurveillance, treating watching oneself watching as a form of freedom; this watching, unlike the grateful escape from the claws of death, does not name a coercive power whose presence one is never allowed to forget, so much as the very figure of consent. Consent, the fundamental ingredient to the Gramscian formulation of hegemony, is the means to organize the terms of opposition. Consent is not an agreement to be constructed out of thin air; it requires the material basis to generate a framework of participation within a given terrain of dominance.

Put in simpler terms, the consent that issues from hegemony could be understood as the power to say yes. Such power is not simply held by the state to disburse as social expenditure (a simple formula would be tax revenues spent on public institutions to assimilate the demands of social movements), but ceded to its citizen-consumers. When stably installed in the body politic, consent grants the impression that one can always say yes to oneself. The urge to gather, to assemble that the coercive state drew its power from is thereby repressed as consumption appears as a purely individual decision. Accordingly, one individual, no matter how close to another, could never offer interference with a consumption decision because each relation of viewer to viewed assumes mutual exteriority.

As Nicos Poulantzas understands it, the capitalist state is active in generating a homogeneous space of monads within which each individual body can assume its particular difference.[7] To the extent that the powers of the simulacra hold, what is in actuality an entire edifice of social reproduction winds up generating a dispersion of individuated subjects through the material fabric of consent. Here too, dance is helpful in making this process legible. Contact improvisation can be viewed as a subversion of narrative to social kinesthetic and therefore disruptive to the cathartic function that invests performance with an operation of the state. On the other hand, contact also allows one to see choice in the making as a property attributed to individuated bodies that enter into relations of codependence to create shared movement.[8]

*The Nation Unbound*

The most dramatic effect of the twin processes of mimesis and simulacra is to maintain the web of dualisms that underwrite modernity in relations of mutual exteriority. The list could be extended indefinitely but the key terms of opposition could be summarized as follows: coercion and consent, art and popular culture, state and civil society, citizen and subject, production and consumption, politics and economics, public and private, mind and body. While modern political theory has occupied itself with accounting for the content of each of these conceptual couples, more recently critical analysis has turned its attention to what sustains the structure of binary coupling itself.

Rather than rehearsing this critique, developed most thoroughly under the rubric of deconstruction, I contextualize the criticism in social and historical terms that return us to the politics of theory and its evaluative criteria. In other words, rather than simply noting that the couples named above are arbitrary and ultimately not logically sustainable—in which case theory has suddenly discovered a world that was unknown to itself—it makes more sense to inquire into the conditions that had sustained that particular logic that by changing now renders what was once so thoroughly taken for granted as now being merely arbitrary.

Hence, it is the very ground that had sustained the opposition between what had hitherto appeared as distinct domains that now begins to erode. These grounds are not the actual terrain upon which dance is produced or spectacle consumed but rather the ideological means through which identity is framed and constituted. Hence it is not dance that comes to an end but certain of its ideological investments and political location. And just what had these entailed? The opposition between mimesis and simulacra, and all that follows from it, presupposes a certain spatial relation that is mapped onto the imaginary geography of the nation-state. What had sustained this dual process of identity and alterity was rooted in the connection between state and society moored to the national scene. As has now been widely discussed under the notion of globalization, the scale and dynamics of economic transactions are increasingly incommensurable with the political units through which they had once been organized. This does not mean that nation-states as such disappear, but that the investment between citizen and state is displaced.[9]

The world divided into nation-states is a legacy bequeathed by colonialism. The putative political equality of sovereign nations permitted relations of uneven exchange to inhere. Within the nation, citizens could be adhered to the political will of the state, and subjects could fix their gaze upon the objects that passed through the national scene. Needless to say, the universalism of such assertions, and of the very juxtaposition between the mimetic citizen and the subject of simulacra, conceals a double exclusion, of the Third World by the first, and of all those not identified by the ideal citizen-subject, particularly along lines of race, class, gender, and sexuality. These last four categories become reconsolidated along the lines of freedom, which allocate persons to mimic the movements of capital and assign places at performances and access to the market.

Clearly, the amphitheater gathered citizens to the exclusion of those who were not, and the market logic of consumptive spectacle prices people away or omits their particular subjectivity. The simulacra can be quite forgiving; one only need be able to watch to participate. Yet the whole question of what one looks for and how one sees is precisely what cannot be assumed as a universal gaze. It is within the power of the universalizing logic to dismiss all departures from the law of the gaze as irrational and therefore irrelevant to the proper organization of society.

The detachment of the state from its commitment to develop the conditions of society for populations defined by its boundaries marks the end of neither coercion nor consent, merely the reorientation of their imaginary topography. The flight of capital from its historic national bases does not eradicate the physical existence of nations; it does, however, attack the state's commitment to portraying itself as the guardian of the national universal. As such, the present critique of universalism is less the discovery of others who were always already there than a challenge to the ability of the state to monopolize the recognition of identity claims.

As government withdrawal from arts sponsorship (what had always been minimal funding aimed at legitimation) in the United States indicates, the state now seems to have less interest in forcing belief upon those in the amphitheater—or even getting people into it.[10] The neoliberal state's language of deregulation, of downsizing, of governmental self-dissolution, not only facilitates the movement of capital away from its prior national commitments; it leaves dance and its double to stake out their own terms of identification. Here the movement of capital must be appreciated as the very basis for the configuration of society: in its movement, its efforts at accumulation, ever emergent contours of human association (socialization), are constituted. Capital, therefore, is never simply an economic relation, but the representation and the effect of the social forces that it sets—and that have set it—in motion. This motion is described by Marx as the revolutionary process inherent to capitalism that transgresses hitherto existing boundaries and means of association in order to constitute new ones.[11] Thus, the principle of socialization as the unwelcome partner of accumulation never abates, but its actual material conditions are constantly being reinscribed. This context is the most robust for appreciating the nation unbound in the face of globalization, a political economy that flees its own prior successes.

The tragic catharsis has moved to the television screen where the murder of others is enacted on the nightly news. As spectacle, public political performances increasingly assume a comic role aimed more at producing disgust and lack of interest than dread in the grip of the state, which even as a form of coercion demands more reciprocity than the state seems willing to offer. Coercion itself, meanwhile leaves the stage and enters civil society more broadly, as the exsanguinating machinations of state foment a generalized violence misrecognized as crime. It is worth exercising some restraint, however, in how far to go with such sweeping pronouncements so that what emerges from these ashes is not obscured by the dust left by capital's hoofprints.

Acknowledging that all is not well when the state aids the abandonment of the national scene, it is nonetheless helpful to reflect upon what possibilities are opened up when the wall between mimesis and simulacra is left to crumble. While the state had maintained an interest in a certain institutional separation between the identification with its powers of coercion and consent, the great divide that had bounded the political itself dissolves in tandem with the effacement of the nation as a societal boundary. It is because politics is unbounded, relative to its prior conditions, that it is crucial now to check the urge to apply all energies toward an inventory of what has been lost; rather, we must apportion some critical attention to what might be gained.

## Proliferations of Dance and Socialism

Every proclamation of crisis presupposes some normative condition of evaluation from which present circumstances are said to have departed. The crisis of identity for dance and socialism does mark a certain loss of reference for how their respective historical forms might have been recognized. Yet with the nation-state unbound it is the fixity of reference that has been lost rather than the means for producing identity per se. The burden of such productions now becomes, By whom or what are they authorized? What powers do they promote? What principle of association do they assume?

One particular episode of a dance and its critical reception is most instructive here, appearing after a decade of attacks of aesthetic decay. It is unusual for a contemporary concert dance to garner attention beyond the pages of a dance review. The 1994 choreography by Bill T. Jones *Still/Here* was an exception. The reviewer for the *New Yorker*, Arlene Croce, explained that she refused to view the dance because she felt "excluded by reason of its express intentions," which she termed "victim art." Her accusation was that the piece transgressed the codes of representation by incorporating the really dying. Tragedy was literal and no catharsis would be possible. Ironically, she missed a work that exuberantly danced against death. She traces the "mass delusion" of victim art to the 1960s, which led to art of the 1980s being held hostage to "community." By addressing the critical reception of his work choreographically, Croce hears Jones silence her: "Jones' message was clear. . . . No back talk!" The loss of monopoly over who speaks and who is spoken for "[has] effectively disarmed criticism."[12]

The critic's anxiety at being rendered unnecessary is transferred into a pronouncement on the death of dance for its failure to separate itself from its referent. The critic withholds the gaze and the critical reception of the work literally proliferates in a whole series of essays and articles in major print media—which often mirrored Croce in their defense of the work's experiential reference beyond the stage. The dance uses community members discussing death cathartically, and the absent choreographer Jones on a television screen mimetically. It is also linked to the narrative of the AIDS crisis (the disease that felled Arnie Zane, Jones's partner) such that the dance is explicitly linked to external worldly reference. The dancing itself, however, is anything but somber and assembles a global array of movement protocols that include capoeira, martial arts, street dance, as well as improvisationally based concert forms.

An earlier work, *Last Supper at Uncle Tom's Cabin / The Promised Land* (1990) employed onstage nudity that drew ire and fire from government-based funders; thus Jones's choreography is already connected with a contestation (without denial) of its relation to the state. As a single dance, *Still/Here* is hardly capable of undoing the conventions of mimesis and simulacra, but it does operate against the divide that sustains them. It is a dance against death in the face of death; it also defies the logic of transference leading to closure in the way it marshals dance to produce a desire for further dancing as well as a kinesthetic of self-representation, of movers who speak for themselves, and are, in that sense, anything but victims. Hence, rather than presenting a crisis for dance, a stilling of life in the fixity of death onstage, *Still/Here* refused the representational allusion of its title to draw upon a capacity to make the movement of life excessive in a manner that spills out beyond its frame. The crisis of critical perspective blames the dance it cannot see for its own loss of self-reference.

From one point of view, it could be said that the effacement of the boundary between mimesis and simulacra—or the theatricalization of daily life—signals the demise of live performance as an autonomous domain of activity. Concert dance is the most economically fragile and publicly marginal of the performing arts. Corollary to this, the ever more tremulous quality of national borders as containing the largest unit of societal transactions, has been applied selectively to account for the collapse of socialism in a national frame. While the failure of boundaries does tend to emit what they had once contained, what now circulates in the name of theater and socialism still depends on the reference (both historical and societal) from which it departs. The loss of fixed reference therefore does not assume the disappearance of all historical referents; quite the contrary, the conditions for reinvoking them are only exacerbated.

Typically this reinvoking takes the form of a negative comparison. Politics as mere theatrical performance without substance. Economic policy that cannot sufficiently rid itself of its socialist specters. But perhaps such negative references are not merely rhetorical. They refer to things that reappear despite their stated death, and to have effects, without naming any identifiable agency. The collision of forces on a global scale that brings together the world's peoples and foregrounds their very conditions of production and reproduction, identification and differentiation, returns the question of society and its order to what might simply be considered the newly expanded dominion of capital. Globalization refers then not only to the subordination of national populations to the prerogatives of capital's transnational movement, but also to the socialization of collective identities, and the explicit constitution of society itself in global terms.

Despite attacks on its institutional edifice and the fiscal immiseration of its public, dance persists. By the late 1990s, more people were employed as dancers in the United States and fewer were registered as unemployed.[13] But as the state relinquishes its hold on dance, dance itself becomes increasingly responsible for offering up its own demand, not by finally conquering market discipline, but by continuing as a site of self-recognition. The collective mimetic faculty assembled in performance does not cease as the state invests in other coercive enterprises. Dance itself, however, is now in a position to copy what had once belonged to the state, the power to give authority to a law of recognition like citizenship.

The mutual insinuation in a body politic that dance still occasions addresses less a national-state contract than a citizenship that aspires to global participation, even when this impulse continues to bear a national brand. It could be said that even as the tragic poetics continues to be performed on stages, neither the initial intensity of identification with the protagonist nor the departing catharsis from that other, bear the same reference. For a public in which difference and transgression are now seen as the condition for having an identity, the Aristotelian tragedy's protagonistic role cannot be seen as eliciting the same empathic response. Further, if state performances themselves are an object of derision that can occasion an escape to the dance or other performances, then relief at surviving the death of the protagonist can hardly secure further allegiance to a state that seems incapable of surviving itself.

Granted, the state's mockery of its own former universalist pretensions can offer a populist face to neoliberal policies that claim, however disingenuously, that populations are now free of its authority. But to the extent that the state now claims to have released the citizenry from its universalizing hold, dance remains a place where the values of self-mastery before the law meet a certain measure of doubt. Dance underscores this doubt by showing what lies beyond narrative regulation. Identification can be sought through the compassion of moving bodies, but it is less clear that a public can come away with a named identity. Identity is no longer an investment that can be deposited with the state's powers of recognition, and citizenship can no longer be conferred but must be generated by the very acts of assembly and association that live performance provokes.

While such a situation does not assure that the identities formed by attending to dance will reflect a demand for global participation, the theatrical locale, no longer held in place by the state, can now pursue such affiliations. The context for these linkages is rendered more concrete by the specific impact of globalization in the circuits of festivals, tours, and the transnational careers of dancers and choreographers. In each case, the dance-set-in-motion may retain its national reference at the same time that it is an emission of the nation. Those who tour the world serve not simply as national emissaries, but living proof that the national idea can circulate where it is absent. The theatricalization of this process indicates that *nation* is no longer simply a territorial referent, of people bound to place, but rather of publics affiliated with an idea of association, an identification better captured by the term *society*.

Dance still gives pause to these global motions while presupposing that they have taken place. By means of performance, diverse publics gather, separated only by what brings them in touch with one another—the activity that passes behind the lifted curtain while a certain mass can only know itself in the anonymity of darkness. That dance can still mediate such diversity in contact, accounts in no small measure for its persistence under conditions whose strict economy might call for its certain demise.

The persistence of dance beyond its coercive instrumentality, and unmoored from its state identification, is suggestive of certain avenues for the development of socialism as well. The dance in question is not free from the constraints of the market, any more than socialist nation-states had been, nor is it free to give up the battle for subvention or support of infrastructure that can seek no other address but that of the state. While national states may be abdicating their monopolies over what recognizes and authorizes identification, they remain pivotal to the maintenance of the global political economy (to say nothing of the centers of performance activity). But the very suffusion of the market everywhere also means that markets policed by states can no longer serve as the horizon of progress. Neither can they serve as the rationalizing standard that every human exchange must attain.

The development of the market has underdeveloped much but its forces have still brought together a common reference for reflecting difference; that is, the market is also a medium of socialization. That dance, and socialism more broadly, retain a commodity aspect, does not mean that they are reducible to it. The present circumstance of some dance in the United States is to foreground association to reflect on the identity of gathered publics. This reflection might be taken as the very question posed by the specter and interest in socialism today in the face of a neoliberal-market usurpation of historical logic. As a basis of political affiliation and orientation, socialism poses the question: How do we recognize society (or more specifically, our expanding capacity to identify with it)?

This problem is rendered all the more complex because the state now appears as that other mimetic faculty that must perform its own legitimacy in contention with a global circulation of identities that all participate in the production of what had once been fixed by the national citizen-subject. Just what replaces the old means of recognition in this drama of perpetual motion can make what is excessive—human associations and their attendant identifications—appear scarce, at least in form. If the expectation remains that identity must be fixed by a singularity, then public gatherings of any sort, whether face-to-face, or linked by local attendance at a shared event or predicament, will always seem deficient and generate reports of a missing person (or people), or even a dance that refuses to be death even as it speaks with and of the dying.

At the same time, however, the conditions, the terms, the occasions, thematics, interests—in short, the politics of association and affiliation— have only been exacerbated, and this swelling of the desire for the social must now be recognized as fundamental to socialism itself. These emergent politics, like those confined to matters of citizenship before them, have not yet been formalized in a polity. That the identification of all this politics seems so excessive to those who had once expressed such resentment toward revolution, suggests a certain equivalence that can be ascribed to movements which recognize that the national state, while still unavoidable, is no longer the prize that it once was. To affiliate these politics with socialism may seem to come too early or too late, if the idea of socialism remains tied to a fixed social base. But if the history of socialism is internal to and set in motion by capitalism, then its own social bases will necessarily change with its context.

What to look out for in the present that continues to gesture toward socialism requires an eye practiced in noticing what is moving in the darkness around it as well as what acts in full illumination. If it is the case that what had separated darkness and light, mimesis and simulacra, has given way, where we sit and what we see can increasingly take account of each other. The irony of watching that which has no pretension to truth induces the self-consciousness of a world of make-believe that must itself be framed by the user. What had seemed the simulacra's absolute relativism of the gaze now forces upon the viewer the question of self-evaluation. This is the very criterion of which self will be projected upon the screen of identification. Choice in this regard is no longer free-floating but becomes reattached to the process of self-recognition in the very process of attending to acts of identification as work done together—precisely what an audience provides.

With dance that audience is particularized and made to recognize that whatever efficacy there will be of the moment is contingent upon seizing those resources mobilized to make for public assembly, the diffuse energies given momentary focus through performance. Whatever the choreographic idea is to be, it is unrealizable without this critical presence; in that sense the critic is more at risk of being rendered incidental in dance than in other media. The fragility of dance as a minor cultural practice is also itself a resource. What gets concentrated onstage as an apparent purity of movement is an abstraction of techniques and kinesthetic sensibilities from an entire historical corporality. While concert dance in the modernist tradition is sequestered within the world of art, it is linked increasingly to what would conventionally be seen as outside the aesthetic domain. The rubrics of risk, of in-your-face performance styles, strip away the ethereality of the sylph without draining away the seductive powers of the wili to tempt death in pursuit of desire. The resources needed for bodies to gather and make use of themselves as ends-in-themselves winds up being what is exchanged in the performative economy of dance.

Labor as sheer physical capacity without ends, as sensuous activity that produces itself, refigures the meaning of movement serving its own ends at a time when technical prowess appears to subordinate all means to a dizzying spectacle. In the face of an all-consuming market rationality, a movement that has no other purpose than to allow people to gather to reflect on what they can be together is perhaps the supreme figure of an ongoing desire for socialism. Desire, while always occasioned in the face of certain fixities and constraints, bears a measure of transcendence. The desire for socialism in the United States, grounded in particularities of practice and location, nonetheless produces a generalized concept of dance and the state.

It has become difficult to deny that the world's peoples, however separated, know that they face the struggle for survival, against repression, and abandonment of their collective wealth. Perhaps it will become easier to recognize the shared predicament of making their disparate identities together, by common means. For this last identification with others suggests as well that it is a process of producing not only selves, but society—a matter that lies at the heart of both dance (that makes itself out of those who gather for it) and the socialist project.

# 4 || The Black Beat Made Visible

## Hip Hop Dance and Body Power

Outside tight communities of dancers, the dancing black body routinely arouses extraordinary wariness and fascination. What drives the movements? How are similar dances known so thoroughly by dancers who have never met; who have had no cause to collaborate? How is the body able to so easily contain narratives of transcendence through dances of physical eccentricity? How are stories of sexuality linked to competition revealed in bold assertions of expertise, of resilient virtuosity, in the inscrutable realm of the nonverbal? What is the power of the body in hip hop?

Black social dances[1] contain dual transcripts of "public" and "private" meaning. These transcripts mirror constructions of outwardly entertaining and secretly derisive rhetoric articulated by black cultural theorists including W.E.B. Du Bois, whose 1903 theory of "double consciousness"— articulated as "two souls, two thoughts, two unreconciled strivings . . . in one dark body, whose dogged strength alone keeps it from being torn asunder"—suggests a doubling of desire contained by the tenacity of the black body and released in dance.[2] Black social dances enact this duality in divergent resonances available to dancers and viewers.

Anthropologist Roger Abrahams extends Du Bois's argument to suggest a split along lines of cultural literacy:

Performers in this tradition know that they may be playing to two audiences simultaneously—the black community and the white hipsters or weekend trippers. . . . Black performers constantly recognize that the very performance that is conventional within the black community will be seen as strange, as pleasurably exotic to the hipster. Thus they operate out of a kind of double consciousness, knowing that they are called upon to present an image which will be interpreted as exotic to the outside world and not to the blacks in the audience.[3]

Drawing his argument from an analysis of minstrelsy, Abrahams assumes that the audience for performance by African Americans includes whites who are not conversant with submerged layers of communication. Whether hipsters in the audience "understand" the performance of black social dances interests me less than the presupposition of a doubled functionality encoded within the performance. Does this doubling disappear without a white audience or larger white context? Is Abrahams only talking about performances that include white audiences? Are black social dances designed to be performed *and* watched at once?

Historian Robert Hinton assumes that the dual audience for dancing black bodies stems from the construction of slave society:

Early in the slavery experience, Afro-American dance split into two basic streams. The first stream was the dance that black folk created for themselves during those few precious hours of sacred and secular celebration. This first stream was the more "African," in part because of the movement quality and vocabulary, but also, because the dance was created for the benefit of the dancers. The experience of any observers (the audience) was secondary. The second stream was the dance that black people created for white people. This second stream was more "European," both because of the technique and because the dance was created under differing degrees of duress for the pleasure of the audience. The experience of the performer was secondary.[4]

Labeling the first stream "dance of celebration" and the second stream "dance of performance," Hinton draws an argument that assumes only participants in its first stream, and a politically privileged but culturally illiterate audience in its second stream. According to him the two streams do not meet until after the renaissance of African consciousness, which occurred during the Pan-Africanist movement between the world wars.[5]

In both of these essentialist configurations, "the black community" is assumed to be a coherent group of participants in dance performances holding a largely unmodulated connotation of celebration. Performances viewed by cultural outsiders are likely born of duress and discomfort; ironically, they also provide a largely unmodulated measure of pleasure for an immobile audience. The transcript of protest in social dance remains "private," read and understood only by dancers initiated into black social dance styles. According to these writers, it is only during the twentieth century, amid burgeoning civil rights activism, that the dancing black body is allowed a self-conscious ability to celebrate and protest simultaneously. Only at this historical juncture can an immobile (white) audience adequately comprehend the transcript of protest inscribed within black social dance movement. But for their (black) performers, black social dances are constructed like verbal games of rhetoric such as toasting and signifying, which simultaneously celebrate and criticize. Although an immobile audience viewing hip hop dance forms may still misread movements of personal transcendence as erotic or simply sensational, I think that the palpable presence of physical pleasure, bound up with a racialized cultural history, makes the dances powerfully compelling. This dynamic amalgamation of pleasure and critique form the basis of power present within hip hop dance forms.

All African diaspora dance, including black social dances, may be likened to verbal language most in the dance's conspicuous employment of "call and response" with the body responding to and provoking the voice of the drum. In a *Dance Encyclopedia* entry titled "Primitive African Dance (and Its Influence on the Churches of the South)," choreographer Pearl Primus asserted African orality as a defining feature of dance performance. After conducting research in the early 1940s, Primus wrote of the linguistic features of African diasporic dance and the relationship of dance to drum: "On my trips south of the Mason and Dixon line in 1944 I discovered in the Baptist Churches the voice of the drum—not in any instrument, but in the throat of the preacher."[6] She concludes that in "emotional impact, group reaction, rhythms, tempos, actual steps and the exact precision with which they were done, dance in the Southern Baptist Churches so closely resembles the dance in Africa as to leave no doubt in the mind that the American form emerged from the African."[7] Her essay suggests a triangular configuration of orality, dancer, and drum as guiding precepts of African diaspora dance.

If we can accept that the dance responds to the drum, not solely in a reactive manner, but within a configuration of communicative collaboration, we can understand how dance is performative, mirroring the way in which speech may be equated with action. Dance movements convey speechlike qualities that contain meaning beyond the formal, aesthetic shapes and sequences of movement detailed by the body in motion. African diaspora dance conveys the same sense of performative utterance as those cited by cultural theorist Eve Sedgwick: "[they] do not merely describe, but actually perform the actions they name: 'J'accuse'; 'Be it resolved . . .'; . . . 'I apologize'; 'I dare you.'"[8] Within black social dance constructions, dancing black bodies express actionable assertions.[9]

In general, black expressive cultures value the process of signification over the signified, the performance of spirituality over scriptural exegesis, talking *by* dancing over talking *about* dancing. As of the year 2000, the forms of black expressive culture generating the most scholarly interest are probably gospel music, the performed African American sermon, and hip hop culture (with rap music as its central focus). Within this lineage of orality, the implications of social dance as text forms an important site of entry to understanding black performativity. Following Sedgwick, I define black performativity here to be gestures of black expressive culture, including music and dance, that perform actionable assertions. In terms of black social dance, these performative assertions do not "describe" dancing; rather, they are the physical building blocks of a system of communication we may term *corporeal orature*.

*Corporeal orature* aligns movement with speech to describe the ability of black social dance to incite action. In this articulation, social dance may contain performative gestures that cite contexts beyond the dance. These citations are read and acknowledged by other dancers who respond in kind with actions or decisions about, at least, the efficacy of the dance gesture. Black social dance thrives within a structure of corporeal orature that presumes the possibility of efficacious performative gesture.[10] But black social dance in general, and hip hop dance in particular, resist inscription and interpretation from an exterior, immobile microanalytic perspective. Working from outside the dance accesses only a portion of its communicative ability: its visual effects. Like literary analyses, which cannot contain the physical embodiment of a performative speech act—the sensuality of releasing the action "I apologize" to a lover—theorizing the dance from the eye of an observer sidesteps the dynamism of the body that drives the form. Dance, like music of black expressive culture, can only be partially present here.

Writing about the construction of "funk," cultural theorist Cornel West articulates a linkage between physical ephemerality and corporeality: "This funk is neither a skill nor an idea, not a world view or a stance. Rather, it is an existential capacity to get in touch with forms of kinetic orality and affective physicality acquired by deep entrenchment in—or achieved by pretheoretical styles owing to socialization in—the patterns of Afro-American ways of life and struggle."[11] I take issue with West's argument that black expressive culture can be "pretheoretical" which, to my mind, foregrounds an intellect/practice split. For me, the capacity to embody patterns of black life is simultaneously kinetic and theoretical, and constantly negotiated by a kinetic and intellectual understanding of its formal properties.

The notion of a pretheoretical or entirely experiential understanding of African American culture contributes to the ahistorical, moorless conception of black expressive culture as an inevitable by-product of the Middle Passage.[12] Of course, theory is, and has always been, embedded within practice; on the whole, black expressive culture has been egregiously neglected by theorists. As African art scholar Robert Farris Thompson offers, black expressive culture performance practice accounts for more than fifty percent of American popular music even though African Americans are no more than twelve percent of the population.[13] Acknowledg-

ing and exploring a theoretical dimension to black social dance performance practice might help us understand how these statistics work, and how
black pleasure and black power foster hip hop dance forms.

Black expressive culture incubates social dance forms that speak to
several audiences of American dancers. But dance, especially as a physical component of popular music, is viewed warily by scholars, who often
seem most comfortable discussing lyrics as the literal, explicitly communicative dimension of music. Walter Hughes's essay "In the Empire of the
Beat: Discipline and Disco" attempts a reading of disco music as a form
that "foregrounds the beat, makes it consistent, simple, repetitive," and
is built on "the emptying out of language which parallels the refusal of
narrative structure in the song overall."[14] Hughes looks through the lens
of the white male outsider—a hipster, of sorts—at the process of disco,
and details links between [white] gay culture and black performance
practice contained by disco music.[15] Along the way, he encounters prominent Africanist features of disco music, although he doesn't identify them
as such. Writing about the foregrounding of the drum in the form, he
notes that "disco mystifies its authorial origins, as we see in the obscure
collective names given to disco 'groups' (such as Hughes Corporation,
Machine, or Black Box) or in performers such as the Village People or
Shannon, who are patently the 'creations' of their producers."[16] I argue
that these collective origins emanate from a theoretical/kinetic Africanist assumption that dance music—music that can provoke and sustain
dance—carries performative qualities like those of language. For dancers,
it isn't necessary to seek authorial origins in the use of this performative
language, as in the physical assertion of "I dare you." This language is not
emptied of meaning; on the contrary, it is full of tangible affect. Disco
music provokes and responds to the action of dance. That provocation
and response are neither unmodulated nor pretheoretical.

If conversation occurs between music and its dancers, and between
dancers, the subtleties of that conversation are missed in the separation
of participant and observer. Still, most analyses of black social dance are
designed from the perspective of an immobile observer. This follows the
unfortunate colonialist construction whereby locations of being "within
the dance" or "without it" operate simultaneously and autonomously. A
society in which bodies can be objectified and marked as 'black' is one
comfortable with watching without understanding; it is one used to observing dance without the ability to decode its communicative value. As
we move from inside the dance to the audience, and movements are
viewed without concern for their performative implications, meaning is
indeed emptied out. Subsequent reproduction of the dances by people

looking only from the outside leads to the flat, militaristic repetition commonly viewed in the commercial music video sphere.

## Interrogating Africanisms in Hip Hop Dance

Several authors have articulated an array of formal characteristics common to dances of the African diaspora, most notably Robert F. Thompson, Marshall and Jean Stearns, Delores K. Cayou, Katrina Hazzard-Gordon, Jacqui Malone, and Brenda Dixon Gottschild.[17] The formal qualities of motion perceived vary slightly according to each author, but all build on the categories articulated by Thompson in 1966 to include "the dominance of a percussive concept of performance; multiple meter; apart playing and dancing; call-and-response; and, finally the songs and dances of derision."[18] In 1983 Thompson expanded on these principles slightly, to include an "inner pulse control" and "suspended accentuation patterning," two principles that aid in understanding complex meter and the layering of rhythmic accent central to African diaspora dance and music.[19]

Building on Thompson's work, Gottschild articulates a series of intertextual "processes, tendencies, and attitudes" of Africanist performance practice.[20] Her work explores the intangible essence of performance through concepts that stress its theoretical hallmarks: embracing the conflict ("a precept of contrariety, or an encounter of opposites"); high-affect juxtaposition ("mood, attitude, or movement breaks that omit . . . transitions and connective links"); ephebism ("power, vitality, flexibility, drive, and attack . . . that recognizes feeling as sensation, rather than emotion"); and the aesthetic of the cool ("an attitude . . . that combines composure with vitality").[21]

Taken together, these categories of Africanist tendencies are broad enough to accommodate several generations of music and movement styles, from nineteenth-century plantation dances to twentieth-century hip hop forms. Thompson's principles provide the formalistic "how" of dance practice, drawn from qualities that may be observed by a viewer outside the dance. Gottschild's concepts offer a sense of the conceptual "why" of dance practice, teasing out theoretical underpinnings experienced by dancers. An additional quality identified by Cayou as "functionalism—becoming what you dance—the art of real life" aligns dance movement to personal identity, a maneuver with implications for dancers and audience members.[22] I argue that this quality of black social dance performance underscores all the others. A hallmark of social dance practice in the African diaspora is the communal valuation of the dancer's ability to speak in the imperative through dance movement. Social dance is inevitably tied to the construction of personal identity, by dancers and the participating audiences who observe them.

The most prevalent theoretical assumptions concerning qualities of black social dance derive, in part, from a corpus of literary descriptions created by immobile cultural outsiders fascinated by the mysterious power of black dance. These writings draw a rich portrait of dance's potentially actionable meanings, even when those meanings are consistently misread by [white] audiences. Consider the performance of a dancer thought to be Master Juba, a champion dancer, witnessed by author Charles Dickens in 1842, and chronicled in the author's oft-cited *American Notes*: "He never leaves off making queer faces, and is the delight of all the rest, who grin from ear to ear incessantly."[23]

### Dances of Celebration

Dickens continued:

Single shuffle, double shuffle, cut and cross-cut: snapping his fingers, rolling his eyes, turning in his knees, presenting the backs of his legs in front, spinning about on his toes and heels like nothing but the man's fingers on the tambourine; dancing with two left legs, two right legs, two wooden legs, two wire legs, two spring legs—all sorts of legs and no legs—what is this to him?[24]

### Dances of Subversive Performance

And in what walk of life, or dance of life, does one ever get such stimulating applause as thunders about him, when, having danced his partner off her feet, and himself too, he finished by leaping gloriously on the bar-counter, and calling for something to drink, with the chuckle of a million counterfeit Jim Crows, in one inimitable sound?[25]

### Dances of Actionable Assertion

To answer Dickens's rhetorical question, what all of this might be to Juba is an expression of musicality, a confirmation and expression of himself, and a sounding on Dickens's amazement. To be sure, Dickens wrote his *American Notes* to an abolitionist ideology condemned slavery and valorized formidable and exotic black cultural processes like Juba's dance. The description of Juba's breakdown comes in the midst of a chapter on New York, sandwiched between disagreeable visits to various public institutions: prisons, orphanages, and insane asylums. In context, Dickens intimates how Juba's dances are subversively eccentric and kinesthetically powerful—expressive qualities that Dickens does not find elsewhere in his New York adventure. And surely the dance was simultaneously celebratory for the dancer as an confirming exercise in physical mastery. It is this conflation of inner and outer aspects of African diaspora dance that I interrogate as the basis of an aesthetic of body power palpable in hip hop forms.

## How Hip Hop Dance Contains Power

Power in hip hop is most apparent in the aggressively layered, dynamic array of shapes assumed by the dancing body. Hip hop dances contain an assertive angularity of body posture and an insistent virtuostic rhythmicity. This is the power of what can be seen, and then inscribed, without being embodied; what Dickens saw in the dances with no legs, the 'virtual' dances performed by a mercurial black body.

How surprised Dickens might be in 1997 to see dancing white bodies moving with a directed unpredictability similar to Juba's, as suburbanites on ESPN use hip hop music and dances to confirm their mastery of imperative body talking in national cheerleading competitions. Hip hop, like much of African American expressive culture, attracts what theomusicologist Jon Michael Spencer calls "resentment listeners"; cultural outsiders who seek to invest their lives with meaning through the power of hip hop dance and music.[26] These listeners and dancers come, I think, to physically invest in the enactment of cool dissension; they learn the dances for the obvious associations of physical power contained within the dancing body magnified by the crucible of race. If these dances can empower impoverished black bodies of the inner city, surely they might offer dynamic celebration to young dancers in the vanilla suburbs. Power is what is seen in the form, and power is what these dancers mean to channel by their performances.

Hip hop dances also gain power from their subversive [black] stance outside the moral law of [white] America. The black body in America has long been legislated and controlled by political systems both legal and customary. In social dance, the black body achieves a freedom from traditional American strictures defining legitimate corporeality. The dancing black body, responding to and provoking the drumbeat, acts performatively against the common American law of black abjection. "Speaking well" in terms of black social dance defies—temporarily—systematized oppression.

In a seminal essay on African diaspora dance titled "An Aesthetic of the Cool," Thompson asserts that hot is always balanced by cool, and that all the aesthetic canons work toward social and artistic synthesis.[27]

This synergistic notion may help us understand the seriousness, or "attitude" of hip hop. The cool facial mask dancers employ in hip hop is a symbolic reference to hip hop's attitude, which reflexively claims direct descendence from African aesthetics of facial masking. The inscrutable facial mask is a symbol of focused energy; an embodied creative gesture that forces attention from the mouthpiece to the whole body, which talks in the dance. The cool, hard face works with the hot, busy body; alternately, a composed, stretched body may be finished by a hot, yawning face. It is also a performance strategy that has to do with competitive strains of black expressive culture. Focused energy in the battle dictates the composed facial mask.

But notice how the separation of audience from performer across cultural and racial lines disperses the power of hip hop dance as a tool of battle. The ESPN cheerleaders smile aggressively as they work to rouse the crowd. Performing similar movements in another context, black dancers in a nightclub hold their faces seriously, dancing an impromptu battle with a focused facial mask. Dance that is designed to please or rouse an audience is different from dance of protest or personal expression. But because dancing black bodies in America are inevitably taken to be performing dances of celebration by cultural outsiders, their dances, as viewed by an immobile audience, are not necessarily actionable. Audiences may sense the submerged political transcript of hip hop dance, but what, they wonder like Dickens, what is this to them? Consider Hazzard-Donald's assertion that "hip hop's outwardly aggressive postures and gestures seem to contain and channel the dancer's rage.:[28] To what end? Channeling rage into dance so as to disperse anger? Or to express anger? Hip hop theorist Tricia Rose suggests that "oppressed people use language, dance, and music to mock those in power, express rage, and produce fantasies of subversion."[29] In this, hip hop dance prepares its black dancers to do battle with oppressive societal forces. Can it accomplish similar goals for its white dancers? Can it fulfill the competitive ambitions that arise in cheerleading competitions; ambitions beyond the physical release of movement driven by "rage"?

## Sacred Dimensions—Groove Is in the Heart

Black power in social dance structures is a sacred holding, a trust of rhythmic legibility and cultural responsibility. We "represent the real" through the dance, accessing its common speech like denominators; making phrases that can be understood by others; becoming the dance. Honesty and eloquence in body talking are linked to a purity of intention in motion. Theomusicologist Jon Michael Spencer calls this ever present spiritual quality "the untouchable rhythmicity of black music and dance [that] have always helped connect people of African spirituality with the cosmic forces that enable healing and sustenance."[30] In this model, the forces that drive the dance are intangible, and power in the dance is attained by aligning ourselves with the submerged rhythmic and linguistic potentials of the beat. Working in the service of a communal conversation with others, the dancer creates dialogue by making the beat visible and shaping its accents into coherent phraseology. Ironically, the body creates the movement, but the body as a physical entity disappears in the midst of its own statements.

As Abrahams suggests, expert social dancers who enter the realm of entertainment for an integrated, but mostly white, audience become the object of a bifurcated gaze. In an essay on theatrical dance and religion, Royster discusses M. C. Hammer as a "griot with shamanic skills, whose singing and dancing show black folk how they can not merely survive but thrive in a spirit of praise."[31] Hammer's short-lived but significant popularity as a dance artist spoke to a core audience of African Americans familiar with the spiritual dimension of his dance, as well as an international audience amazed by his virtuosity. The connection of spirituality and social dance is not casual, as Malone reminds us, and the best dancers in the black tradition are considered to be those who can tap into the spirituality of the dance: "African American musicians, dancers, and singers all testify to the spiritual dimension of their art."[32] In other words, serious "body talking" dancers manifest aspects of spiritual strength displayed and understood as such by their collaborating audience.[33] If spirituality is accessed by good dancing, religiosity may, then, be the unspoken subject and source of the dancer's action, its root. Again, the dancing body disappears in the creation of motion, but here, in the service of spirituality.

The dancing body is itself considered the generative force of movement only through the act of stylization. In this process of personal invention, the dancer approaches a goal of purity, of expressing the self by manipulating basic movement utterances. This process provides the dynamic underpinnings of hip hop as "a never-ending battle for status, prestige, and group adoration, always in formation, always contested, and never fully achieved."[34] The social process that gives rise to black social dance will never be ended; hip hop offers only the contemporary manifestation of that cultural and political process.

## Formal Aspects of Hip Hop—Jinglin' Baby

The formal characteristic most obvious to dancers and viewers of hip hop dance is the bounce. The bounce in hip hop is a recoil, a triage before the next skip. Body power draws from the illusion of physical weightiness, of neediness, of the voracious consumption of space. Physical virtuosity is also a function of the hip hop sound, present in the skill of the mixmaster's arrangement of preexisting music into an interlocking wall of beats. For dancers, weightiness and aggressive physicality—unchecked virtuosity—lead us into the beat.

Hip hop virtuosity is an alignment of physical tension [hardness] with politicized blackness unique to the post–civil rights era. This is a virtuosity of precision and attack; of finish joined to flow. The movement startles the viewer with angularity and asymmetry; with an outwardly explosive directness of precision unknown to earlier black American social dances. According to West, rap music "Africanizes African American popular music—accenting syncopated polyrhythms, kinetic orality, and sensual energy in a refined form of raw expressiveness—while its virtuosity lies not in technical facility but rather street-talk quickness and linguistic versatility."[35] This raises an alternative issue: is softness unwelcome in hip hop dance?

Perhaps. To dance hip hop, the body is held "tight"; that is, focused, with strong weight, and capable of an explosive suddenness. Because the body dances a complex array of interlocking rhythms, percussive accents of isolated body parts pop out in unexpected phrasing. These performed accents help to ground alternative rhythmic conceptions of the beat; to keep it fresh; to allow the dancer to reenter the same beat in many different ways. To my mind, it is the tightness of the body that speaks most to a hip hop dance aesthetic. These dances are fundamentally concerned with controlling the body, holding it taut, making it "work" in a fragmented manner that echoes the sampled layering of hip hop music. These dances look different from their predecessors, because of their unabashed hardness, their visible intimations of complex meter at work, and their palpable projection of a physical dynamism.

Hip hop dance is also fun, which offers its dancers a mechanism to express kinetic musicality with a bravado that is easily consumed by an immobile audience. Consider the strange, short-lived popularity of break dancing, an elaborate social dance form originated by teenage Latino and African American males in the South Bronx of New York City, circa 1970. Break dancing began as a form of fighting, a mixture of physically demanding movements that exploited the daredevil prowess of their performers, and stylized punching and kicking movements directed at an opponent. A descendant of capoeira, the Brazilian form of martial arts disguised as dance, breaking developed as the original movement aspect of rap music when break-dancers filled the musical breaks between records mixed by disc jockeys.

The elaborate spins, balances, flips, contortions, and freezes performed by break-dancers required extreme agility and coordination. Real physical danger surrounded movements such as the "windmill," in which dancers spun quickly supported only by the shoulders, or the "suicide," in which an erect dancer would throw himself forward to land flat on his back. The competitive roots of break dancing encouraged sensational movements such as multiple spins while balanced on the head, back, or one hand. Dancing crews met on street corners, subway stations, or dance floors to battle other groups with virtuosity, style, and wit determining the winner. In these style wars there were no "judges" per se; rather, the dancers agreed on the winner at the moment of victory. In competitive strains of black social dance, there is no balloting or predetermination of the winner; victory is conferred intuitively by all the participants.

Clearly, break dancing possessed an inner logic that grew from its competitive background, and a simultaneous outer flamboyance that engendered its popularity for nonparticipating audiences. But what is lost in the shift from a social form with actionable consequences—the confirmation of victory or defeat—to a repeatable form admired by a crowd? How is the power of the body or of the dance diminished in this transference? If the audience doesn't know how to "read" the dance, can the dance speak? According to Hazzard-Donald, movement from a black social sphere to a [white] mainstream defused its expressive capacities: "Breaking's introduction to the general public by the mass media in April 1981 surely marked the beginning of its decline as a functional apparatus for competitive challenge among rival groups or individuals."[36] But does the commodification of the form for an audience of cultural outsiders somehow unmark break dancing as an invention of the black diaspora and a manifestation of body talking? As Rose notes, "for many cultural critics, once a black cultural practice takes a prominent place inside the commodity system, it is no longer considered a black practice—it is instead a 'popular' practice whose black cultural priorities and distinctively black approaches are either taken for granted as a 'point of origin,' an isolated 'technique,' or rendered invisible."[37] But what is taken for granted in the movement from the realm of expressive social dance to commodity for hip hop dance forms?[38]

If unique, individual authorship is assumed as a component in the creation of dance style, then the amplification of hip hop style may not be possible through the simple magnification of dancing bodies moving in unison. In other words, copying steps only achieves a repetition of outward shapes, as opposed to a rearticulation of the communicative desire that drives the dance. We may repeat what is done by the body, rather than what is willed by the act of dancing—personalized speech. In this repetition, the intimations of actionable assertion may still be present, but the ability of the dance to tap into religiosity or generate action—its core power—becomes stalled in a stuttering through phrases repeated incompletely and without modulation.

Black social dances physicalize a continuity of performative oratory for Africans in diaspora. Dances offer greeting and debate; a mode of cultural identification and recognition that links African Americans in corporeal orature. Participation in the larger black culture involves the successful attainment of social dances and the invention of individual movement style as a marker of identity. According to Malone, collaborative body talking through social dance "automatically ensures a certain degree of dynamism because the demands of the audience for dynamic invention and virtuosity prevent the performer from delivering static reproductions of familiar patterns or imitations of someone else's hard-earned style."[39] The call and response mode of performance embraces an inclusionary aesthetic of creativity and invention, in that "call-and-response implies that every part of the community is important to its continuity and richness, that every one has a voice and, through it, the power to act, enact, react."[40] For hip hop dancers, this participatory call and response mode also provides generous space for weighted male and female presence in the dance.

The basic vocabulary of hip hop dance—its stylistic mandates of taut body positions that could mirror tensely honed electronic drumbeats—emerged alongside technological developments in music. Films and music videos cemented the public vocabulary of hip hop dance quickly. In the realm of break dance, for instance, while Charlie Ahearn's film *Wild Style* (1982) offered a window to burgeoning break-dance culture, this independently produced effort was eclipsed by a thirty-second breaking sequence in *Flashdance* (1983), which pushed the form to international attention. Other major studio releases quickly cashed in on break dancing's sensational appeal, including *Breakin'* (1984), which starred Shabba Doo (Adolfo Quinones), an important break-dance choreographer from Chicago; and Harry Belafonte's *Beat Street* (1984) which featured the New York City Breakers. Although these films offer predictable formulaic narratives of hip hop culture as adolescent exotica, they capture the urgency and immediacy of corporeal oratory contained by hip hop social dances.

These films also contributed to the movement of hip hop dance from the competitive, masculinized realm of ritualized battle to an integrated social space that accommodated dancing by men and women. According to Hazzard-Donald, "In its early stages, hip hop rejected the partnering ritual between men and women; at a party or dance, hip hop dance was performed between men or by a lone woman."[41] If early hip hop dancing in the social sphere "aggressively asserted male dominance,"[42] movement of the dance into the commercial region marshaled its availability for women. The films allowed women access to hip hop's hard edges. For example, in *Flashdance,* the heroine accomplishes her dance audition for the local ballet company by copying the break-dance moves she witnessed performed by a group of young men. The popular television dance group The Lockers, an early proponent of hip hop dance styles, included women and men among its numbers from its inception. It may be argued that all social dance contains roles for men and women defined by gender; as a solo form, however, hip hop dance generally resists this sort of gendered categorization.

## The Academy Breaks

Hip hop has inspired movement beyond the dance floor, and some of the sharpest breaks and flamboyant versionings of hip hop style have occurred within the academy. This response to hip hop has been at least two-pronged: younger scholars, who typically begin their careers following a path of study set forth by their mentors, find themselves creating new points of entry to African American studies building on their experiential awareness of cultural processes in action; while established scholars of literature and cultural studies work to connect social dance and music with their larger areas of humanist inquiry. For older scholars, the powerful dancing body in hip hop appeals to the nostalgic desire for physical action; it offers a physical confirmation of cultural sustenance and generational rebirth. Younger scholars who have grown up fired by hip hop's technology-strewn landscape embrace the physical release of the dance forms even as they migrate from house party to nightclub to television, and its music moves from turntable to radio, to magazine op-ed pages, and finally the courtroom. As Dyson notes, "Rap has almost single-handedly reignited popular and academic interest in black oral practices, spawning articles, books, journalism, conferences, and impassioned conversation across a variety of racial, sexual, ideological and class boundaries."[43]

Little of the scholarship referring to hip hop culture is grounded in any of the creative disciplines that give rise to its forms. Often, manifestations of hip hop culture are used by scholars to construct arguments about race. For example, literary and cultural theorist Houston Baker admits in the introduction to *Black Studies, Rap, and the Academy* that he initially set out to draw a history of black studies, but the imperative power of rap intervened, and large, block-styled letters spelling RAP define the cover of his book. In the text Baker uses rap as a call to arms for black studies, a call for a hybrid pedagogy for the 1990s that can enact a "black stud-ies sounding of form."[44] But in writing from outside of hip hop's dances, Baker's analysis seems to fetishize the recorded music and its agent, the disc jockey, over the dances and dancers that inspire them.

For example, Baker argues for the foregrounded presence of a per-forming body in hip hop: the emceeing rapper. Technological develop-ments "produced a rap DJ who became a postmodern ritual priest of sound rather than a passive spectator in an isolated DJ booth making ro-bots turn. . . . The high technology of advanced sound production was re-claimed by and for human ears and the human body's innovative abili-ties."[45] In some sense, then, hip hop's disc jockey restored the primacy of live performance to black popular music. In another passage, Baker con-firms the centrality of oral performance in hip hop, as "technology can create a rap disc, but only the voice dancing to wheels of steel and pro-ducing a hip hopping, responsive audience gives testimony to a full-filled *break*. You ain't busted a move, in other words, until the audience lets you know you're in the groove."[46] Evoking hip hop style in his very phraseology, Baker suggests a participatory connection between music and dance that black expressive culture, in effect, demanded of hip hop.

An obvious response to hip hop's aesthetic provocations is Jon Michael Spencer's *The Emergency of Black and the Emergence of Rap.*[47] Essays in this groundbreaking volume focused almost exclusively, and myopically, on the lyrics of recorded raps. Still, rap music, as a compo-nent of hip hop culture, provided the impetus for a survey of the political emergency of contemporary black life. Stressing commonalities in impera-tive speech, Spencer's preface acknowledged that "the black scholar can-not afford to be separated from the black rapper, and vice versa. Neither can we allow the audiences of these two 'teachers' to be divided, lest di-vided they fall."[48] Connections between academicians and performers are key as "both the rapper and the engaged scholar seek to provide the black community with a Wisdom that can serve as the critical ingredient for em-powering the black community to propel itself toward existential salvation, that can overcome disempowering, genocidal, hell-bent existence."[49] For Spencer, the distance from the rapper's podium to the scholar's podium is short, separated only by "differences of style and strategy: the black scholar's 'insurrection of subjugated knowledges' is carefully calculated, while the rapper's insurgence is wholehearted and absolute."[50]

In a separate volume, Spencer revisited the connections between rap music and corporeality with an enlightened awareness of the music's physical components: "Despite its aspect of intellectual insurgency, rap is first and foremost exhausting to the body; for it is the body, not the rational understanding, that is the absorber of rap's rhythms."[51] Although Spencer, like West, denies a rational understanding *of* the body, the connection of the music to its physical provoker and respondent predicts theoretical work that aligns the components of black expressive culture. The performative aspects of music, dance, and orality in black expressive culture are intertextual, rational, and theoretical.

## Conclusion

Black social dance structures offer a site of performative body talk inhabited by several audiences simultaneously. As Malone asserts, among African Americans, "the power generated by rhythmical movement has been apparent for centuries in forms of work, play, performance, and sacred expressions."[52] Contemporary versions of these dance structures— hip hop dances—continue this construction of actionable physical expression that belongs to the realm of art as life. While stationary audiences may sense the imperative power of hip hop dance, they often fail to interpret the movements effectively; they fail to read the dances as actionable. Without recourse to the spiritual vocabulary that inspires movement, without talking back with the body, it may be impossible to interpret and write about black social dances effectively.

Considered within a frame that includes an immobile [white] audience, the prevalent underlying action of movement in hip hop dances, is "j'accuse," spoken by young people of color to those in power who would ignore them. These are emphatic dances of presence that belong to the realms of the lucid and the ludic. The body in these forms dances about unequal power relations, self-awareness, and kinetic fun; it creates pleasure in the personal layered statements of rhythmicity. These dances implicate all who would perform them to be in the pursuit of an efficacious corporeal orature. Their mastery can be achieved by any dancer—not only by black bodies—willing to investigate their powerful communicative potential. Ultimately these dances generate a physical statement of pleasure, inextricably bound up with the political frames of race continually surrounding modes of black performance in America.

## Select Bibliography

Abrahams, Roger D. *Singing the Master: The Emergence of African-American Culture in the Plantation South*. New York: Penguin Books, 1992.

Baker, Houston. *Black Studies, Rap, and the Academy*. Chicago: University of Chicago Press, 1993.

Cayou, Dolores Kirton. *Modern Jazz Dance*. Palo Alto, Calif.: Mayfield, 1971.

Cross, Brian. *It's Not About A Salary . . . : Rap, Race + Resistance in Los Angeles*. London: Verso, 1993.

Dickens, Charles. *American Notes* [1842]. Introduction by Christopher Lasch. Gloucester, Mass.: Peter Smith, 1968.

Du Bois, W. E. Burghardt. *The Souls of Black Folks*. New York, Dodd, Mead, 1961.

Dyson, Michael Eric. "Rap Culture, the Church, and American Society." In *Sacred Music of the Secular City: From Blues to Rap*, edited by Jon Michael Spencer. A Special Issue of *Black Sacred Music: A Journal of Theomusicology*, 6, no. 1 (Spring 1992). Durham: Duke University Press, 1992.

Gottschild, Brenda Dixon. *Digging the Africanist Presence in American Performance: Dance and Other Contexts*. Westport, Conn.: Greenwood, 1996.

Hazzard-Donald, Katrina. "Dance in Hip Hop Culture." In *Droppin' Science: Critical Essays on Rap Music and Hip Hop Culture*, edited by William Eric Perkins, 220–235. Philadelphia: Temple University Press, 1996.

Hazzard-Gordon, Katrina. *Jookin':The Rise of Social Dance Formations Among African-Americans*. Philadelphia: Temple University Press, 1990.

Hinton, Robert. "Black Dance in American History." In *The Black Tradition in American Modern Dance*, edited by Gerald Myers, 4–7. American Dance Festival Program, 1988.

Hughes, Walter. "In the Empire of the Beat: Discipline and Disco." In *Microphone Fiends: Youth Music & Youth Culture*, edited by Andrew Ross and Tricia Rose, 147–157. New York: Routledge, 1994.

Malone, Jacqui. *Steppin' On The Blues: The Visible Rhythms of African American Dance*. Urbana: University of Illinois Press, 1996.

Primus, Pearl, "Primitive African Dance (and Its Influence on the Churches of the South)." *Dance Encyclopedia*, edited by Anatole Chujoy, 387–389. New York: A. S. Barnes, 1949.

Rose, Tricia. *Black Noise: Rap Music and Black Culture in Contemporary America*. Hanover: Wesleyan University Press, 1994.

Royster, Philip. "The Rapper as Shaman for a Band of Dancers of the Spirit: 'U Can't Touch This.'" In *The Emergence of Black and the Emergence of Rap*, edited by Jon Michael Spencer, 60–67. *Black Sacred Music* 5, no. 1 (Spring 1991).

Sedgwick, Eve Kosofsky. *Tendencies*. Durham: Duke University Press, 1993.

Spencer, Jon Michael. *The Emergence of Black and the Emergence of Rap*. In *Black Sacred Music* 5, no. 1 (Spring 1991).

————. *Protest & Praise: Sacred Music of Black Religion.* Minneapolis, Minn.: Fortress, 1990.

————. *The Rhythms of Black Folk: Race, Religion, and Pan-Africanisms.* Trenton, N.J.: Africa World Press, 1995.

Stearns, Marshall, and Jean Stearns. *Jazz Dance: The Story of American Vernacular Dance* [1964]. New York, Schirmer Books, 1979.

Tate, Greg. "Diary of a Bug." *Village Voice,* November 22, 1988, p. 73.

Thompson, Robert Farris. *African Art in Motion: Icon and Act.* Berkeley and Los Angeles: University of California Press, 1963.

————. "Dance and Culture, an Aesthetic of the Cool: West African Dance." *African Forum* 2, no. 2 (Fall 1966): 85–102.

————. *Flash of the Spirit: African & Afro-American Art & Philosophy.* New York: 1st Vintage Books edition, 1983.

————. "Hip Hop 101." *Droppin' Science: Critical Essays on Rap Music and Hip Hop Culture,* edited by William Eric Perkins, 211–219. Philadelphia: Temple University Press, 1996.

West, Cornel. "On Afro-American Popular Music: From Bebop to Rap." In *Sacred Music of the Secular City: From Blues to Rap,* edited by Jon Michael Spencer, 282–294. A Special Issue of *Black Sacred Music: A Journal of Theomusicology* 6, no. 1 (Spring 1992). Durham: Duke University Press, 1992.

# 5 ‖     Danced Spirituals[1]

The history of danced spirituals reveals a striking turn at midcentury: whereas modern dancers both black and white staged spirituals during the 1930s, danced spirituals became associated almost exclusively with black choreographers after World War II. Moreover, the spirituals performed by Euro-American dancers during the depression era received more exposure and more critical acclaim than the spirituals performed by African American dancers. Although many black choreographers working during the 1930s—Edna Guy, Hemsley Winfield, Katherine Dunham, Charlotte Moton Kennedy, Wilson Williams—staged spirituals neither individually nor collectively did their danced spirituals achieve the renown of Helen Tamiris's *Negro Spirituals,* accorded more than one hundred performances during the decade, or Ted Shawn's *Negro Spirituals,* accorded more than 250 performances. Based on the extant documentation, the nearly four hundred performances of danced spirituals by Tamiris and Shawn exceed the roughly forty performances of danced spirituals by African American choreographers by a factor of ten. And these numbers do not count the spirituals staged by other Euro-American dancers during the period—Edith Segal, Catherine Littlefield, William Bales, Valerie Bettis, Barton Mumaw, La Meri (Russell Meriwether Hughes).[2]

During and after the Second World War this pattern of production and reception radically changed. After 1944 white modern dancers rarely essayed the form. In contrast, most of the black choreographers who came of age in the 1940s and 1950s—Pearl Primus, Janet Collins, Talley Beatty, James Truitte, Louis Johnson, Geoffrey Holder, Alvin Ailey–staged spirituals.[3] Although production figures are not easily compiled, Ailey's *Revelations* probably has achieved more performances than any other single work by a modern dance choreographer, black or white. (Judith Jamison once estimated the number at "thirty thousand, forty thousand, maybe fifty thousand times.")[4] In the decades immediately following World War II, it became nearly unthinkable for a white dancer to choreograph a spiritual and nearly unthinkable for a black dancer not to.

More recently, the association between black choreographers and spirituals has begun to break down. Not that white choreographers are returning to the precedent set in the 1930s and essaying the form again. Postmodern choreographers who are black, however, are less drawn to the danced spiritual than were their predecessors. Although on occasion black postmodernists have set spirituals, most have not.[5] The attitude of Randy Duncan seems typical. He once remarked that although he could "whip up a spiritual as fast as anyone," he had not simply because black themes interest him less than they did his predecessors. In other words, Duncan associates danced spirituals with expectations for African American choreographers from which he deliberately takes his distance.

As choreographers such as Randy Duncan challenge the association between spirituals and the African American dancer, it becomes possible to historicize the emergence of the association, to ask why the danced spiritual in effect became taboo for white choreographers and de rigeur for black choreographers during the immediate postwar years. In this essay my intent is not to elaborate an encyclopedic stage history of the form, as my opening recitation of names and statistics may have suggested. Rather, I shall focus on the danced spirituals most widely performed during their periods—Helen Tamiris's and Ted Shawn's *Negro Spirituals* before World War II, Alvin Ailey's *Revelations* after World War II—as a case study for changing representations of race, gender, sexuality, and nationality in American modern dance. Through close readings of works by Tamiris, Shawn, and Ailey, I shall demonstrate that shifting images of whiteness and blackness at midcentury cannot be understood apart from shifting images of masculinity and femininity and shifting images of the nation.

To anticipate my conclusions: in 1930s modern dance the Euro-American body served as a privileged site for the circulation of culturally marked bodies—whether marked as oppressed worker, pioneer settler, Spanish freedom fighter, primitive native, or Negro. Thus modern dance of the period defined Americanness through the overlay and encounter of culturally marked bodies. Consider, for example, how Martha Graham's *Primitive Mysteries* (1931) performed Americanness through the Euro-American dancers' representation of Native American and Hispanic religious practices. Such performances allowed the mostly female dancers who practiced the form to undermine the sex-gender system of cultural representation at large; that is, to stage the female body not as an eroticized object but as a social subject. Similarly, the layering of culturally marked bodies enabled the few male dancers who practiced the form in the 1930s to perform queerness at the same time as they performed the athlete, the Oriental, the clown. Consider, for example, how Charles Weidman's solo *On My Mother's Side* (1940) showed the male body alternately taking on gender identities both masculine and feminine. Performing America through the superimposition of diverse identities, the Euro-American body in 1930s modern dance performed feminist and queer politics.

During the 1930s black dancers aimed to participate in the articulation of an American modern dance. Yet more often than not, their attempts were undermined by white critics, who could not perceive the African American body as a national body or, for that matter, as a feminist or queer body. Rather, white critics located the African American dancer as a site of aesthetic failure. On the one hand, if black modern dancers staged themes perceived as Africanist, then white critics considered them "natural performers" rather than "creative artists." On the other hand, if black modern dancers staged themes perceived as Eurocentric, then white critics considered them "derivative" rather than "original" artists. The presumed performativity of the black body rendered the African American modern dancer illegible to most white critics.

After 1940 critical perceptions and conventions for representing race radically changed in American modern dance. Resolving the critical contradiction scripted by white critics during the 1930s, black modern dancers acquired artistic authority through their performance of diasporic identities, of shared cultural memories. On the modern dance stage the black body came to figure the social identity of blackness, to signify a common history of racial oppression and racial uplift, and to demonstrate the continuity between African, Afro-Caribbean, and African American movement styles. At the same time white modern dancers redefined their artistic authority by rejecting the culturally marked body in favor of a psychologized, mythologized, or formalized body. On the modern dance stage the white body came to signify the Freudian or Jungian psyche, to enact archetypal figures from Western myth and legend, and to demonstrate the formal possibilities of movement in time and space. Differently stated, after 1940 the African American dancer became the culturally marked body of modern dance as the Euro-American dancer became the newly privileged unmarked body.

As conventions for representing race were transformed in American modern dance at midcentury, so too did conventions for representing gender and sexuality. The performance of heterosexism, of male-female difference and complementarity, eclipsed the earlier performance of feminist and queer politics, of (white) women as social subjects and of (white) men as inscriptions of gay desire. Yet the expression of female subjectivity and gay desire did not disappear altogether from American modern dance.

Rather, heterosexist performance became a closet for both feminist and queer politics during the postwar era, a period that revalorized the familiar opposition between a feminized private sphere and a masculinist public sphere.

How can one explain these interrelated shifts in American modern dance: from the Euro-American body as the vehicle for the circulation of diverse national bodies to the binary of culturally marked (black) and unmarked (white) bodies; from feminist and queer body politics to heterosexism? At the risk of oversimplification, I would point to the influence first of wartime patriotism and then of cold war liberalism. Mobilization for war occasioned a suspension of the social critique that had animated 1930s modern dance, and the rise of McCarthyism led to the outright suppression of political dissent. As is often noted, cold war culture intensified the homophobia and heterosexism of American life. It is perhaps not surprising that many modern dancers rejected their earlier advocacy of leftist politics while closeting their earlier performance of feminist and queer politics.

Yet cold war culture also witnessed the emergence of the civil rights movement. After all, if the United States had decided to "make the world safe for democracy," the question arose of why it could not guarantee democracy for all its citizens at home. And so black self-representation became a contested issue for both artists and politicians: black modern dancers were newly legitimized through their performance of a shared social identity and white modern dancers were newly reluctant to represent black subject matter.

Such connections between changes in the practice of modern dance and in the sociopolitical milieu seem self-evident. Less obvious are the interconnections between the tendencies within cold war culture that, on the one hand, suppressed Communists and queers—to quote part of the title of one study on postwar theatre (Savran)—and, on the other hand, prompted activism for civil rights. Were the cultural currents that put black self-representation on the national agenda, both politically and artistically, related to the cultural currents that led to the blacklisting of so many artists and activists and the criminalization of homosexuality? It's a question that seems a long way from the history of danced spirituals. Yet it is a question that my research demands I ask.[6]

At its most reductive, my case study of danced spirituals suggests a simple correspondence: that black modern dancers acquired artistic authority at precisely the moment when the performance of leftist critique and of feminist and queer politics became deauthorized. In other words, the cultural pressures supporting black self-representation also supported the suppression of leftist critique and of gay culture, at least within the arena of modern dance. Yet I am not satisfied with this reductive scenario. As my reading of Alvin Ailey's *Revelations* shall demonstrate, American modern dance during the cold war era destabilized the very binaries of racial and sexual difference that grounded its practice.

From 1928 to 1944 Helen Tamiris choreographed nine dances set to spirituals, mostly solos, which she performed in varying combinations and in diverse venues in New York City: Broadway and Off-Broadway theaters, Lewisohn Stadium, the Rainbow Room. Over the course of more than a decade she shifted the framing of her spirituals, presenting them first as exemplars of a self-conscious modernism, then as vehicles of social critique, and finally as a type of patriotic Americana. Yet in all these differing guises Tamiris's *Negro Spirituals* presented the Eurocentric body as the vehicle for Afrocentric expression. Or, differently stated, Tamiris's *Negro Spirituals* relied on the representational strategy of universalizing the other. In Tamiris's work and in the work of many of her contemporaries, this strategy worked to legitimize the performance of the white female modern dancer, to transform the white female body from a potential object of the erotic gaze to a potentially universal subject.

The best visual evidence of this representational strategy is a film of *Negro Spirituals* Tamiris made fourteen years after she had stopped performing the dances onstage.[7] (Following the precedent of her performances after 1937, the film was accompanied by singers performing musical arrangements by Tamiris's collaborator Genevieve Pitot. Before 1937 Pitot had accompanied Tamiris's performances on the piano, playing arrangements scored by J. Rosamond Johnson and Lawrence Brown.) In the 1958 film Tamiris does not play the minstrel and impersonate an African American type. Rather, she sets in motion choreographic oppositions— interiorized versus exteriorized focus, gesture versus locomotion, weighted versus buoyant movement—and corresponding thematic tensions between bondage and freedom. As captured on camera, Tamiris moves from the weighted gestures, interiorized focus, and tragic feel of "Go Down, Moses" to the vibrant locomotion, exteriorized focus, and almost comic quality of "Swing Low, Sweet Chariot" and "Git on Board, Li'l Chillun." She then returns to the opening emphasis on interiorized focus and gestural movement in the somber "Crucifixion" and ends with a reprise of the outward-focused qualities in "Joshua Fit de Battle ob Jericho." In effect, Tamiris abstracts the qualities of the music and lyrics and creates a multivocal dance text that alternates between themes of suffering and jubilation, themes that resonate with the historical experiences and religious beliefs of African Americans, Jews, and Christians of all ethnicities. The dancer's body becomes a vehicle for a universalized subjectivity, a site of circulation for culturally marked bodies. Thus what I term the feminist body politics of 1930s modern dance cannot be separated from the genre's articulation of Americanness through the Eurocentric body.

The stage history of Tamiris's *Negro Spirituals* from 1928 to 1944 reveals a nearly complete acceptance of the convention that granted the white dancer, and only the white dancer, the privilege of universalizing the other.[8] In one telling instance John Martin, critic for the *New York Times* and self-appointed arbiter of the emergent modern dance, compared Tamiris's performances of the spirituals to performances of Bahamian folk dances on a shared program at Lewisohn Stadium. Martin wrote:

Although the stadium is perhaps as trying a place for a solo dancer as anybody could suggest, it was Tamiris who walked away with the honors of the occasion. . . .The group of Negro spirituals assume a certain new validity when seen at close proximity to actual Negro movement. . . .There is not such a favorable tale to be told of the Bahama dances. Such formless cavorting has rarely graced a concert program.[9]

What is the logic of Martin's response? Apparently that Tamiris was able to perform black subject matter more effectively than the Bahamian dancers because she possessed a necessary aesthetic distance that the folk dancers lacked. Yet then, how would it be possible for black dancers to perform black subject matter? Martin never says; he cannot transcend his perception of the black dancer's presumably natural performativity as an obstacle to achieved artistry.

In 1938 an interviewer asked Katherine Dunham what she thought about white dancers performing spirituals. (Four years earlier Dunham had choreographed two spirituals for her Negro Dance Group in Chicago.) Dunham replied:

I think she [the white dancer] should if it is within her background and emotional understanding. For instance, I am a Negro, but I was reared in the North, and in white schools with white associates. Naturally, I heard spirituals, but until I was fully grown, I probably heard them much less than a white girl in the South. Why then, should I dance them and she not? Some dancers, however, attempt them for the exotic, for publicity, *or to satisfy some vague longing to champion the oppressed*. Motives such as these speak for themselves.[10] (emphasis in original)

Given the timing of the interview, it is likely that Dunham alluded to Tamiris's performances of her spirituals in the mid-1930s in the context of a leftist social critique. Significantly, Dunham does not object to white dancers performing spirituals per se but only to what she perceives as Tamiris's (or other leftist dancers') patronizing attitude toward black folks. In other words, Dunham assented to the defining convention of

1930s modern dance: that the dancer's performance circulates a diversity of culturally marked bodies.

Yet, in contrast to the dominant paradigm in 1930s modern dance, Dunham believed that the Afrocentric body, as well as the Eurocentric body, could function as the site of circulation. Other black modern dancers of the period concurred, although many white critics did not. In 1931 Hemsley Winfield and Edna Guy presented a concert billed as the "First Negro Dance Recital in America." The program included two solo spirituals choreographed by Guy, *Get on Board, Little Chillun* (a year before Tamiris premiered her version) and *Weeping Mary;* along with works that Guy had learned while studying at Denishawn in the mid-1920s, *A Figure from Angkor Vat* and *Temple Offering.* Reviewing the concert in the *New York Times,* John Martin once again articulated critical assumptions that excluded the black dancer from the category of high art, a category implicitly defined as white art. Martin wrote:

It is not these dances which echo and imitate the manner of the dancers of another race [*A Figure from Angkor Vat* and *Temple Offering*] that the Negro dancers are at their best, but in those in which their forthrightness and simplicity have full play. Miss Guy's group of "spirituals" . . . can be counted in this category. [11]

Although Martin never questioned the prerogative of Ruth St. Denis to represent Oriental subject matter or of Helen Tamiris to represent Negro subject matter, he criticized Edna Guy and the other black dancers involved in the concert for "[imitating] . . . another race." Better, he suggested, for black dancers to perform (his) stereotyped images of blackness, the dancers' presumed "forthrightness and simplicity," as in Guy's danced spirituals.

As John Perpener has noted, Martin's response typifies the no-win situation for black modern dancers scripted by many white critics during the 1930s:

All that was generally agreed upon was that black dancers who were attempting to enter the concert field were stranded somewhere between Africa's rituals, Harlem's "high jinks," and the leaden seriousness of modern dance. But they were searching for a way out. The dance spirituals—a form which by then had become almost standard fare for black concert dancers—were one way out, one way of creating a serious theatrical expression of Afro-American culture through dance.[12]

Praised for their natural performativity and damned as original artists, black modern dancers could avoid double jeopardy only through their performances of danced spirituals, where performativity and artistry became reconciled.

Yet although black modern dancers received more praise for their danced spirituals than for other works staged in the 1930s, their danced spirituals never received the critical acclaim accorded the versions staged by Tamiris and Ted Shawn. Reviewing Charlotte Moton Kennedy's danced spirituals for the Hampton Institute Creative Dance Group, Walter Terry summarized what he believed was the "problem" of black concert dance:

It seems incredible that the spirituals of Ted Shawn and Tamiris are better and closer to the actual quality of the music than are the danced spirituals of this Negro group. . . . The Hampton spirituals are cast in a highly stylized form. They are studied, accurate in design and smoothly performed, and all the freedom, the wealth of emotional content and the beautiful shadings of the songs themselves are completely gone. Why can't they dance them as they sing them? Why can't the cold technical problems be hidden, and the great beauty of the spirituals allowed to shine forth? It can be done. The Negro must develop a technique that is so broad and malleable that the sense of improvisation, the emotional freedom, the lustiness and naturalness of the Negro expression are never obscured, for these enviable qualities highlight the Negro character.[13]

Like Martin, Terry articulates stereotyped notions of "the Negro character." But whereas Martin posits the presumed performativity of the black dancer as an obstacle to achieved artistry, Terry believes that black dancers' performativity possesses the potential for African American artistry. Yet both Martin's proscription and Terry's prescription rest upon the same assumption: that the Euro-American body was more suited for modern dance expression than was the African American body.

Indeed, the stage history of danced spirituals in the 1930s reveals the tenacious hold of the convention that granted the white body the privilege of representing the other. Nowhere was its hold more evident than in the company of Ted Shawn and his Men Dancers. And just as Tamiris's *Negro Spirituals* had participated in a widespread reconfiguration of the white female body in performance, so Shawn's' *Negro Spirituals* participated in an attempt to reconfigure the white (gay) male body in performance.

From 1933 to 1939 Shawn criss-crossed the country on tour with his group of white male dancers. His stated intent was "to convince public, press and educators that dancing is a legitimate profession and life's work for a he-man."[14] Thus Shawn's choreography projected an image of masculinity deliberately designed to counter the stigma of effeminacy carried by the male art dancer since Nijinsky's Parisian debut in 1909. Although Shawn himself was involved in a homosexual relationship with dancer Barton Mumaw, the lovers made sure that their liaison did not become public, as Mumaw recalls, lest it "destroy the image of the Men Dancers as 'respectable' artists."[15] In other words, artistic respectability demanded the projection of heterosexist masculinity.

Yet Shawn's choreography was doubly coded: the choreographic strategies he devised to project "true" masculinity carried a homosocial, even homoerotic subtext. Dramatizing a range of masculine personae drawn from diverse historical and cultural contexts, Shawn's choreography implied not one, but many subjectivities. Developing dance sequences based on movement drawn from male-associated activities such as manual labor, sports, and war, Shawn's choreography presented men joining together in close, even intimate formations. Featuring dancers whose athletic physiques were often costumed to suggest near nudity, Shawn's choreography made reference to the Greek ideal, an ideal that had legitimated Western art since the Renaissance and had served as an important identification for gay men since the construction of homosexuality as a social identity at the turn of the twentieth century.

It is impossible to determine whether Shawn consciously intended to create such double-coded dance texts, but the company's reception made clear that at least a few spectators perceived the subtextual address. As Mumaw recalls in his memoir:

We were constantly made aware of a more subtle response to our work by young men, students mostly, each of whom confided that his Old Man preferred him to run the risks of injuries in a football game rather than accept the challenge of an art that was equally strenuous, vowing that "I'll see you *dead* before I'll let you be a dancer!" Many of these frustrated boys were proficient in different fields of athletics. Some dared knock on stage doors, or come back to the locker rooms of college gyms to talk to us about dancing. Others approached us on campus or on small-town streets, pathetically pretending a fascination with our streamlined De Soto in an attempt to disguise their real interest. Only a few were furtive. The rare spats I had with Ted during periods on the road were triggered by my meeting someone who had become infatuated with me. None of these superficial encounters ever in any way threatened my love for or commitment to Ted.[16]

Although most reviewers perceived only Shawn's intent to present images of heterosexist masculinity, some spectators clearly recognized the subtextual staging of gay desire.

Shawn's *Negro Spirituals,* performed on cross-country tours from 1933 to 1936 and again in 1938, reveal the double-coding characteristic of Shawn's repertory as a whole. As recorded on silent film, the work follows a trajectory from individual isolation to group unity, emphasizing the choreographic oppositions of soloist and group, counterpoint and unison, low level and high level. (In performance Jess Meeker, musical director for the Men Dancers, accompanied the group on the piano, playing his own arrangement of the spirituals.) In an opening solo, "Nobody Knows de Trouble I've Seen," Shawn struggled to rise from kneeling to standing before kneeling again in despair. Three men join him for the middle section, "Go Down, Moses," and he and the men dance contrasting patterns, as if unable to join together. The group doubles in size for the ending section, "Swing Low, Sweet Chariot," and in the closing tableau Shawn and the six men finally unite. They all lean back in unison and, body against body, they form an image of the chariot to heaven, with Shawn as its support and Mumaw as its figurehead.[17]

Always placed last on the program, *Negro Spirituals* closed a series of "Religious Dances." Thus the frame of "Religious Dances" lent legitimacy to the danced spirituals as a representation of religious worship and religious community. However, as was characteristic of Shawn's double-coded choreography, the imagery of *Negro Spirituals* both supported its legitimating frame and suggested a homosocial and homoerotic subtext. Baring their chests, Shawn and his Men Dancers joined together in an image of ecstatic communion that could be read in erotic as well as religious terms. Displayed groin against buttock, the dancers' formation suggested one subcultural meaning of "Greek" among gay men at midcentury, anal sex.[18]

Of course, Shawn himself would never have acknowledged choreographing such a homoerotic image. Rather, his program note for the work sounded a common trope of the African American as a metaphorical other within Western culture. The souvenir program for the 1936–37 tour read in part:

[*Negro Spirituals*] draw their substance from one of the richest emotional fields of all—the American Negro and his songs, wedding Africa with Western Christianity. In these three spirituals familiar now to all, the object has been to preserve the rhythm, the simple emotional abandon and intensity, and something of the meaning of the content of the songs themselves.[19]

In Shawn's scripting of the program, the expressivity of the spirituals serves as a vehicle through which the Men Dancers may mend the split in Western Christianity between dance and religion. Thus the African Americans who created the spirituals become ciphers for an "emotional abandon and intensity" that Shawn, as a publicly closeted homosexual and Euro-American man who came of age in the era of Teddy Roosevelt, desires. For Shawn, qualities associated with blackness—emotionalism, physicalized religiosity—become figures for what Western culture lacks and needs to become whole. Textually, blackness becomes a figment of the white imagination. Subtextually, blackness—and all the other varieties of otherness foregrounded in Shawn's repertory—become vehicles for the expression of gay desire, the performance of queerness.

In 1940 Shawn disbanded the Men Dancers, as most of its members faced the prospect of the recently legislated military draft.[20] As the United States entered World War II, American modern dance entered a period of change that in retrospect constitutes a paradigm shift. The single-sex companies that had predominated during the thirties gave way to mixed-sex companies. Just as Shawn disbanded his all-male troupe, so Tamiris and Hanya Holm disbanded their all-female troupes, and both Tamiris and Holm turned to the mixed-sex casts of the Broadway musical. Martha Graham invited Erick Hawkins and Merce Cunningham to join her previously all-female ensemble. Only the mixed-sex company of Doris Humphrey and Charles Weidman made the transition from the thirties to the forties relatively intact. This shift from single-sex to mixed-sex companies accompanied a shift from the performance of feminist and queer politics to the performance of heterosexism or, more accurately, to the closeting of feminist and queer politics within a heterosexist frame.

Performances by Martha Graham's company in the 1940s exemplify the change. Once Hawkins and Cunningham joined Graham's company, the choreographer and her female dancers no longer represented a universalized subjectivity, but danced the Jungian feminine in relation to the newly inserted presence of male dancers (Manning). On the one hand, the mixed-sex casts supported a clear choreographic distinction between "masculine" (outward-focused) and "feminine" (inward-focused) movement qualities, what I term a heterosexist frame. On the other hand, this heterosexist frame supported a reorientation of Graham's feminist politics: her mixed-sex choreography emphasized the point of view and subjectivity of the female protagonist. Moreover, the heterosexist frame provided an effective closet for the (gay) male dancer, who no longer could risk the blatant double-coding of Ted Shawn's choreography for his all-male ensemble in the 1930s.

During and after the war years the closeting of feminist and queer politics in American modern dance accompanied a retreat from leftist politics. In 1939 the Dies Committee, precursor to the House Un-American Activities Committee, had dismantled the Federal Dance and Theatre Projects in response to allegations of participants' Communist sympathies. Although some leftist dancers continued to stage works of social protest, most either stopped producing or altered their focus.[21] Not only leftist dancers but also politically more moderate dancers shifted their orientation, moving away from the circulation of culturally marked bodies and claiming the culturally unmarked body—whether psychologized, mythologized, or formalized—as the site of artistic authority. As Euro-American modern dancers eschewed the legitimizing frame of culturally marked bodies, African American modern dancers finally attained legibility through this frame. Yet the newfound authority of African American dancers altered the frame, as the black body became a site of circulation for diasporic identities. Thus emerged a binary of the culturally unmarked (white) body and the culturally marked (black) body that defined American modern dance during the immediate postwar years.

The history of danced spirituals vivifies the paradigm shift in American modern dance at midcentury. After 1944 the dominance of Euro-American dancers performing spirituals gave way to the dominance of African American choreographers. In 1945 Pearl Primus presented her first danced spirituals, and over the next decade she continued to add more to her repertory. In 1947 Janet Collins premiered her solo spirituals on the West Coast, and Talley Beatty premiered his group work, *Southern Landscape,* set partly to spirituals, on the East Coast. In 1951 Katherine Dunham returned to the form after a nearly twenty-year hiatus and included a danced spiritual in her *Americana Suite.* In 1958 James Truitte premiered a suite of spirituals for the Lester Horton Dancers, and two years later Alvin Ailey premiered *Revelations,* also set as a suite of spirituals, at the 92nd Street YMHA in New York City. (Hall Johnson and Howard Roberts contributed the choral arrangements for the spirituals, originally performed live. Within a year of the work's premiere in 1960, however, recorded music had replaced live accompaniment.)[22]

To a greater extent than any other danced spiritual from the postwar period, Alvin Ailey's *Revelations* established the black body as the culturally marked body in American modern dance. Yet at the same time as *Revelations* renders "danced spiritual" and "black modern dancer" nearly synonymous terms, the work challenges the binary of blackness and whiteness. The challenge results from the work's choreographic structure as well as from its mixed-race casting: both structure and casting fuse postwar conventions for staging blackness and whiteness in American modern dance. Thus Ailey's work eludes any simple reading of its meaning, significance, or influence.

Framed in the first instance as Ailey's autobiographical memory—reiterated through numerous published interviews over the years—*Revelations* recalls scenes from the choreographer's boyhood in rural Texas. As Ailey told an interviewer in 1961:

These are dances and songs I feel very personally about—they are intimately connected with my memories of the Baptist Church when I was a child in Texas—baptismals by tree-shrouded lakes, in a lake where an ancient alligator was supposed to have lived—the holy-rollers' tambourines shrieking in the Texas night.[23]

From Ailey's perspective (and from the perspective of many of his spectators) his choreographed autobiography shades into the "blood memory" of all African Americans. Introducing a film version of his work, Ailey links his "blood memories about Texas and blues and spirituals and gospel music and ragtime music" to his desire to "celebrate the black experience" and "to make a social statement . . . about the beauty of black people."[24] Framed as the choreographer's autobiography and as racial uplift, *Revelations* presents the dancers' bodies as marked by African American culture and history.

At the same time as *Revelations* stages the culturally marked (black) body, the work gestures toward the unmarked (white) body by framing the action in mythic terms. The three-part structure of the work traces a mythic progression from despair (the opening three sections titled "Pilgrim of Sorrow") through baptism or initiation (the middle three sections titled "Take Me To The Water") to rebirth (the final three sections titled "Move, Members, Move"). Recalling the structure of many of Martha Graham's works from the same period, the frame of mythic abstraction distances the dancers' bodies from the social location of African American culture and history. As Ailey noted in his autobiography, "The tune and texture of the spirituals speak to everybody."[25]

How do spectators read the multiple frames of autobiography, cultural memory, and mythic abstraction? The published responses of critics suggest that black and white spectators may well attend to different frames when viewing the work. Whereas many black critics emphasize the frames of autobiography and cultural memory, many white critics emphasize the frame of mythic abstraction. Typical of white critics' praise is Edward Thorpe's assessment: "*Revelations* transcends any specific time and place and achieves a universal expression of the spirit of mankind."[26] Compare the praise of black critic Zita Allen: "[*Revelations*] can transport me to Sunday services at John Wesley Methodist Church. Body language can sometimes speak tomes of history."[27] For Thorpe, the work's significance lies in its generalizing power; for Allen, in its particularizing force. In other words, just as Shawn's *Negro Spirituals* addressed gay and straight spectators in distinct ways, so *Revelations* addresses black and white spectators in distinct ways.

Does the doubled address reinforce the postwar binary of the culturally marked (black) body and culturally unmarked (white) body? Or resist the binary? And how does the mixed-race casting of the work contribute to spectators' diverse responses? Although the 1960 premiere featured only black dancers in the work, Ailey regularly cast Euro-American, Asian American, and Hispanic dancers from 1962. During the heyday of the Black Arts movement in the 1960s, peers often criticized Ailey for casting dancers from diverse ethnic backgrounds in the work. In his posthumous autobiography Ailey baldly states the rationale for his casting decisions: the "presence [of nonblack dancers] universalizes the material."[28] Thus Ailey's own defense of his casting choices supports the postwar conception of the white body as the body that universalizes, in contrast to the black body as the body that bespeaks culture and history.

Yet the performance of the work does not necessarily support Ailey's conceptual division between the specifying function of black dancers and the generalizing function of nonblack dancers. On the contrary, *Revelations* presents dancers from diverse backgrounds together creating a stage world framed by both Ailey's personal memory and by the structural progression from suffering to jubilation. Moreover, the progression translates not only Ailey's autobiography into the cultural memory of African Americans but also African American culture into universal myth. Blurring any perceptible distinction between black and nonblack dancers, fusing the frames of autobiography, cultural memory, and mythic universality— *Revelations* undoes the binary of culturally marked and unmarked bodies even as it reiterates the binary. The work plays off spectators' preconceptions about the differences between black and white bodies even as it breaks down their perceptions of racial difference.

Does *Revelations* undermine not only its own performance of racial difference but also its own performance of sexual difference? I would argue that it does. Here my analysis emphasizes not the work's multiple frames and mixed-race casting but rather its sequential structure. The opening image of despair in "I Been 'Buked"—the dancers' deep second-position pliés pushing their lower bodies into the ground while their arms and upper torsos strain upward and outward against the force of gravity— does not differentiate male and female dancers. All share in the image of self-division, of body part pulled against body part. Over the course of the work the opening image of male-female sameness gives way to varied images of male-female difference. Gender difference becomes especially clear in passages when the men dance alone and the women take the lead in community-building. A trio of one man and two women in "Didn't My Lord Deliver Daniel" and a male-female duet in "Fix Me, Jesus" initiate the transformation from despair to celebration. In "Processional" and "Wade in the Water" a young man and young woman undergo baptism (or, perhaps, initiation), watched over by a mature woman in the group. In "I Want to be Ready" a lone man dances a solo, struggling to rise from the floor and finally succeeding before falling to the floor again. In "Sinner Man" three men dash across the stage, each in flight from himself, and join together in jumps and falls as if attempting to expurgate their sin. (What is their sin, I wonder? A desire to remain apart from male-female community?) Then in "The Day is Past and Gone" and "You May Run On" the women come onstage, first gossiping among themselves and then turning to the men and admonishing them for their trans-

gressions, demanding that they join the group. The passage toward celebration culminates in "Rocka My Soul in the Bosom of Abraham" as the
ensembles divides into male-female couples and reassembles in a group
celebration that invites even the spectators to participate. It is as if the
achievement of community requires male-female difference and complementarity: male apartness and female interrelatedness. In other words,
nation building—whether defined as an African American community or
a universal brotherhood—requires the performance of heterosexism.

But does the ending performance of heterosexism erase the men's earlier waywardness, their subtextual queerness? I suspect that Ramsay Burt
would answer that it does. In his groundbreaking study *The Male Dancer:
Bodies, Spectacle, Sexualities,* Burt argues that American modern dancers
from Ted Shawn to Alvin Ailey deployed heroic images of masculinity as
anxious defense against cultural suspicion of male bodily spectacle.[29] Although I do not dispute his thesis, I do believe that the performance of
masculinity in American modern dance at midcentury was more complex
than Burt allows. For choreographers from Shawn to Ailey created double-
coded dance texts that both valorized heterosexist masculinity and affirmed subtextual queerness. To be sure, Shawn's subtextual performance
of queerness was more vivid than Ailey's. Yet in the context of the height-
ened homophobia of the cold war period, Ailey's queer subtext perhaps
was no less daring in its time than Shawn's in its time.

At once constructing and deconstructing racial and sexual difference,
*Revelations* suggests the complexities of American modern dance in the
cold war era. Performing race as both an essentialized identity and as a
social construction, performing both heterosexism and queerness, *Revelations* challenges any simple assessment of its originating context. Just as
surely as the postwar era suppressed leftist critique and closeted the feminist and queer politics of American modern dance, so the era enabled
African American modern dancers to establish their artistic authority.
However much we might want to separate what appears to us as the pro-
gressive and reactionary dimensions of cold war dance culture, the history of danced spirituals suggests otherwise.

# 6 ‖ Breast Milk Is Sweet and Salty (A Choreography of Healing)

*For Bill T. Jones*

June 1990: I am staying in the compound of a house of Candomblé on the periphery of Rio de Janeiro. It's an evening ceremony and I am slowly shuffling in a counterclockwise circle with several other women, our arms softly washing from side to side. In the center of the circle, the Mother of the house, Mãe Aildes, gently guides a little girl, Lumidé, as she dances the ritual choreography of Yemanjá, the maternal goddess of the sea. Lumidé, discreet but sure of her moves, takes several plunging steps forward, then douses herself with imaginary waves. Finally, she kneels down and dips her head and arms forward, and pulls back wave after wave over her face, neck, and torso. Despite her tininess—she is six and very fragile—in that moment she invokes oceans.

February 1992: Silvana Magda, the director and choreographer of the New York–based Afro-Brazilian dance company Viva Brazil, is teaching me and other members of her company a stylized choreography (later to be performed at the American Museum of Natural History as part of the museum's Black History Month celebrations) dedicated to Yemanjá.[1] Slowly, we bend forward in a deep second-position plié, and Silvana guides our hands up our bodies, passing over our breasts and then flowing outward toward what was to be our audience. She reminds us that Yemanjá created the oceans from her unending flow of breast milk. As we repeat the gesture, I feel the incongruity of my hands running over my own diminutive breasts, trying to make this momentous, oceanic gesture. I have simultaneously the sense of my own smallness, and the magnitude of the movement in spite of that.

This is an essay about breast milk, and about the fluidity of the body, literally and choreographically. It is also about the capacity of the fluid body both to infect, and to heal. And it is about the individual dancing body's simultaneous insufficiency, smallness, insignificance *and* the magnitude of its gesture to move beyond itself.

I am returning to two topics I have dealt with at length in separate places. My first book, *Samba*,[2] was an extended meditation on both religious and secular Afro-Brazilian dances. The second, *Infectious Rhythm*,[3] dealt, on a more theoretical level and across a broader range of genres and geopolitical sites, with the European configuration of African diasporic culture as epidemic. Each of these studies might be read as a kind of subtext of the other: in the former, I touched on the political implications of the cross-racial and transnational transmission of performance practices. In the latter, I gestured toward the importance of dance—and particularly "possessional" dance—in the paradigm of cultural contagion. Here, I want to make the links very clear, even as I shift the emphasis from the "infectious" to the curative capacities of dance. The essay is an attempt to engage recent work in medical anthropology in thinking about dance. In writing it, I am returning to the specific scenes in which I first acquired a bodily understanding of the fluidity of cultural forms, as well as alternative models for understanding literal bodily fluids. I am also returning to a methodological and writerly question that I have previously broached in different ways: the insufficiency, the meagerness of individual experience in grappling with political questions, and the significance of the gesture to move through and then beyond one's own embodied perspective.

"African culture . . . by contagion was to enrich the Brazilian."[4]

The metaphoric depiction of African diasporic culture as infection or contagion has a lengthy and complex history. Often the figure is invoked in apparently benign ways: "infectious rhythms" and "contagious dances" might even be celebrated as "enlivening" the national cultures of multiracial societies. One of the most stunning examples of such an apparently benign figure is the case of samba, the (unofficial but widely acknowledged) "Brazilian national dance." Hermano Vianna has traced the ascendance of samba to a station of such evident cultural nobility through the philosophical trajectory of Gilberto Freyre, Brazil's most influential social scientist. While Freyre's postulation of the realization of a "Brazilian racial democracy" has since been widely critiqued, his celebration of racial mixing—both at the levels of literal miscegenation and of cultural hybridity—continues to inflect much political and intellectual debate. Vianna points to a particular evening in 1926 when Freyre attended an informal samba performance at an outdoor bar in Rio. Later that year he composed an essay, "On the Valorization of Things Black," in which he argued that "black songs, black dances, mixed with traces of *fado* [a distinctively Portuguese musical tradition] . . . are perhaps the best thing Brazil has to offer."[5] Vianna hypothesizes that the miscegenist ideology developed in dialogue with popular music and dance: Freyre's privileging of racial and cultural admixture assumed nationalist dimensions even as samba was achieving its status as national symbol.

Samba has long been—and continues to be—discussed as a musical and choreographic form that parallels the literal admixture of the races in Brazil. The association is reduced to a word, to the name designating the representative dancer of samba: the *mulata*.[6] But metaphors of miscegenation also mix with metaphors of contagion. In *The Masters and the Slaves,* an early and extremely influential text, Freyre wrote of the "contagion" of African culture which "was to enrich the Brazilian."[7] After elaborating on the specific cultural and "eugenic" contributions of diverse African populations to the constitution of the nation, Freyre turns to "the more intimate aspects of this contagious influence."[8] By "intimate" he means sexual, and Freyre is interested not merely in the racial mixing consequent to interracial coupling, but also in sexually transmitted disease. While Freyre celebrates the former effect, he understands the latter as evidence of the structural violence of the institution of slavery, which made every such sexual encounter inherently sadistic. Countering the blaming narratives of "African sexual depravity," Freyre posits that Africans in Brazil evidenced "greater moderation of the sex appetite"[9] than Europeans, and he argues his point by citing their "aphrodisiac dances": for Freyre, choreographed eroticism (such as that often remarked in the samba) *displaces* literal sexual excess. This cultural analysis stands as part of Freyre's insistence that Europeans were the primary vector of syphilitic and gonorrheal contagion.

Doubtless Freyre's reasoning was provoked by the prevalence of racist stereotypes of African sexuality—stereotypes linked to historical depictions of "sexual" dances. While Freyre still reads the dances as "aphrodisiac," he reads their significance as evidence of "moderation." But an even more stunning inversion of the assumed trajectory of contagion follows, when Freyre considers another kind of interracial "intimacy": that between white children and their African wet nurses: "[M]any a Negro mother who was a wet-nurse was infected by the infant at her breast, thus conveying from the Big House to the slave hut the blight of syphilis."[10] Freyre cites an 1877 publication by a Dr. José de Goés e Siqueira who recommended punishment for the "unscrupulous" entrusting of syphilitic children to previously healthy wet nurses because of the high incidence of infant-to-breast transmission.

Of course the nursing infant–as-vector argument is again, in part, an effort to counter literal epidemiological narratives that would cast blame on Brazil's African population for the prevalence of certain diseases. But it also works against figural narratives (rampant in the earlier sociological treatises on and from Brazil), which cast Africans as the origin of Brazil's *moral* ills. Most interesting, it recomplicates any project of cultural "vectoring." If the very embodiment of source—the lactating breast—can be understood as vulnerable to infection by the sucking infant, all flows, literal or figurative, are shown to be multidirectional. This notion of a multidirectional flow is, ultimately, perhaps more radical than Freyre's assertion that the "contagion" of African culture "enriched," enlivened, vitalized the Brazilian nation.

Epidemiologists, in trying to trace vectors of disease and in formulating strategies of prevention, must attend to cultural issues. These cultural issues have occasioned particularly intense debate in discussions of the AIDS pandemic. I have elsewhere reviewed some of the early "scientific" literature on the pandemic that attempted to draw causal connections between African and African diasporic cultural practices and the transmission of the virus. I argued that such hypotheses (which ultimately proved epidemiologically implausible) could not be separated from the historic proliferation of depictions of cultural practices as being, themselves, contagious.[11]

While there is no end in sight to the AIDS pandemic, epidemiological theses and strategies continue to shift. Among the most significant global strategy changes was the 1998 shift in recommendations on breast-feeding issued by the U.N. Program on AIDS: according to the most recent guidelines, women in the developing world found to be HIV-positive should be counseled to consider giving up breast-feeding their babies. This recommendation was made in regard to European and North American HIV-positive women very early on in the epidemic. But until August 1998, poor women in Africa, Asia, the Caribbean, and Latin America were advised to feed their children breast milk, regardless of their HIV status. In a *New York Times* account of the shift in policy, dateline Kakulu, Uganda, the chief of obstetrics and gynecology at Makerere University Medical School of Uganda clarified why the recommendation of infant formula presented complications:

"Oh sure it could be great," said Dr. Francis Miro. . . . "Do you know what I would love to counsel every HIV-positive mother about her choices in life? I would love to tell her about breast milk and about formula. Then I would love to have a conversation with her about what would happen to her in her village if she stopped breast-feeding. What would her mother-in-law say? What would her husband do? And of course I would love to make sure she understood the rules for keeping formula sterile and that she complied with them. I would love to do all that," he concluded wearily. "But then I wouldn't be living in Uganda and I wouldn't be talking to my own people. I would be living in America and I would be talking to your people." Asked if he thought it was always foolish to recommend formula to women living in villages, he closed his eyes and reeled off the numbers. "Twenty-seven percent of babies born to infected mothers become infected from breast-feeding," he said. "In rural areas 85 percent of babies will die from dirty water used in formula. I know what they are trying to do, and I applaud the effort. But you don't need a medical degree to figure out which of those odds to take.[12]

In fairness to the U.N. Program on AIDS, the current guidelines take these kinds of statistics into account, which is why they urge counseling women to consider their options, and to weigh the relative risks according to their circumstances. Of course all HIV-positive mothers should have the opportunity to nurture their children without risk of exposing them to the virus. The U.N. guidelines stress the need for infrastructural support if artificial infant feeding is to be recommended. In most of the world, and certainly in the communities hardest hit by the pandemic, such support seems highly unlikely anytime soon.[13]

Dr. Miro invokes not only his patients' lack of an infrastructure to support bottle-feeding, but also cultural resistance (embodied in the surveillant mother-in-law and husband). Interestingly, such resistance has proved, in the past, all too easy to undermine. This is another reason that the U.N. AIDS guidelines had to be so carefully worded on the issue. One of the most extended and poignant documentations of the undermining of the culture of breast-feeding is Nancy Scheper-Hughes's *Death Without Weeping: The Violence of Everyday Life in Brazil.*[14] Part of the poignancy of the book is that Scheper-Hughes was, herself, a vector of contagion of the culture of artificial milk: she worked as a Peace Corps volunteer in the 1960s, and distributed powdered, processed cow's milk in an impoverished area of northeastern Brazil. At the time, women were "'suspicious' of 'American milk' and fearful of giving it to their fragile infants and small babies."[15] When she returned, some twenty-five years later, to research infant and child mortality in the same area, she found that artificial infant formula had been embraced virtually to the exclusion of breast-feeding—with catastrophic results. Mortality rates for exclusively bottle-fed infants were fourteen times those for breast-fed infants.

Scheper-Hughes recounts that when the Food for Peace program's distribution of powdered milk ended in the 1970s, "charitable" organizations had fostered a "culture" of powdered milk dependency, then exploited by Nestlé and other formula producers and distributors. "But why," Scheper-Hughes asks, "did the women of the [area] give up their original resistance to powdered milk? How were they turned into avid consumers of a product that they do not need, that they cannot afford to buy, and that contributes to the death of their children?"[16] Misleading advertising was only a part of the problem. An international boycott of Nestlé products in the 1970s led to more "responsible" marketing practices in both developed and developing countries, but in some parts of the world, the cultural adoption of bottle-feeding had already become thoroughly entrenched. This shift was not only a question of exploitative marketing: it coincided with changes in the global economy and labor markets that forced many more mothers of nursing children to leave them during the day as wage laborers. In Donna Haraway's words (referencing Scheper-Hughes' observations): "Labor patterns, land use, capital accumulation and current kinds of class reformation might have more to do with the flow of breast milk than whether or not Nestlé has adopted policies of corporate responsibility in its third world infant formula markets."[17]

Haraway, in 1991, observed that shifting labor patterns were not only affecting women. Men's labor, too, among the working poor of the world, was becoming increasingly "feminized": "To be feminized means to be made extremely vulnerable; able to be disassembled, reassembled, exploited as a reserve labour force; seen less as workers than as servers."[18] Haraway argued that these labor patterns were creating "new sexualities." Interestingly, shifting labor patterns in poor Brazil—where both women and men share vulnerability if not always parenting responsibility—have created new associations between gender and milk. Scheper-Hughes notes that part of the social cachet of bottle-feeding is that it evidences assumed paternity:

The definition of father . . . is the man who arrives at least once a week bearing the prestigious purple-labeled can of Nestlé. . . . In fact, this is how a woman's current lover and father of her child is often greeted. As he sheepishly enters the door of the hut, a woman will say to her newborn, without looking up at her man, "Clap your hands, little one; your milk has arrived!"[19]

Scheper-Hughes more recently has made explicit the ways in which this scenario shows the confluency of gender roles and bodily fluids: "Father's milk, not his semen, is the poor man's way of conferring paternity and establishing legitimacy on the child in many poor single-parent households."[20]

*Mama África, a minha mãe, é mãe solteira,*
*E tem que fazer mamadeira todo dia . . .*

Mama Africa, my mother, is a single mother,
And she has to prepare the baby bottle every day . . .

–Chico Cesar

Chico Cesar's "Mama África" was an enormously popular hit in Brazil in 1998. International audiences were introduced to the song as part of the soundtrack of the film *Central Station,* which received unanticipated attention abroad. The choice of this song for the soundtrack of this film might seem incongruous: none of the major characters in the film are black, and African identity, whether racial or cultural, isn't even touched on. One might argue (but it would be a stretch) that the story of a markedly unmaternal woman who assumes responsibility for a destitute child invokes the same kind of shift in social structures for nurturing that I have just touched on. One would have to lean heavily on the figure of "Mama Africa" as a maternal ideal to make the reading work.

But I suspect the song found its way into the film for another reason altogether: it is infectious. Like much contemporary Brazilian popular music, it draws stylistically on various African diasporic rhythms, principally reggae, even as it celebrates diasporic identity under postmodern circumstances. The lyric describes a cultural genealogy and maternal ideal that is remarkably embedded in social realities: this Mama Africa makes up a bottle of artificial infant formula before running off to her job wrapping packages in a discount store. Cesar pleads with her kids to have patience with her, to understand that even if she has to get up and go to work, "she never really leaves you behind." Her "kids" are the carnival groups banging out a thoroughly hybrid samba-reggae, a raucous jazz. And if she's not always in the mood to play, one has to understand the demands on her time: "Kid, give her a break, it's so much polyrhythm / This rhythm of a mother's life . . ." Mama Africa has to contend with, and adapt to, changes in the global music industry *and* in the local economy. And she has to prepare the baby bottle. If "Mama Africa" is a romanticized notion of cultural heritage transmitted lovingly, at the breast as it were, Chico Cesar's lyric demonstrates simultaneously the artificiality of the notion, and its continuing relevance and capacity to nurture and sustain. It shows that African diasporic culture has been fully absorbed into the global market, but that it can still retain political significance *as African.*[21] In fact, it is by acknowledging the specific "artificial" conditions of underclass women of color in Brazil that the song makes their Africanness significant.

I am of course mixing metaphors: of culture, and of milk. But just as "natural" Mama Africa is shown to be a cultural and political (and nurturing!) construct, Scheper-Hughes reveals that "natural" breast-milk is, in fact, cultural—and political—as well:

> Breast-feeding is a form of body praxis. Like swimming, dancing, or making love, breast-feeding must be learned, and the knowledge of "how" to do it comfortably and well (though with many cultural variations) can be lost.[22]

This argument is not new: Marcel Mauss spelled it out quite explicitly in "Body Techniques," first published in 1935. Mauss says he came to understand "the techniques of the body" by "expanding" Plato's teachings on the technique of dance. His "biographical list of body techniques" begins with the choreography of birth and breast-feeding, and ends with the observation that "nothing is more technical than sexual positions."[23] In between, he urges European readers to denaturalize their understanding of a variety of cultural forms, including swimming, and social dance: "we should realize that dancing in a partner's arms is a product of modern European civilization, which demonstrates that things we find natural have a historical origin. Moreover, they horrify everyone in the world but ourselves."[24]

Breast-feeding is like dancing. And dancing—be it ballroom, samba, or the oceanic choreography of Yemanjá—is like breast-feeding. That is, it *is* a potentially nurturing, sustaining activity, an act of transmission. It can be configured as cultural purity, contagion, or as cure. Breast-milk, of course, is also ambiguous, as we have come to understand all bodily fluids to be.

December 1993: I find myself with a superfluity of breast milk. My baby has traveled to Brazil with his father and I am pumping bottle after bottle of the stuff. I read in the *New York Times* a story about a breast-feeding mother who was asked to donate milk to a medical study: researchers were attempting to use the maternal antibodies from expressed milk to augment immunity in AIDS patients. This is meaningful to me in a number of ways. I quickly call St. Vincent's Hospital to see if they have a milk bank, and to ask if they are aware of any such studies currently under way. When I ask the woman on the other end of the line if the hospital accepts breast-milk donations, there is a long silence. She doesn't try to disguise her revulsion at the idea "in this day and age, given what somebody could have . . ." I suddenly realize that despite my sero-negative status, if I *could* find a milk bank, because of my history, my milk, like my blood, would probably not be acceptable—even if it were cultured and found to be uninfected. Even if it were cultured.

What makes mother's milk bad? Paul Farmer, who has written the most compelling analyses of the confluence of economic exploitation, racism, and sexism in the AIDS pandemic, published an early paper on the pathology of breast milk among Haitian women. The article doesn't mention AIDS, but foreshadows Farmer's later work on the topic in an uncanny way. He describes a common malady among poor rural Haitian women, *move san* (bad blood), which, when it afflicts pregnant or nursing mothers, can result in *lèt gate* (spoiled milk). *Move san,* Farmer argues, is "a somatically experienced disorder caused by emotional distress."[25] Women typically seek herbal treatment, but the process of seeking treatment lays the circumstances of their private lives—particularly abusive relationships—open to public view. This very performative publicizing of private pain may, in effect, be part of the cure. When afflicted by *move san,* many women will determine that they should not communicate their *lèt gate* to their children.

Farmer cites other researchers who have hypothesized that the prevalence of *lèt gate* (and consequent weaning) is linked to economic forces—the same forces that led Mama Africa to prepare her baby's bottle. Farmer argues that the syndrome is more complex, but concurs that *lèt gate* "cannot be understood apart from the economic pressures that make emotional stability so elusive."[26] Still, he goes further, questioning the specific bio-symbology of the problem:

Viewed as a cultural artifact, the most striking thing about *move san* disorder is the lurid extremity of its symbolism: two of the body's most vital constituents, blood and milk, are turned to poisons. The powerful metaphors serve, it may be inferred, as a warning against the abuse of women, especially pregnant or nursing ones. Transgressions are discouraged by their publicly visible, and potentially dire, results. As somatic indices, "bad blood" and "spoiled milk" submit private problems to public scrutiny. The opposition of vital and lethal body fluids serves as a moral barometer.[27]

The relative vitality or toxicity of the blood and the milk is a measure of forces *acting upon* the afflicted women. The violence they experience is often domestic, but always structural. The performative diagnosis makes it visible.

In the *lèt gate* model, blood and milk are not merely made toxic: they are also confluent. Farmer says that the bad blood / spoiled milk syndrome is understood as pathological *mixing* or confusion of the fluids in the mother's body. Leonard B. Lerer writes of a similar explanatory model among impoverished black township mothers in South Africa. Lerer notes that the repressive and violent social policies of apartheid have left behind a "fluid and abnormal family life for many South Africans," particularly in the townships where women often shoulder the burden of sustaining children alone. Some turn to prostitution, which is often seen as the cause of a pathology known in Afrikaans as *vuil melk:* dirty milk. Lerer cites a local healer who explained to him that infant mortality in the area was high because the mothers were "'sleeping around and thereafter breast-feeding infants who then sucked this bad blood.'"[28]

In Brazil, Scheper-Hughes also heard diagnoses of toxic milk:

> I was told by dozens of women that their breast milk was "bad." They described it as salty, watery, bitter, sour, infected, dirty, and diseased. . . . When they refer to their own milk as scanty, curdled, bitter, or sour, breast milk is a powerful metaphor speaking to the scarcity and bitterness of their lives as women.[29]

Neither Farmer, Scheper-Hughes, nor Lerer makes connections between these diagnoses of body fluid pathology and the specific pathology of HIV infection (although, as I said, Farmer has written extensively elsewhere of the relationship among poverty, race, gender, and HIV). To say that many poor women in Haiti, Brazil, and South Africa understand their own breast milk to be toxic is not, of course, to imply that the toxicity of body fluids is only ever figural. Body fluids can be dangerous as well as life-sustaining. In fact, Farmer even goes so far as to concede that an analysis of *lèt gate* might indeed show some detectable irregularity that could be articulated in biomedical terms ("for example, neuromodulatory inhibition of oxytocin letdown or prolactin rise").[30] He questions, however, the necessity of such an alternate diagnosis given "the possibility that *move san* might be just what it is said to be: a blood disorder [with consequent changes in breast milk] caused by malignant emotions." Farmer's informants do not exhibit "a great deal of Cartesian anguish as to whether it is more somatic than psychological." Nor does Farmer exhibit much anguish as to whether the condition is more literal or figurative. The breast milk of an HIV-positive woman *is* dangerous. But what does it mean—at both literal and figurative levels—to acknowledge that the conditions of her poverty make artificial milk even more dangerous? "Salty, watery, bitter, sour, infected, dirty, and diseased. . . ."[31]

"Viewed as cultural artifact," as Farmer writes, breast milk, like blood, is teeming with significance. So is artificial milk. They are teeming with culture, that is. They *are* cultural. Breast-feeding, bottle-feeding, are both a complex choreography of mothering. The lactating father, with his prestigious tins of Nestlé, is choreographing a new way of attempting to nurture, despite ever more daunting odds. Scheper-Hughes expresses some suspicion of "deconstructionist and postmodern" approaches to gender politics "where the categories of 'woman' and 'mother' are rigorously problematized and deconstructed out of existence."[32] Interestingly, she specifically references Haraway in this regard, although Haraway, in turn, finds in Scheper-Hughes's work evidence of the very bodily recon-figurations that changing labor patterns and political relations enact.

What would they both make of a man dancing the choreography of women's fluidity? Could that scene of the "performativity" of gender hold together the particularity of mothering with the fluidity of bodies? Tânia Cypriano's 1997 film *Odo Ya!* (Life with AIDS) is a moving docu-mentation of a nurturing response to the AIDS crisis through African cul-tural forms in Brazil. For over a decade, many houses of Candomblé have participated in an AIDS education campaign that uses African cosmology and ethical thought to illustrate safe sexual, social, and ritual behavior, and to encourage support of those living with HIV and AIDS.[33] The cam-paign has distributed comic books depicting stories of the *orixás*, African deities, as they address issues of the potency (both vital and toxic) of blood, semen, and other bodily fluids, and the importance of taking care. They mix these narratives with explicit, graphic instructions for sterilizing rit-ual instruments for scarification, and for putting on a condom. And they invoke the praise name of Yemanjá, who not only created oceans from her overflowing breasts, but also adopted an abandoned child, Obalu-aiyé, a sickly baby born covered with sores so ghastly his own mother couldn't love him. Yemanjá's nursing was so effective, the child grew to become the master of all infectious disease.

Cypriano's film depicts a number of nurturing individuals who relate their caretaking capacities to the example of the *orixás*. But it is a man who appears dancing a choreography of fluidity and maternity. Pai Laér-cio, a Candomblé priest, established a crèche for HIV-positive children in São Paulo, eliciting outrage, threats, and acts of violence from fearful neighbors. Although in recent years he has concentrated his efforts on caring for the children, rather than on his ritual practice, he continues to hold a yearly feast for his matron *orixá*, Oxum, after whom he named the crèche. Oxum, like Yemanjá, is a female divinity, associated with fresh waters, the tributary rivers that flow into Yemanjá's ocean. She is also as-sociated with bodily flows: the circulation of blood, and the flow of nu-trients that sustain life in the fetus. Like Yemanjá, she douses herself with her own waters as she dances. *Odo Ya!* documents Pai Laércio's feast, in which he embodies this fluidity.

Cypriano told me that she struggled with the footage of Pai Laércio dancing. While she knew it had the capacity to communicate something very important about Candomblé's fluid understanding of individual identity, and about the religion's celebration of the capacity to nurture, she worried that it might be read differently by audiences for whom "drag" performance was inherently parodic. Of course, this dance is anything but parodic; in fact, it has the capacity to reveal to audiences the political, ethical, and spiritual dimensions possible in other transgender performances.[34] It might even have the capacity to resolve the apparent differences between the gender politics of a maternalist feminism and a cyborgian deconstructionism.[35]

March 1994: I receive an urgent telephone call saying that L. has been hospitalized and is probably dying. As I stand by the phone in my office absorbing the shock of a moment I have long anticipated, tears begin to flow down my face, and then, uncannily, milk begins to flood my breasts. I hold my hands against them to try to stanch the flow, but it won't be held back. My body is acting on its own. I am not moving, but I am performing a dance, a choreography simultaneously more "natural" and more culturally significant than I can hope to explain by virtue of my own experience of it. It didn't, I regret to say, effect a cure. But it enacted an ethos of fluidity that I had only glimpsed in other dancers, and I continue to strive to embody.

Perhaps the most literal—and strangest—ethnographic account of the choreography of bodily fluids occurs in Maya Deren's *Divine Horsemen*. The episode, interestingly, presents another, opposite, moment of gender inversion and apparent exchange of the figures of milk and semen. In a section of the book detailing the qualities of the Afro-Haitian deity Ghede,[36] Deren notes that his "dance is broadly sexual."[37] But though Ghede's choreography may manifest the "aphrodisiac" qualities Freyre attributed to Afro-Brazilian dance, his embodied performances can also be acts of healing. In the ceremony Deren recounts, a dying child, unresponsive to various "injections and treatments, both medical, herbal and ritual," [38] is visited by Ghede in the body of a priestess. After anointing the child with the blood of a sacrificed goat:

Singing fervently, he reached down between his legs and brought forth, in his cupped palm, a handful of fluid with which he washed the child. It was not urine. And though it would seem impossible that this should be so, since it was a female body which he had possessed, it was a seminal ejaculation. Again and again he gave of that life fluid, and bathed the child with it, while the mambos and houses sang and wept with gratitude for this ultimate gesture. . . . And though there is no reasonable way to account for this, the child lived.[39]

The nurturning capacity of Ghede is expressed through a woman's body, but not in the form of milk. The "gesture" is Ghede's, as is the fluid it communicates.

Ghede and the seminal priestess, as well as the political history of Haiti, are behind the performances of the cultural transmission of Africanness with which I began. As I have argued elsewhere, the European and

Euro-American pathologizing of such transmissions became particularly virulent at the time of the Haitian revolution. Haitian popular accounts of the uprising often attribute the slaves' surprising military success to cultural practices—the inspiriting music and choreography of Vodou.[40] Music and dance *can* communicate political consciousness, and so, from a colonialist perspective, the danger they represented was real. Of course, to pathologize the spread of political consciousness indicates one's own stake in maintaining a particular model of the "healthy" body politic. Fortunately, cultural transmission continues to infect not only exclusionary notions of individual identity, but also of national identities. South Africa, Haiti, Brazil (and for that matter the U.S. underclass), share infrastructural inequities and political challenges—but also cultural practices that both politicize and sustain life.

February 1993: I am eight months pregnant, and I am performing in a piece choreographed by Sandra Stratton for three very pregnant dancers, including herself. She has asked me to compose a small text for my section of the piece, and I have written it around Deren's story of the seminal priestess. For me, these fluid stories keep circulating through my big watery body: water, the child, dancing, sickness, the woman, dancing, blood, semen, the baby, dancing, healing, the man. . . .

In 1987, Scheper-Hughes and Margaret Lock published a "prolegomenon to future work in medical anthropology," in which they proposed a model of "the three bodies" relevant to cross-cultural research in sickness and healing. The first is the "individual body-self," understood in phenomenological terms. The second is the "social body," a "natural" symbol for thinking about the social world.[41] The third is the body politic, "an artifact of social and political control."[42] Interestingly, Scheper-Hughes and Lock argued then that medical anthropology needed to look to foundational works in the "anthropology of the body" (among which they cite a number of studies of dance) in order to problematize certain biomedical assumptions. In short, what I have tried to do here is to make the counterargument: that recent work in medical anthropology actually speaks in interesting ways to dance scholarship. My own desire to bring together conversations about dance and about sickness and healing are obviously inflected not only by my interest in dances that have been configured as disease, but also those that are performed toward explicitly curative ends. More than that, however, it is precisely the confluence of the phenomenological, the social and the political bodies in dance that reveal the choreographic nature of our most "natural" acts.

# III || ONTOLOGY'S EVENTS

MARK FRANKO

# 7 || Given Movement

## Dance and the Event

*Life exchanged for death ["given back to" (rendue à) death] is the very opera-tion of the symbolic* —Jean Baudrillard[1]

This essay progresses from the question of artistic responses to 9/11—the lack of which represented a kind of secondary civil crisis here in 2001–2002—to a consideration of event theory and the philosophy of the gift in relation to the dilemma of response. This consideration shall entail a discussion of the poststructuralist critique of speech act theory. The actual performance materials to which I shall refer may seem a little out of date, but I believe they are theoretically and to some extent also historically relevant. To approach the issue of the transmission of move-ment I shall turn to the Bateson/Mead film *Learning to Dance in Bali* (1936–39), and shall conclude with Tatsumi Hijikata's butoh perform-ance in the film *Navel and A-Bomb* (1960).

I am concerned with the obverse of heroic response and the possibility of dance as a ritual of incorporation. As is well known, in a classic text of ritual analysis, *The Rites of Passage,* Arnold Van Gennep determines "the necessity to express by actions the idea of passage from one state to another."[2] Rather than envision incorporation as the enlistment of the in-dividual in a corporate identity, I wish to imagine the incorporation of the event into the individual and collective body. Here again, I shall find the notion of the gift with and since Mauss useful with respect to movement as incorporative donation.

I

"The event," writes Stephen C. Foster of art practices, "was adopted as a theoretical reference point, or medium of artistic action, and became a major component of twentieth-century aesthetic activism."[3] Indeed, twentieth-century aesthetic activism also managed to blur the boundaries between performance and other arts as a way of underlining its own eventfulness. But what constitutes an event for avant-garde practice may require revision in the post–9/11 world. "The event," specifies Foster, "served the artists as an instrument for achieving, in reality or by illusion, a positioning of themselves and their audiences in a hostile and self-destructive world and as a potential instrument of change."[4] Because the performative event has been turned against itself as the disaster, has not its instrumentality for performative positioning been indefinitely suspended? How can performance respond to events while abandoning the essential engagement to itself as an event?

Calls for performative response to the events of 9/11 have been issued in profusion. But have they been acknowledged, let alone acted upon? The subject came up for discussion, albeit not directly in the context of dance, at the Performance Studies International conference "Theatres of Life" (New York University, April 11–14, 2002). Coco Fusco cited the "calls from so many sectors to make art about the tragic events." She sketched the possibilities for performance as testimony and acts of witnessing.[5] Anne Cubilie recounted the gathering of testimony of female survivors in Afghanistan as an ethical obligation, and counterposed it to (mediatized) spectacle and other forms of viewing.[6] Barbara Kirshenblatt-Gimblett's analysis of the phenomenology of reception at the World Trade Center and across Manhattan Island envisaged the disaster as always already spectatorship through the tropes of snapshots and flashbulbs. "Photography," she stated, "was one of the most powerful responses to the attack."[7] Kirshenblatt-Gimblett restored a performative dimension to event as spectacle entailing its own replay. The impact of viewing could not be detached in this case from the reception of the event itself, which seemed to have been "designed" for vast visual consumption across Manhattan Island and the surrounding areas, as well as through the media.

Without precluding mourning, testimony, and witnessing, my question is tangential to these axes of inquiry. I address the call for and to dance. Can dance "respond" to the event? Is "response" (in the terms of a dance) actually what is called for?[8] Has 9/11 ushered in the place of "the event" as that which "comes after"—in the sense of supersedes—the performative. And I ask specifically: Can dance render (perhaps better than "respond to") the disaster? What kind of "giving back" would this rendering entail? Which logic of performative exchange are we engaged with here, in the wake of the event? Here I would recall Baudrillard's statement: "Life exchanged for [given back to] death is the very operation of the symbolic."

The need for performance to reappropriate eventfulness as a condition of response, is the very problem posed by the gift. There is a kind of debt at work in this call for response that seems to stand between the event to which something is owed and the performance as payback. From Marcel Mauss and Georges Bataille to Maurice Blanchot, Jacques Derrida, Jean Baudrillard, Pierre Bourdieu, and Jean-François Lyotard, the gift has obtained a contradictory status between performance and event. This essay attempts to think the place of dance between performance and event.

II

> *This place, this will be precisely* what happens, *what we are arriving at or what happens to us, the event, the place of what takes place, which mocks the perfor-mative, performative power.* —Jacques Derrida, L'Université sans conditions, 24.

These words of Jacques Derrida, first pronounced in a 1998 lecture but published only in September 2001, take on an almost prophetic tone in the wake of September 11th.[9] The arrival of "what happens to us" as the events of 9/11 and its pressure on performance and performance theory invite a reconsideration of Derrida's work on performativity, the gift, and the event. A brief survey of these topics can help us to situate the gift in its pivotal position between performance and the event. Derrida's progress from the examination of performative power to event theory is framed by the period of the early seventies (the Iran hostage crisis) and the present moment (the war against terrorism). To examine this intellectual "progress" suggests that some historical necessity or causality leads from the performative to the event, a suggestion that is disabling for the power of performance. I wish to show, however, that its power can be recaptured through the gift whose contradictory status undermines any supersession.

Any such historical or causal progress would necessarily begin with J. L. Austin's speech act as "something done" by an intending subject. "If issuing the utterance is doing something," wrote Austin, "the 'I' and the 'active' and the 'present' seem appropriate."[10] Derrida critiqued Austin in 1971 for restricting the effectiveness of the speech act to the context vouched for by the I, the active, and the present of the performative enunciation.[11] Instead, he aligned the performative utterance with writing as a *mark* inevitably severed from its original context in the speech act. Derrida's critique is founded on the conventional nature of the performative utterance as duly noted by Austin. "But this relative purity [of the performative for Austin] does not emerge *in opposition to* citationality or iterability, but in opposition to other kinds of iteration [such as theatrical performance] which constitutes a violation of the allegedly rigorous purity of every event of discourse or every *speech* act."[12] The speech act, as Austin states, relies on conventionality for its effectiveness.[13] But Austin does not allow that this conventionality endows the speech act with the structure of writing as an inscription because such an admission would compromise the speech act's intentionality.

The Derridean inscription is a mark that exists *in the wake of* I, active, and present. It is something like a relic of the I, the active, and the present. This afterlife is, in other terms, *iterability,* generally referred to in the literature as citationality, and also central to a philosophical concept of performativity. The citation is a kind of verbal *artifact,* no longer speech, but thing (mark, text, inscription).[14]

Let us jump ahead to the "event." The event engages neither with intentionality underwritten by the context of the speech act's live enunciation (Austin) nor with the performativity of the mark whose conventionality guarantees a citational chain reaching well beyond the immediate context of its original production (Derrida). Now the event that "happens to us" "mocks" *both* such understandings of the speech act. The event, in other terms, is neither conventional, logocentric, nor iterative. The singular presence of "what takes place" *takes the place of* the performative, and mocks it, displaces it, and supersedes it. In other terms, the event disarms the performative by effectively removing its capacity to respond. The event leaves the act "speechless."

III

> Before it is there, no one awaits it; when it is there, no one recognizes it: for it is not there—the disaster. It has already diverted the word "be," realizing itself to such a degree that it has not begun.[15] —Maurice Blanchot, The Writing of the Disaster, 36

This third historical moment (our own) in which the event supersedes both the speech act and the performativity of the mark is also that of the gift. To be "arriving at" "what happens to us" is to to arrive at what Heidegger called the giveness of Being. "To think Being," he wrote, "explicitly requires us to relinquish Being as the ground of beings in favor of the giving which prevails concealed in unconcealment, that is, in favor of the It gives. As the gift of this It gives, Being belongs to giving."[16] By the same token, "Time *is* not. There is, It gives time."[17] The English "There" as subject of the verb translates the German "es" (es gibt die Zeit) and the French impersonal "il" (Il y a le temps). The capitalization of *It* indicates this impersonal and fundamentally mysterious agent *Es* or *Il* that "gives" Being and time.

Derrida began his first seminar on the gift in 1979–1980 at the Ecole Normale Supérieure, with this quote from Heidegger: "Die Zeit ist nicht; es gibt die Zeit." ("There is no time; time is given"). The power of the event is its *giveness* as it arrives, which power is sustained by the secretiveness surrounding its original intention (it is "concealed in unconcealedness").[18] The source and intention of 9/11 are at the time of this writing far from being unequivocally identified in political discourse. Just as it is difficult if not impossible to respond to Being and time by subjecting them to representation (they don't exist as the ground of beings), so the event poses an analogous crisis. The event is in some way transparent or invisible. The gift's contradiction or impossibility (Derrida calls it "the very figure of the impossible") is that it must not call forth reciprocation if it is to sustain its being as gift.[19] Derrida: "If he recognizes it *as* gift, if the gift *appears to him as such,* if the present is present to him *as present,* this simple recognition suffices to annul the gift."[20] Derrida derives this dictum not from Heidegger, however, but from the sociological and anthropological investigations of Marcel Mauss.

As Mauss observed through his fieldwork in Polynesia, Melanesia, and the American Northwest in the 1920s, the gift incurs debt in that it obliges the countergift. Despite this systemic process suggesting circulation and exchange, Mauss also discussed the impossible impulse in gift giving. The *potlatch* shared across these cultures is sumptuary and agonistic gift giving whose excessiveness (even madness) attempts the foreclosure of reciprocation. For Mauss, the cultural logic of giving in archaic societies is not the precursor of economic logic in mercantile exchange, because its actions do not prefigure the restricted economy of circulation. The philosophical problem of nonsubjective donation and the socio-anthropological evidence of *potlatch* as sacrifice and destruction together recast the gift as variety of event. Every gift aspires to the structure of the event in its aspiration to disable response, to block the competitive impulse to reciprocate. Indeed, Mauss accrues evidence showing how reciprocation entails competition, sumptuary destruction, and thus profound antagonism.[21] The gift aspires to escape the political economy of any gesture.

I emphasize now an aspect of Mauss that Derrida does not accentuate. There is always an obligation to return the favor, an obligation that is imposed by rank and power but also—and most important according to Mauss—by virtue of the force *in* the things that circulate. This force is the result of a nondifferentiation between persons and things. It is precisely such nondifferentiation that could be useful in grasping the inscription as relic. The *force* of the gift is not based on the I, the active, and the present.

What does the force circulating in gifts mean? As Lyotard has written: "There is a dimension of force that escapes the logic of the signifier: an excess of energy that symbolic exchange can never regulate, excess that 'primitive' culture thematizes as debt."[22] Lyotard goes on to theorize the event as follows: "One could call an event the impact, on the system, of floods of energy such that the system does not manage to bind and channel this energy; the event would be the traumatic encounter of energy with the regulating institution."[23] An event happens by passing through the body without the body's ability to contain, bind, or channel its energy. The force of this passage works on the body—dead or alive. I suggest we consider this process as transmission.

First: transmission in/as communication. As Derrida establishes in "Signature Event Context," communication cannot be limited to "the transmission of a *meaning*."[24] "To say that writing *extends* the field and the powers of locutory or gestural communication presupposes, does it not, a sort of *homogeneous* space of communication?"[25] Inscription and transmission become interchangeable sites of verbal and kinetic communication. Some communications occur without evident intention: "A tremor, a shock, a displacement of force can be communicated—that is, *transmitted*."[26] The process of transmission itself is what links the force of the event to the force of giving. Further, transmission links dance and writing, as we shall see.

Dance as expressive communication is also rarely if ever thought (at least in contemporary Dance Studies) to correspond to "meaning" or "signification." That dance "communicates a movement" (what this means awaits determination) has been theorized as occurring outside the discursive field, even if many logocentric qualities can be associated with the production of its gesture: immediacy, presence, and often the seriousness concomitant to "liveness."[27] Much postmodern dance has responded to, or perhaps even prompted, the poststructuralist critical perspective wherein dance as mark can be seen to emerge: "the non-present remainder of a differential mark cut off from its putative 'production' or origin."[28] But what are the historical conditions of the production of dance as mark? As my final example shall suggest, the conditions may be those of Hiroshima in 1945.

The transmission of dance movement is generally apprehended within a pedagogical perspective. But movement contains the double property that distinguishes the gift: it is personal as it doesn't exist without a personal manifestation, but it is also a cultural object in that it derives from a tradition. Transmission is rarely—if ever—thought about from a theo-retical let alone from a hermeneutic perspective. That dance can perform this marking in/as transmission (even in/as the transmission of an aes-thetic tradition) may remain divorced from the fact that its means of pro-duction rely on the logocentric qualities of liveness. There is sometimes a need to distinguish between the dancer and the dance. But this is the very tension explicit in the encounter between performative action and the event. The event implies a hyperbolic reduction of agency such that the event's status as gift appears to negate dance as communication.

But what of the transmission of dances, which refers primarily to the performance of their learning? What of their learning as gift? And what in the structure of this pedagogical transmission corresponds to eventful-ness? How does the reception of an aesthetic (even a newly invented one) imply the learning implicit in the radical sense we are giving to the term *response?* Can we resolve the contradiction between performance and event by thinking of dance as transmission? Consider first transmission in its most prosaic instance as dance pedagogy.

## IV

Margaret Mead introduces a Balinese dancer and teacher in Gregory Bate-son's film *Learning to Dance in Bali* (1936–39): "This is Mario, the most famous dancer in Bali who already was reputed more as a teacher than a dancer."[29] We are shown Mario dancing the kebiar solo form in a short sequence, after which we see him instructing a young boy, Murda, whom he meets "out for a stroll" and who has "never had a lesson before." I wish to pause over this "informal lesson"—a gratuitous gift—of the dancer/teacher to the unsuspecting student. The narrative setup is trans-parently fictional, but this does not invalidate what the film has to tell us about the transmission of dance techniques, which we can see with our own eyes. In fact, the fictive elements may be there precisely to convey a point of view on technique and its transmission.

Mario positions himself behind his pupil whose arms and torso he ma-nipulates into the positions and through the trajectories of the choreog-raphy he imparts. As Sally Ann Ness noted of a Balinese dance lesson she took in Bali in 1992: "I felt like a tree with branches that she [the teacher] arranged."[30] In the film as well in Ness's more recent experience, the teacher "gives" the choreography to the pupil in a way that renders giv-ing difficult to visualize, as giving means shaping the other's gesture while remaining unseen. Invisible, Mario offers no image to mimic.

According to the film's narrative, this instruction is an unexpected gift, and the sense of that fortuitousness is echoed in the pedagogical technique through which it is imparted. Murda is fortuitously enlisted to receive Mario's instruction on a whim, as the film would have it. Mario transmits the gesture's shape to Murda inasmuch as this shape is realized directly in/by Murda's body. This gesture, derived from an aesthetic tradition personified by the teacher's, is not transmitted across a mediating space of observation and interpretation. Whatever doubts one may have about the documentarity of the film itself, there can be no doubt that the performance and pedagogical techniques are closely hewn to one another. Using Laban movement analysis terminology, Ness remarks that "the amount of Bound/Quick needed for these actions was extraordinary."[31] This lesson, however fictional, contains marks of technical communication that in themselves cannot be falsified.

We should also say that Mario gives Murda nothing and, following Derrida, that he preserves in this way the integrity of his gift. Mario's movements are presenced in Murda's body at the very moment Murda "learns" them, or is *given* them to learn. Other eyewitnesses noted: "The dancing teacher in Bali does really communicate *himself* and not merely his instruction. He literally inspires the body he is training."[32] Teaching a movement is giving something of oneself, and this gift of movement indexes the force inhabiting the gift as described by Mauss.[33] This force makes it impossible to discern between what is given and who is giving. Mauss: "Yet it is also because by giving one is giving *oneself*, it is because one 'owes' *oneself*—one's person and one's goods—to others." ("Mais aussi c'est qu'on *se* donne en donnant, et, si on *se* donne, c'est qu'on *se* 'doit'—soi et son bien—aux autres)."[34] This force—the motor of posteconomic circulation—involves the "circulation" of self as mark, which is analogous to the philosophical necessity of abandoning the "I," the "active," and the "present." Paradoxically, this is the way a dance form is transmitted and is able to survive culturally.

With this pedagogical example I am proposing that we think of this "self-force" as transmission. *Learning to Dance in Bali* provides a striking image of this transmission, which it sets up as the communication of a dance as gift. The two figures hover close to the ground. Mario is positioned behind Murda to manipulate the pupil whose "will and consciousness," as Mead notes, are almost "in abeyance."[35] It would seem he is poised to receive the gift of the other. But this is not in reality a manipulation in the conventional sense because the teacher, unlike the puppeteer, uses no analogical code. Both bodies move fully and share the same kinesthetic experience: an impulse is transmitted. In this way, movement is transmitted from one body to another.

This same pedagogical method is displayed later in the film with Mario's more seasoned pupils. As the teacher sits on the sidelines, an older student manipulates a younger trainee. In this tripling effect of transmission, what emerges is a danced figure of performativity in the realization that fixed gestures are passed down to sustain the dance form's fragile cultural identity. I call attention to the interaction in this example between gift/event and performativity that the film allows us to glimpse in the transmission of a dance in Balinese culture. In this transmission, we can also glimpse a possible structure of "response" to the event whose potential is grounded in the operations of transmission. But they are not limited to Bali in the 1930s.

The process of transmission contains within it the structure of the event. It is the performative basis of dance (and to this extent of performance in general) that the event cannot mock. Aesthetic traditions, more than any other kinds of movement, are generated by the It of It gives.[36] But their transmission from body to body is the mode of their reinscription, which is itself a kind of event constitutive of the inscription of tradition on bodies—that is, of cultural traditions.

This part of the film allows us to see and understand, in other terms, the reception of the event as an unsolicited form of transmission qua training. The disciplining imposed by the event generates its own performativity; "a tremor, a shock, a displacement of force can be 'communicated.'" What this account of transmission makes evident is that dancing can be a particularly efficacious form of giving in the philosophical sense. What the philosophical tradition (even that of deconstruction) underplays, however, is the simultaneous self-donation required to render this giving efficacious, and which, in the absence of any object, fills the role of intentionality that Derrida sees as inseparable from the gift.[37] The invisible intentionality of the event resides in (its) movement and in the transmission of its movement.


V


> To make gestures of the dead, to die again, to make the dead reenact once more
> their deaths in their entirety—these are what I want to experience within me.
> A person who has died once can die over and over again within me.
> —Tatsumi Hijikata[38]


I shall conclude with a brief discussion of the film shot by Eikoh Hosoe in 1960 with Tatsumi Hijikata, *Navel and A-Bomb*.[39] Hijikata (1928–1986), one of the originators of the postwar Japanese dance form *ankoku buto* (dance of utter darkness) establishes a visual relationship between the attacks on Hiroshima and Nagasaki at the end of the Second World War and buto. Early in the film we see a flash in the sky followed by a plume of rising black smoke. The film is in a sense an agglomeration of marks—white on black, black on white—by virtue of the cinematography, the formality of framing, and the relation of composition to montage. Buto undoubtedly entertains a privileged relation to the status of dance as mark.

The first shots of *Navel and A-Bomb* suggest an ambiguity of forms: an apple perched on one of five mounds of earth resembles the fleshly contours of a supine body, with the crashing waves of the sea as backdrop. Into this scene come two hands from either side of the frame that dialogue over the apple. Here, as elsewhere in the film, the frame acts to isolate parts of the body and to give them autonomy as moving objects, whether they be a back, a stomach, hands, an elbow, or feet. The first scene establishes a conversation between a hand and an elbow in which these body parts are endowed with intentionality, yet deprived of organicity. As with the headless bodies seen repeatedly in the film, relation is presented as intentionality without subjectivity. As with the apple, each body part appears self-contained. The frame never suggests isolation, as if these body parts were extensions of a proximate and adjoining whole. The dancers' partial bodies belong to the organic world of the apple and the sand mound except for their autonomous mobility. Movement itself is a gift whose source is obscured by the body-object. The performing partial bodies stand in stark visual contrast to the cow on the beach. The partial bodies are organic forms with smooth surfaces and orifices whereas the bovine body is "complete," but for that reason a static and weighted body almost devoid of motion and consciousness. Of course, the dancers have feet, but we see them tied together and only below the knee; they have heads but these are wrapped in white fabric or out of view thanks to the composition of the shot; they have arms but these are rarely seen connected to shoulders. The partitioned totality is dead although still in motion, like the white chicken carcass that floats in the waves and "gestures" involuntarily with its claws in the air. The dancer's arms iterate these clawing gestures. The human body is "iterated" in/as the organic but inanimate object, and in the dead animal. The dying carcass describes white marks or blots against the dark sea, intercut with a close-up of Hijikata's chest inscribed with white marks. Given the chicken's claws in the surf, this marking seems to be a transmission visualized by association through editing. "Even as it consigns," remarks Derrida, "inscription produces a new event."[40] Inscription as event is the performative act of response we are inquiring after.

Hijikata's torso is scratched with white chalk marks. His hands do the marking and reorganize or reinscribe the marks. His is a body of the event in the sense that it is at once a witness to atomic explosion and a body already in pieces. His fingers discover his navel and appear blindly to seek entrance there. This body fragment, site of the mark, displays the intention to rediscover itself in the process of its own decomposition. Transmission occurs between parts with no governing subjectivity; it occurs as the advent or occurrence of self-inflicted marks. The mark stabilizes a set of connections (a communicating network) between body and event, navel and A-bomb. In the end, a child's navel is marked with a black X: a navel both crossed out and reinscribed on the skin's surface. A rope is pulled from the navel, the child shields its eyes from the glare in the sky, and the nuclear explosion reappears in a blinding white flash.

The body in *Navel and A-Bomb* is marked by the event and becomes the mark of the event. It lies on the shores of time. But that mark, like the navel, is also a place: the place of performance. The experience of dying takes place again, as Hijikata said, "within me." In saying, "a person who has died once can die over and over again within me," he refers neither to mourning nor to witnessing. Instead he describes the giving of movement to disaster as event. This is the performance of what Baudrillard has called "symbolic exchange": "a death given and received, thus reversible in social exchange ("une mort *donnée* et *reçue*, donc réversible dans l'échange social").[41]

I shall venture to say in conclusion that transmission is necessary to the production of "responsive" dance, and thus that the performative cannot be severed from the way dance is "given." That is, dance as an event has always already preceded its (Austinian) performativity. It takes place before and after the I, active, and present. Without feigning to prescribe any particular imaginable response (who could possibly do so?), I would also venture this hypothesis. Response can be said to require a *form* (mark), not just a choreography but a *dance form,* even if (and indeed especially if)—as in the case of *ankoku buto*—it was invented uniquely for the purpose of response.[42] To perform a response to the event is to bring forth the contradiction of the gift as a reappropriation of eventfulness.

Perhaps the problem has been in calling for a response when what should be called for are gifts of a sort—gifts whose marks are choreographic. Such choreographic giving might serve to redefine the event's reception in the wake of 9/11.

# 8 || Inscribing Dance

*For Elsa and Tobias*

Where lie the limits between body and text, movement and language? Within the historical tradition that shaped Western modernity, answering this question implies not only considering the new art form of modernity par excellence, dance, but directly confronting ourselves with two components interstitially inscribed in the very cultural perceptions and definitions of dancing. I am referring to the (almost spontaneous) parallels habit and language have forged between dance and writing (as explicitly manifested in "choreo/graphing") and between dance and femininity (as explicitly manifested in the perception of dancing as threat to masculinity).[1] The intertwining of dance, writing, and femininity in Western theatrical dance since the Baroque period suggests that any attempts to define the limits between body and text, between movement and language, must inevitably start with identifying the grounds where (what is understood by) dance and by femininity stand. The problem with such a project, however, is that one soon discovers that those grounds are boundless. The streaming of signification, the passing of movement through time, the dissolution of the body—all propose that categorical distinctions, closed units, fortified boundaries are constituted less as monads than as circuits of exchange, spaces of friction, where, as Gaston Bachelard once noted, "formal opposition refuses to remain calm."[2] The spaces of friction constituted by the restless tensions between body and text, movement and language, indicate precisely a limitless contiguity among dance, writing, and femininity. Shared ground: dance cannot be imagined without writing, it does not exists outside writing's space,[3] just as dance cannot be perceived without the apparition (even if by a negative ghostliness, a reactionary disavowal) of the feminine. If this is the case, then a question emerges, wildly, almost unreasonably, certainly hysterically: could both writing and femininity ever happen without dancing? Could one separate the threads that bind such a powerful triad without betraying the ontological grounding through which each of its elements finds its stance? To answer the unreasonable question, it is necessary to trace the history of the interstitial, insistent inscription of writing, dancing, and femininity upon one another. For it is within the folds, crevices, and fissures such continuous inscribing carves that dance makes its appearance and finds its presence through its most intimate accomplices: writing and femininity.

## Dance's Lament

Despite the theoretical emphasis on disappearance and trace brought about by deconstruction, the perception of dance as an art of self-erasure is contemporary with the foundation of dance theories that inaugurate both modern choreography and dance studies.[4] Jean-Georges Noverre, one of the founders of the modern conception of choreographing, as well as of what can be properly denominated as dance theory, lamented in 1760 on the subordinate position of theatrical dance within the arts, brought about by dance's specific materiality. In the first of his *Letters on Dancing and Ballets* Noverre identifies the materiality of dance as ephemeral and deplores its evanescence in the following terms: "Why are the names of *maîtres de ballets* unknown to us? It is because works of this kind endure only for a moment and are forgotten as soon as the impressions they had produced."[5] Noverre's perception of dance as an art in self-erasure, echoes earlier voices of dance masters, already turning toward the page to articulate the possibility of dancing within the novel project of modernity. Thoinot Arbeau, in the late sixteenth century: "As regards ancient dances all I can tell you is that the passage of time, the indolence of man or the difficulty of describing them has robbed us of any knowledge thereof."[6] Before this predicament, Arbeau will propose writing as archival commandment.[7] For Arbeau, dance's unfortunate ephemerality can be overcome by writing, dancing felicitous supplement. But note how this archival force commands not only the living bodies presenting the dance but also the spirits of the dead. Arbeau's narrative starts by proposing how the embrace of masculinity and law is the first condition for the re/presentation of dance in a body ready to be filled with the steps of the dead. His interlocutor and student, the young lawyer Capriol, responds to Arbeau's lament by urging: "Do not allow this [dance's disappearance] to happen, Monsieur Arbeau, as it is within your power to prevent it. Set these things down in writing to enable me to learn this art, and in so doing you will seem reunited to the companions of your youth."[8] Standing before dance, writing emerges with a double function: it turns the dancer's body into a medium for temporal exchange; it cures dance's somewhat embarrassing predicament of always losing itself as it performs itself. Within the homosocial dialogue depicted in Arbeau's book, this double function of writing casts dance as unruly, light-headed, slippery—the negative attributes femininity is accused of. Nonetheless, Arbeau's *Orchesography* (literally, the writing of movement) still demonstrates trust in a semiotic symmetry between writing and dancing that guarantees the unproblematic traffic from one and the other. This trust would not last long.

Noverre's use of writing differs from Arbeau's in the sense that Noverre believed firmly on the excessive aspect of dancing as that which could never be fully grasped, nor fixed by notation. Thus, his letters inaugurate writing as mournful performance within choreographic imagination—a performance in which writing announces and indicates dance's ungraspable excess. Noverre's suspicion of notation yet trust in writing inaugurates a whole new relationship between inscription and dancing, text and embodiment. Jean-Noël Laurenti noted how Noverre's project radically differed from (and harshly critiqued) the earlier dance-notation methods. The early French academicians were bound to Raoul-Auger Feuillet's notation method (systematized in his influential *Chorégraphie ou l'art de décrire la danse, par caractères, figures et signes démonstratifs* [first published in 1699]). With this notation code, dances could be created even without the presence of a moving body. Laurenti describes how, in the seventeenth century, "the city's dancing masters are shut up in a room with paper, writing desk, 'mathematical case, etc.,' as if for a written examination; they compose choreographies [ . . . ] which are then sent to Paris to be judged and classified by the Academy; only afterwards comes the practical test, or 'execution.'"[9] Inscription preceded dancing; the space of writing prefaces the performance of the steps. Moreover, both notation and steps were harmonized within the luminous planar space of Cartesian rationality, manifested in linear geometrism and the perception of the body as machine.[10] Laurenti locates the drive behind the development of dance notation more as a political project than a mournful lament: writing not only allowed centralization of power with the Royal Academy "replacing the privilege of the guilds"; it also allowed for "imposing French influence [ . . . ] on foreign nations"[11] by the means of the dance manual. One could argue that this political project is predicated upon the development of an archival structure of command responding to an ontological understanding of dance as a lamentable art that can neither remember nor be remembered.[12]

Such structure of forgetting attributed to dance will have an enormous impact on the gendering of dance as an art form within the disciplinary project of modernity. Forgetting will shape the understanding and perception of what constitutes the presence of dance. Still, according to Laurenti, Noverre's critique of Feuillet's notation methods signals for the first time in dance writings the identification of a central problem in dance's ontology: that of a presence that ontologically resists and escapes those boundaries codification and inscription as temporal arrest try to impose. Laurenti summarizes Noverre's attitude by invoking the choreographer's stance before the problem of dance's ephemerality, of dance's vanishing presence from the field of representation. According to Laurenti, the problem of dance's materiality for Noverre can be summarized as follows: "how can the presence of the object be regained through that which decomposes it?"[13] This becomes the fundamental question for dance, dance's paradox, its curse. From the moment the question of dance's presence began to be formulated as loss and temporal paradox, dance was transformed into hauntology and taxidermy—and choreography cast as mourning.

Jean-Georges Noverre announces the formation of a perceptual and ontolinguistic ground where dancing and writing, body and text, start detaching and distancing from each other.[14] As Susan Foster writes, "even thought construed as language in Enlightenment thought, the body's gestures begin to signify that which cannot be spoken. This unique role for gesture prepares the way for a complete separation between dance and text that occurs in the early decades of the nineteenth century."[15] This distancing, this insertion of boundaries, immediately sets up a problem for writing on dance. On the one hand, the separation of disciplines follows and charts the by then unfolding project of modernity, anticipating the self-referentiality typical of the aesthetics of modernism. On the other hand, the distancing and splitting are precisely what allow the perception of dance as art in excess. This excess is associated with dance's unruly standing before time and memory, dance's presence as a falling away from an arresting visibility. Once the symmetry between writing and dance is undermined, dance's ephemerality starts posing the problem of dance's presence. Dance's presence as a motion that escapes writing is problematic because it disturbs the project of dance's regulation and registry. Thus, from a perception of dance as unproblematically translatable from code to steps, and from steps back into code again (a peaceful symmetry between inscription and dancing that characterizes, as we saw, Arbeau's and Feuillet's perception), we arrive, with Noverre, to an understanding of dance as elusive presence, dance as the fleeting trace of an always irretrievable, never fully translatable motion: neither into notation, nor into writing. Inscription fails the test of a new regime of perception, which announces and pursues a new ontological grounding for the presence of the dancing body. Within this new visual regime and this new metaphysical ground, what tests both vision and inscription to their limits is presence: presence unfolding as a mode of being whose temporality escapes scopic control, presence as haunted by invisibility, presence as sentencing to absence.

Here, movement starts to share some characteristics of presence: movement is that which becomes increasingly invisible, elusive, filled with blanks, blind spots, nebulous regions.[16] Mostly, movement disappears, it marks the passing of time. Movement is both sign and symptom that all presence is haunted by disappearance and absence. This stepping into invisibility of both movement and presence generates a new nervousness within the project of writing dances and writing on dances. Pierre Rameau, preceding by a few decades the publication of Noverre's *Letters,* authors a dance manual in which this new regime of perception is clearly tied with a model of the body described by Francis Barker as essentially modern.[17] Rameau's *Dancing Master* (1725) is structured around a systemic, Cartesian fragmentation of both body and movement down to their most minute components. The book is divided in several small sections with titles such as "Of the Manner of Holding the Body," "Of the Manner of Taking off One's Hat and Putting it on Again," "A Discourse on the Arms and of the Importance of Knowing How to Move Them Gracefully," "On the Manner of Moving the Wrist," and so forth. Despite the detail in the writing and the breaking down of movements into gestures, steps, body parts, Rameau's book already indicates a quite telling distrust on the capacity of writing to convey movement. Illustrating writing's new asymmetrical stance before the dancing body, Rameau includes in his book dozens of drawings, accompanying each detailed section. He justifies the inclusion of the drawings by arguing that "the eye, which is the mirror of the soul, shall give more force to my [written] powers of expression by affording the reader that clear explanation which I desire to give him."[18] Clarity could only arrive with the supplementation of writing with the image of the body. What is truly telling of changing of perceptual regime and ontological trust in the symmetry between writing and movement, is that for Rameau not even the "mirror of the soul" is such a transparent vehicle for clarity. A few pages into the text, Rameau has a moment of hesitation, a nervous burst of doubt in the unfolding crisis of representation (of which he is both victim and agent). Rameau distrusts his drawings; he will not be not satisfied with their truth value. Thus, his decision to publish the drawings along the text happens only after the author has "submitted them to the criticism of the most skilful persons both in danc-ing and in drawing," and has received from them that guarantee that "in their opinion, they are drawn correctly to rule, both in their relation to the body and to be able to move with ease in the different *pas*."[19] For the dancing master confronted with the faulty nature of both writing and il-lustration to convey movement, nothing less than a plebiscite guarantees the stability of representation before the fleeting body moving toward its own erasure.

Rameau's *Dancing Master*, a book hovering between the inadequacy of language and the inaccuracy of vision, announces Peggy Phelan's in-sight that "writing re-marks the hole in the signifier, the inability to con-vey meaning exactly. The intimacy of the language of speech and the lan-guage of vision extends to their mutual impossibilities."[20] My point is that the identification of an intimacy between the inability of the language of speech and the inability of the language of vision, their isomorphic co-impossibilities, points toward the outlining of a new ontolinguistic regime of sensibility that casts movement and presence as absence. Before an ab-sent presence and an absent movement, the problem dance puts before writing is of how movement and words can be placed under arrest. Dance confronts us with the impossibility of such project. The perception of this double lack is what motivates the mournful energy behind dance. Mourn-ing is the psychic state resulting from the difficulty in acknowledging how presence has slipped or will slip into absence no matter how much effort, love, anger, cathexis we invest and project onto the loved object, or ideal.[21] The whole epistemic-technological apparatus (including later de-velopments in dance inscription, from Laban notation to motion-capture technologies), manipulated by the collapsing of technology as archive, develops from the mourning force that movement as presence and pres-ence as absence propose.

To summarize my points so far: the late eighteenth century sets up the conditions of possibility for an understanding of movement isomorphic with an understanding of presence as invisible, elusive—presence as con-demnation to disappearance. This fleeting presence as that which will not stay put has informed the framing of dance's visibility ever since—dance's constitution of itself as a force-field of absence-presence, a field charged with a lament verging on mourning. Mournful lament emerges the mo-ment writing and dancing become inextricably bound to each other not by a pacific symmetry between word and motion, but by the means of a newfound distancing from each other. It is such a binding distancing that provokes and necessitates dancing to keep building bridges toward writing and writing to bridge toward dancing. I shall now discuss how this distancing and this bridging performs dance as haunting presence of the feminine.

## Photology

It is in this specific sense of mourning, of understanding the necessity of the lack in vision and of the gap between dance and writing initiated by dance as performance of absence-presence, that Noverre's lament is central to modern dance theory. Noverre's mournful energy both delimited dance theory's epistemic field, as well as fueled to the present day the epistemological project of dance studies as photology[22]—one that envisions dance writing as an endless effort to counter dance's self-erasure. Note how Noverre's lament reemerges, almost verbatim, in the writing of influential American dance critic Marcia Siegel when she affirms, one hundred and twenty years after Noverre, that "[dance] doesn't stay around long enough to become respectable or respected. Its ephemerality is mistaken for triviality."[23] Between Siegel's and Noverre's statements the whole project of dance theory can be summarized as follows: dance vanishes; it does not "stay around" (for such is the unfortunate condition of its materiality); therefore, the dance scholar, theorist, critic, must work against dance's materiality by fixating the dance; therefore documentation (whether descriptive writing, movement notation, filming) gives the dance the defense it needs against the accusation of never sticking around, of being too trivial, of constantly loosing itself, of *being* loose. In order to make dance "stay around" longer "to impede the extinction of yesterday's dance,"[24] dance theory has found its model in the highest aspirations of photology: the illumination and arrest of presence for the sake of History. The hope of such a model would be that documentation of dances would "correct," or "cure" dance's flawed materiality. The photological project subjects dance to the archival structure of command.

Dance historian Mark Franko has commented on how the documental response to the ontological relocation of dance as ephemeral established an epistemological deadlock in dance theory.[25] Franko does not contend the notion of dance's materiality as ephemeral but rather the perception of ephemerality as a lack, in need of the supplement of documentation. What he criticizes is the tradition in dance studies that sees dance's materiality as ephemerality as something that must be worked against. Franko argues that the privileging of documentation for the sake of securing dance's presence has historically relegated both dance and dance theory to an apparently hopeless ahistorical, atheoretical, and apolitical realm.[26] Franko observes, however, that recently this same "ephemerality of dance" that launched the documental effort has endured a significant epistemological transformation within dance studies. From a symptom of aesthetic inferiority that must be "corrected," dance's self-erasure has been recently reformulated as a powerful trope for new theoretical (as well as performative) interventions in dance, and in writings on dance, beyond the documental tradition. Commenting on this epistemological shift, Franko states: "dance's change of cast has deconstruction to thank."[27] For Franko, dance's (and dance studies') debt to deconstruction lies primarily in the Derridean notion of "trace."

I would argue that Jacques Derrida's radical reevaluation of the problem of materiality and of presence within Western metaphysics are of relevance for rethinking the relationship between dance and writing in two fundamental aspects: in Derrida's proposition of the "concept" of "trace,"[28] and in his investigations of the "question of woman" in the writings of Friedrich Nietzsche. (That is to say, on the unstable relations between writing and femininity, and dancing and femininity). Derrida's notions of trace and *différance* provided dance studies the theoretical tools needed to engage in critique of the epistemological claims of the documental tradition. Ironically, the only text by Derrida that specifically addresses dance marks the very limits of his contributions to dance theory. I shall briefly outline Derrida's critique of metaphysics in those aspects most relevant to the present discussion. For it was Derrida's critique that established the paradigmatic shift Mark Franko identified as responsible for changing dance's cast. Moreover, it is through Derrida that the specter of femininity makes her reappearance in the scene, to complicate both writing and the possibility of dancing.

If we agree with Gayatri Spivak's statement that, for Derrida, the word metaphysics is but a "shorthand for any science of presence,"[29] then we could say that Derrida's critique of classic metaphysics is an effort to liberate philosophy from the burden of presence at/as the center of philosophy itself. Let us not forget that, for Derrida, the entire history of metaphysics, which he identifies with the "history of the West," has always been structured around a center: that of "Being as presence in all senses of the word."[30] He notes how all the names assigned to that center (from *eidos* to *ousia,* from man to god) designate "an invariable presence."[31] It is only with Nietzsche, Freud, and Heidegger that presence as Truth, presence as Subject, and presence as Being, respectively, are decentered.

However, as revolutionary as these "destroyers" of metaphysics were, their task was not, according to Derrida, fully taken to the limit.[32] To summarize an extended argument, Derrida critiques Heidegger for his longing for a theological Being and his nostalgia for a transcendental signified to which all signifiers refer. He radicalizes Nietzsche's concept of the sign by using the model of the Saussurean sign, unavailable to Nietzsche, in order to further what Spivak calls Nietzsche's "undoing of opposites."[33] Critiquing Freud, Derrida invokes the problem of presence in psychoanalysis. Derrida argues that as soon as we accept a conscious or unconscious subject, as Freud did, we are immediately locating in/as the core of our discourse a substance, a center, therefore a presence.[34] For Derrida, in order to fully critique metaphysics, to escape its economy and its discourse circling forever around presence, one must take one more step. That step is the one of disappearance, of (self)erasure, which is to say, the step of the *trace*.[35] Derrida writes: "the trace is the erasure of selfhood, of one's own presence, and is constituted by the threat or anguish of its irremediable disappearance, of the disappearance of its disappearance."[36] This erasure "of one's own presence" constituted by an "irremediable disappearance" has been influential for the field of performance and dance studies.

Mark Franko affirms that dance's "ephemerality-as-disappearance is a synonym of the Derridean trace."[37] Franko's formulation echoes what performance theorist Peggy Phelan had already defined as the "ontology of performance": that "maniacally charged present" announcing itself at the very moment presence plunges into disappearance.[38] Rivière's, Franko's, and Phelan's writings on the performing, dancing body, because they acknowledge, without lament, the ephemeral tracing of dancing, generate something other than discontent, or the desire to document. By emphasizing erasure as/at the origin of discourse, and by removing presence as prerequisite for "knowledge," their (different) uses of what could be defined as the Derridean trace emerge as that which allows the possibility of writing along (as opposed to "against") ephemerality.

The "slippery" aspect of the trace (derived from the "structure of the Saussurean sign as well as of our psyche")[39] undermines the (heuristic) weight of presence. The trace is always already referring one signifying element to another set of traces of traces, other absences of absences. This motion of the trace along a signifying continuum allows theories of dance (and of performance in general) to free themselves from the visual attachment that has traditionally accompanied them. Dance studies no longer have to serve the eye alone. As Mark Franko suggests, "complexity hinges on asking how much of dance [ . . . ] materializes as visible, or should be understood in visual terms alone."[40] I have discussed already how the purpose of this visual attachment is isomorphic with Noverre's anxiety: to block dance's self-erasure by the means of documentation. With Derrida, we can identify the dynamics of such attachment as a mimetic reproduction of the blindness at the core of metaphysics itself. Derrida's emphasis on disappearance, on erasure, on specters, not only displaces presence from the center of philosophy; it reformulates the very sensorial basis of philosophy. Derrida identifies metaphysics' attachment to presence as a desire to make presence always visible: "the entire history of our [Western] philosophy is a photology, the name given to a history of, or treatise on, light."[41] Therefore metaphysics can only offer dance theory the endless description of what "happened on stage"; this secures the presence of dance, keeps it fixed within a certain visibility. Note how presence, description, and photology collapse in the following passage, where writing on dance is utterly bound to the presence of a scopic body: "None of the documentary devices presently in use is as accessible, as highly developed, or as reliable as good on-the-spot dance criticism."[42] With Derrida, dance studies can finally leave this morbid photology.

What does it mean to write with dance? What happens to the distinction of body and text once one critiques the putative distinctions between writing and dancing? Derrida's critique of metaphysics as "any science of presence," points to a possible answer to these questions, while it illuminates the dynamics of commandment propelling the project of documentation. Documentation works against the trace as it insists on the centrality of presence. Once one applies this principle to writing on dances, the irony emerges in that it is the very documental effort to fixate dance that betrays dance's material promise and hope. Documentation, in its optical-descriptive obsession, withdraws dance from the flow of its own materiality. All documentation provides is a stiff body. Derrida's notion of writing as difference offers dance studies a set of "signs" as elusive as those dance steps to which they refer. Both writing and dancing plunge into ephemerality. With Derrida, dance finally finds a form of writing that is in harmony with dance's current ontological status. Perhaps not since the seventeenth century has the harmonization of writing and dance had so complete a model. The return to symmetry derives from the acknowledgment that both writing and dancing participate in the same motion of the trace: that which will always be already behind at the moment of its appearance.

## Presence

Derrida's critique of presence implies that any signifying element (in a dance, in a text) is always already inhabited by and referring to another set of references, traces of traces of traces, in an endless play of *différance*. Derrida coined this "neographism" to refer precisely to the "movement of the trace" as a deferring-differing detour. This characteristic of *différance* makes any "structure of presence" (although, perhaps a better phrasing would be dynamics of presence) an always fleeting deferral (of itself) by the means of the unstoppable signifying movement of the trace. In this movement, presence differs and defers from itself, thus establishing the epistemological basis for the displacement of "objective" description under the logic of the Derridean trace—not only is the dance fleeting in eternal deferral but the observer is always in difference with his/her own presence.[43] That is to say, it is not only the object (the dance) that is in motion; the writer, the viewer, the spectator, is never, ever fixed as well.[44]

The contributions brought by the Derridean trace for dance studies are powerfully illustrated by Henry Sayre, when he analyzes the work of American postmodern choreographers such as Trisha Brown, Yvonne Rainer, and Anna Halprin. Sayre untangles the choreographic uses of repetition in Trisha Brown's work by stating that, with Brown, "the repetitive gesture is caught up in the dynamics of the Derridean trace."[45] What Sayre means is that both choreographic structure and movement style in some of Brown's pieces from the late 1970s and early 1980s (particularly in *Glacial Decoy* [1979] and *Set and Reset* [1983]), are embedded in a dynamics isomorphic to the one put in motion by the trace—a dynamics predicated upon the dancer's "self-erasure" and the (dramatic) anxiety derived from the possibility of the very "disappearance of disappearance." For Sayre, as Brown's dancers slip on- and offstage, appear and disappear from the wings, inhabit each other's fleeting gestures, they accumulatively create a dance that forbids "that a simple element be *present* in and of itself, referring only to itself"[46] (which is the inevitable consequence of an interpretive model embedded not in presence but in the elusive dynamics of the trace). Sayre's analysis must not be taken as merely an elegant discursive analogy between certain formal aspects of Derridean deconstruction and a certain postmodern approach to dancing. Rather, his analysis of postmodern choreography makes explicit that the motion of *différance* initiated by the trace opens up a whole set of possibilities for dance writing: of considering dance's materiality not only as that physical motility temporally and spatially enclosed within the frame of the stage and the dancers' skins, but also as a symbolically charged imaginary space.

Femininity

I have argued so far that Derrida's contribution for dance studies derive from his proposal of a "writing" whose constitutive sings are as unstable and fleeting as dance steps. It is interesting to note how, when explicitly addressing "the dance," Derrida's writing describes those steps and genders the ephemeral dancing body. Here, we shall find the limits of Derrida's understanding of dance, and therefore the limits of his project for writing. It is important that both limits be marked by femininity.

Derrida's only explicit text on dance, an interview with Christie MacDougall titled "Choreographies," is not a theorization of the question of presence, or of trace. The problematics of this text, staged as a dialogue, is that of sexual difference as an ongoing, unstable, and moving exchange (a sexually tense pas de deux) within the boundaries of history. "Choreographies" collapses a series of Derridean problems. Briefly, Derrida proposes that the materiality of dance is cast as woman. One must turn to Derrida's long essay *Spurs: Nietzsche's Styles,* particularly to the discussion of the "effect of woman," to understand such casting.[47] For Nietzsche, the most powerful effect of woman was that of her distance (in German *Distanz*). Derrida plays with the *Tanz* (dance) contained within woman's powerful effect to state that woman's dance at a distance is precisely the deferment, the differentiation, with which woman "engulfs and distorts all vestige of essentiality, of identity, of property."[48] In other words: woman's *Tanz* is outside any economy of exchange, and within the play of eternal deferral, eternal distancing, and detour that is the play of *différance*, the play of the trace. Woman is such playful tracing; woman's effect is this distancing dance. As opposed to the documental tradition, Derrida's stance regarding dance's ephemerality, dance's self-erasure within the shifting self-deferring realm of the trace, is in fact an embracing of vanishing as that which fulfills dance's own promise. For Derrida, only when dance happens off the record, beyond registration, when it escapes from the trap of documentation, when it vanishes into time properly, when it steps outside history—only then does it generates a powerful disturbance within the field of signification. That is to say: for Derrida, dance must be improvised, must move before writing. The relationship between body and text is against the commanding force of the prewritten. Rather, the dance writes and erases itself as it forgets itself, unpredictably unfolding (at a distance).

Derrida suggests that such dance is not a utopic-theoretical project, but actually took (takes) place within Europe where "the joyous disturbance of certain women's movements, and of some women in particular, has actually brought with it the chance for a certain risky turbulence."[49] Joyous disturbance? Certain women? Risky turbulence? Derrida does not name those women who "actually" disturbed the law of the European house with their improvised dances. This anonymity is problematic. Here, we are at the very limits of Derrida's contributions for dance studies. As provocative as Derrida's arguments might be for the exploration of dance's revolutionary and gendered materiality, Ann Cooper Albright's definitely strikes a chord when she comments in her reading of "Choreographies" that "the question keeps darting through my head: what do Derrida's 'incalculable choreographies' actually look like? Whose body is dancing, and what is it dancing about? [I]t would be hard to translate Derrida's vision onto the stage"[50]

Albright's comment points toward the limits of deconstruction for dance and performance studies. Just as Mark Franko, Henry Sayre, and Peggy Phelan derive their critique of presence from the Derridean model, both Franko and Phelan deviate, in their writing, from a strict Derridean approach on the matter of dance's self-erasure, dance's exteriority to history, and dance's ontology. Franko finds it problematic that the subjectivities of the performers ("in their gendered, cultural, and political distinctiveness")[51] have little place in the Derridean model. Phelan's analysis similarly deviates from Derrida as she relocates the problem of self-erasure in performance within a historic-political realm that inscribes (multiple) effacements upon (historically) subjectified and gendered bodies (notably women's bodies) that are nevertheless very present when they move. Phelan wrote on the specificity of disappearance in dance to propose that dance's "representational frame" works from within a tension between presence, disappearance, and re-presentation.[52]

Phelan's and Franko's attention to the historical materiality of the dancing body proposes a relationship between text and body, dance and writing, where dance's self-erasure is contained within fields of representation, disciplining, and embodiment that must be taken into serious and profound consideration. Configuring the conditions of dance's embodiment destabilizes the play(fulness) of the trace by anchoring the dance in the dancer's historical, material body. Presence returns, with perhaps more weight than Derrida would like, but it returns with the mark of a history on the edge of its own withdrawal, the history the body dances. Such history inscribes itself on and in the body, thus making again dance and writing one.

And yet . . .

Yet, Mark Franko's and Peggy Phelan's somewhat diverging uses and critiques of the Derridean trace still share a similar understanding of what constitutes presence—both in dance and in performance in general. Their understanding of presence is predicated upon an ontology of dance siding with ephemerality and disappearance. What I have been suggesting throughout this essay is that such ontology of dance has a historical grounding. It exists only within the horizons of the mournful lament generated by the splitting of dancing and writing, a splitting propelled by the perception of movement and presence as markedly sentenced to disappearance. My position then, is that one may not single out, attribute to, nor privilege one single materiality of dance over, and in exclusion of, another (be it ephemerality, disappearance, invisibility, trace), without acknowledging the transitory and historical nature of our attributions. This means that to accept *ontologically* that "the moving body is always fading before our eyes. Historical bodies and bodies on stage fascinate us because they fade,"[53] or that "the exuberant present of performance masks an intrinsic absence. . . . by definition transient, [performances] are immediate yet quickly become historical,"[54] is to engage in a theoretical move that must be preceded by a provisional acknowledgment of the historical conditionality and fluidity of the current ontolinguistic grounding of dances' presence as absence and of movement as sentenced to pastness. It also means to throw the presentness of the verb *to be* into the space of friction between writing and dance, a space mediated by gendered bodies as systems of exchange, as practices of counterfeiting, as spaces of troubling restlessness through which dance's presence becomes undecidable, multiple, lawless, a presence whose present can point simultaneously toward yet unthinkable ontological coimpossibilities of pastness, presentness, and futurity.

Yet . . .

Yet, distance remains as problem. A problem for writing *and* dancing, for the two-way bridge the mourning of dance's presence built between writing and dancing. Moreover, as we saw, distance performs the effect of woman. Here, I shall attempt an ending that will perform a return to the beginning. A return to my opening question, the one concerning the hysterical-historical attachment of dance, writing, and femininity. You will remember that the question was an unruly one, wildly unreasonable: could writing and femininity happen without dancing? As for the first element in the question, I shall reaffirm: dance cannot happen without writing just as writing cannot happen without dancing. I shall corroborate this hysterical project with one instance of reversed teleology. The corroboration starts with yet another affirmation: that the conditions of possibility for Derrida's project on writing as *différance* and for his critique of presence are grounded on the imperative insertion of movement in grammatology. For Derrida this movement is called deferment.

All this is well known; but what I don't think has been noticed is how the deferring motion of the signifier both mimics and casts (and reifies, but this must be left for another essay) presence as slippery movement, presence as that which will not be pinned down. In Derrida, it is movement—the motion of deferment, the tracing of the trace, the writing under erasure, the slipping of the tracing—that quietly reintroduces presence in grammatology.[55] Now, the reversed teleology: Derrida's points echo uncannily Jacques Rivière's writings on dance, as when the famous French dance critic wrote, in 1912, on the dancer's presence (he is writing on Fokine): "he travels along a road which he destroys in the very act of passing; he follows a mysterious thread that becomes invisible behind him; [ . . . ] he will not be caught; we shall not be able to hold him fast and pin his arms to his sides, so as to survey him at leisure from head to foot."[56] This passage with all its Derridean nuances begs the question of the copossibility of writing and dancing. What came first? Dancing as writing or écriture as dancing? My point is that both are absolutely codependent, reshaping each other's blindness and ontology in an ongoing ontolinguistic duet.

Yet, as Rivière makes very clear in the quoted fragment, distance remains a problem.

To really end, I shall attempt one answer to the second part of the unruly question: can we think femininity without dancing? Peggy Phelan notes in the introduction to her book *Unmarked* how Luce Irigaray described woman as "the sex which is not one: that is, the sex which is always already a double—or a triple or a quadruple."[57] Doubled, tripled, quadrupled, folded over, squared—woman presents her presence as already being in a multiplicity of self-distancings. This multiplicity was certainly in Nietzsche's mind when he wrote on the effect of woman as a dance at a distance: a troubling telekinesis, a faraway moving that will not be grasped, held, accounted for, arrested. I have shown how Derrida, following Nietzsche, writes on how certain woman's dances (dance as woman's dancing) resist house arrest, their pinning down to the house of the Father. Again, there is a dance that happens away from home, beyond reach, faraway, and that dance is femininity: a materiality that must not be grasped. Once woman's dance is grasped, pinned down, arrested (through documentation, let's say), then she is no longer at a distance. The pinning down of woman's dancing is the debacle of the possibility of thinking distance, of *Distanz,* of dance's femininity. Once she is not at a distance, once she is not distance, she is no longer woman (this is where Derrida sees in Nietzsche a disturbing feminism—that woman's fall within the grasp of man, her approaching of man, is woman's self-betrayal, her domestication, the impossibility of *Distanz*). This formula in regard to critical distances, this asymmetry that puts woman's dance away from the possibility of understanding, of epistemology, is strikingly familiar with the asymmetry Noverre attributed to dance's materiality as resistance to linguistic grasping: the moment dance is arrested, fixated, written down, it is no longer dance. Yet.

# 9 || Embodying Transgression

## Transgressive Intensification

> . . . *the deepest space in us,*
> *which, rising above us, forces its way out*
> —Rainer Maria Rilke, "To Music"

"Transgression," as term or concept, has had such wide and popular currency that it threatens at any moment to become obsolete; indeed, perhaps it has passed into swift obsolescence already. This sense of threat is enhanced by the temptation to regard the transgressive as reactive; as a rebellious response to, and more precisely against, some culturally imposed limit. In this conception transgressive art not only breaks our boundaries but also pushes our buttons (of outrage or delight, depending on who *us* is). This defiance fits nicely with another aspect of the popular sense of transgression: it is somehow violent and rule-smashing. Only what is conspicuously novel, committedly marginal and deliberately disturbing could lay claim, then, to this oddly coveted label.

Without intending the least disrespect for such work (after all, much in our culture does call for some reaction, even if there are other modes of resistance), I note that in fact what transgresses may arise quite differently. Rather than indicating a hostile and intentionally destructive reaction against its object (or the law the boundaries of which it crosses), it may arise as a fluid and highly desirous response to that (or those) object(s) (or laws). In the very act of transgressing, crossing limits, breaking boundaries, this response may, paradoxically perhaps, carry forward and irrevocably alter these very boundaries. "Transgression," as Maurice Blanchot says in *The Step Not Beyond*, "does not transgress the law; it carries it away with it."[1] If things are not the same afterward, it is not because the artwork has smashed things to bits but because it has pushed them into new and constantly mobile admixture with those forces that seem to oppose them. This admixture allows us to view transgression both as integral to art and as a force that is not merely *re*active—giving it a much more positive (and considerably less trend-bound) value. It is of this, I believe, that Michel Foucault wrote, "Transgression opens onto a scintillating and constantly affirmed world, . . . without that serpentine 'no' that bites into fruits and lodges their contradictions at their core."[2]

I propose that it is this latter, responsively desiring, transgression that makes dance, as much in the highly codified stylings of classical ballet as in the sometimes puzzling movement incorporations of postmodern dance. Dance is a love and exploration of motion, arising as the desire for and exploration of movement. In the intensity of this very desire, however, dance takes us beyond the limit of the very conditions for the possibility of movement: space and, still more apparently, time (time and movement having been linked for us at least since Plato and Aristotle).[3] "Beyond" these limits, and yet within them—having borne away the boundaries and changed the space of the game—dance creates not some unmoving, cosmic, transcendent unity but an extraordinary stillness-in-motion (and vice versa), immanent in the dance itself, shifting the limits of our senses of time and of space.

I begin this exploration of dance-as-transgression oddly: by making use of an art that, in its seemingly utter disembodiment, might seem to be maximally distant from dance: literature. There are three reasons why this distance is only seeming. First, literary theory has become (as most of us surely know) amazingly rich, with applications and implications well beyond traditionally "literary" boundaries. (This is true, I think, whether or not one takes the more radical "everything is a text" approach to theory.) Literary theory is, more particularly, where theories of transgression and intensity are well developed, especially by those whose writing is both literary and philosophical—even more so, in fact, than in aesthetic work dealing with other art forms.

Second, it is in theories of literature that philosophy has taken the temporality of art most seriously, though of course there have been questions of endurance, cultural specificity, the desire for immortality, and so on in discussions of the visual arts. (I omit music only because it has until recently received little more attention than dance, and the theory, within aesthetics, is far from being as developed as the theory of literature.) Because a curious temporality is so central to dance, theories of aesthetic time can only help us.

Finally, as Jane Gallop once remarked, "There is a peculiar *calling* relation between language and the body."[4] Dance is of all the arts perhaps the least amenable to discursive or any linguistic description, just as literature seems of all the arts most disincarnate. Yet body and language do call to one another, and perhaps most just *here,* where each pushes beyond the limits that our ordinary understanding has set and our ordinary experience perceived, bringing through dancing body and literary text open spaces that we had not supposed to be there, that are not supposed to be there: spaces of transgressive delight.

## Writing, Time, and Silence

> *Words move, music moves*
> *Only in time, but that which is living*
> *Can only die.*
> —T. S. Eliot, "Burnt Norton"

The discussion of literary theory that follows here may seem a bit lengthy, but the relevance of these points to dance can only be clear if the points themselves have been clarified. Naively, we conceive of writing as an effort to preserve—or even, fictionally, to create—a presence. In this conception, I set down some image, truth, or tale I am unwilling to lose or I desire to share, so that in the future, when I am no longer copresent with it, this image or truth or tale can be re-presented to others (possibly including some future version of myself). Writing presents facts, or ideas, or a story, to be read over and over. Thus pinned down by language this presence is re-presentable to anyone who can read. I write to make of my memory, or of a fictional past (something that has happened, at least imaginatively, so that I could set it down), another's future; I write to be read.[5]

But we know enough of time and writing and the human memory to see that this takes all of them a bit optimistically. When we write, it is not because we have nailed presence down but because we have felt it slipping away. Writing marks the absence that memory makes of presence; Blanchot even suggests that presence and language are in inescapable conflict. What written language "presents" is time as the coming of an absence.[6] Though we write against this sense of time/loss, it is writing's precondition. The very memory that my writing attempts to create demands the loss of the remembered moment.

It is really too facile to say that presence simply cannot be distinguished from absence. Certainly the two are conceptually complex in their relations, and careful thought guards against any easy opposition between them. But everyday experience and ordinary language do set these two apart with relative ease; it is only in the intensification of experience beyond itself (as Georges Bataille joins Blanchot in telling us) and the pushing of language beyond its limits (as both show us) that the meaning of presence and that of absence slip into and fill one another:

> Not that one ought to say . . . that presence would refer back to an always already refused absence, or that presence, the presence of being and as such always true, would simply be a way of warding off lack or more precisely of failing lack—but that there is no reason at all to establish a relation of subordination or any relation whatever between absence and presence, and that the "root" of a term . . . only comes to language through a play of interdependent little signs.[7]

What we find at work in the "literary" works, and the subject of theory in the "philosophical" works of both Bataille and Blanchot is a still more difficult temporal problem, a preoccupation with the *immemorial,* with the precise spaces of what is absent from our knowledge or experience. The role of the already forgotten in language is to intensify the absence inherent in memory; memory does not in fact re-create a present, but brings into the present the already absent past. The immemorial is different from the ordinary-forgotten of our everyday world because in it both presence and absence are intensified: it is an over-fullness of language and experience that bursts the limits of the ability to know or to say. It is necessarily excessive. This is so as much for the delight-in-motion of dance, which seems to be gone before we can remember it, as for the play-of-words in literature. Surely some of the intensity of our pleasure in movement derives from the longing it creates in us, not only to move with it, but to hold it—to have it move before us and yet remain, to have it remain still.

In Bataille the effort to say this excess of intensity brings language into the space of "non-knowledge" (not the lack of, but that which goes beyond, knowing), the unrepresentable inexperienceable of his "inner experience." In Blanchot, it brings out the remarkable disappearing time of the literary. The displacement is in and of excess, a too-much for both experience and language, what Blanchot calls "the quick of life," which "consumes all that is present till presence is precisely what is exempt from the present. The quick of life is the exemplarity, in the absence of any example, of un-presence, of un-life; absence in its vivacity always coming back without ever coming."[8]

Literature, like dance, is overfilled in its time by the immemorial instant. This is not to suggest a sort of extreme version of representational theory, in which language would represent the experiential excess by its own excessiveness: the literary experience *is* essentially linguistic, an experience of the rupture and recurrence of language, of meaning and structure. Such language cannot be merely descriptive. "Descriptive language," Bataille tells us, "becomes meaningless at the decisive instant when the stirrings of transgression itself take over from the discursive account of transgression."[9] Rather, the literature of excess, of intensity, of inner experience; of the disaster, of madness, of the outside[10] is a bringing-into-language of language's impossible, ever "present" opposite, silence. And thus, however gracefully, it is violent, with all of the violence that silencing suggests. (Indeed, Bataille declares that "violence is silent"[11]—and silence, as his fragmented texts demonstrate, is violent.) In this transgressive leap, we read what was always possible: "Writing is per se already (it is still) violence: the rupture there is in each fragment, the break, the splitting, the tearing of the shred—acute singularity, steely point."[12] Foucault remarks upon the techniques by which Bataille attains to such points:

> The juxtaposition of reflective texts and novels . . . the constant movement to different levels of speech and a systematic disengagement from the "I" who has begun to speak . . . temporal disengagements . . . , shifts in the distance separating a speaker from his words . . . ,an inner detachment from the assumed sovereignty of thought of writing.[13]

The introduction of opposition into meaning, then, does not simply mean that writing lacks meaning, nor does it imply a refusal of meaning. It does not even refuse description or representation: it *intensifies* the description/described, intensifies the presentation, until "presence itself is precisely what is absent from presence." It is not simply lacking but also too-much. And so the silence of forgetfulness invades the "presence" that clamors to be remembered, where this non/presence is already immemorial.

Already we can see some of the elements of this theory that will be important to our understanding of dance—and the ways in which dance, the very art of movement, teaches us new ways to listen to language. It is intensification of what is "normal"—in literature, the meaningful efforts or functions of language; in dance the seductive kinesthetic pleasures of the body in space and time—that introduces a kind of temporal rupture through that which is beyond presence (and a rupture of coherence or of space, respectively). We can already see that our ordinarily orderly sense of neatly divisible past, present, and future tenses and geometrically divisible spaces will have to be broken. A second common point has to do with the nature of this breaking: like silence in language, stillness (better conceived, I shall suggest, as suspension) in movement does not merely oppose our understanding or experience but radically disrupts it. Finally, because the opposition arises within intensification, we can begin to understand what it means to transgress out of an excessive desire rather than from a destructive loathing.

A closer exploration of literary temporality will help us to further our sense of this transgressive moment. Both Bataille and Blanchot see in the violent, silent too-much the paradoxical temporality of language, with its dependence upon memory, which is also loss and the possibility of forgetting, crucial to recurrence. Blanchot writes of the impossibility of finding *a place* for silence: "Silence cannot be kept; it is indifferent with respect to the work of art which would claim to respect it—it demands . . . a language which, presupposing itself as the totality of discourse, would spend itself all at once, disjoin and fragment endlessly."[14]

In dance movement, stillness plays the role that silence plays for literary language. Movement is "joined" to movement in a more intentional, self-conscious way than in our less attentive everyday somatic motion; yet it is precisely this jointure that allows division—into steps (sometimes, as in classical ballet, formally identifiable), into shorter phrases and longer variations. Smoothness may be valued, but so too are precision, distinction (the precise division that makes smoothness possible), and the purity of position; (the still instant in every motion) that gives meaning to the movement.

In the impossible, infinitely mobile language that attempts to get beyond its own temporal limits, "when the subject becomes absence" or silence, "the absence of a subject . . . subverts the whole sequence of existence, causes time to take leave of its order."[15] The return of time comes as that which has already passed and so has no present or presence, and no one to say it. The dancer's body is, as Yeats long ago noted, indistinguishable from the dance, but only while the dance lasts—no body retains it.

Vivid as Blanchot's imagery of fragmentation is, Bataille may give us a clearer picture of this radical temporal dissolution of language. Language, he suggests, "cheats" in its efforts to conceal the violent impact of silence: "and if language cheats to conceal universal annihilation, the placid work of time, language alone suffers, language is the poorer."[16] Language, which cheats to hide time's power to undo, is nonetheless inextricable from the passage of time, and this inextricableness too can force it to lie:

if language is to formulate . . . , this can take place only in successive phases worked out in the dimension of time. We can never hope to attain a global view in one single supreme instant: language chops it into its component parts and connects them up into coherent explanations. . . . So language scatters the totality of all that touches us most deeply even while it arranges it in order.[17]

Order for language is order in time, yet this ordering necessarily dismembers each instant, each silent point that is at the same time an explosive force, scattering further the language that attempts to make of it a still point. Order for dance is spatial as well as temporal, holding the still instant-between in the spatial unfolding of musicality. Blanchot links this to the violent fragmentation that silence effects upon language:

Fragmentation is the spacing, the separation effected by a temporalization which can only be understood—fallaciously—as the absence of time. The fragment, as fragments, tends to dissolve the totality which it presupposes and which it carries off toward the dissolution . . . to which it exposes itself in order . . . to maintain itself as the energy of disappearing: a repetitive energy . . . or the presence of the work of art's absence.[18]

Fragmentation, bringing silence to the forefront of language, exposes the lies of coherent thought, but by telling us that there is evocation beyond coherence. Stillness goes beyond the constancy of motion, evoking the impossible urgent desire for the suspended instant.

The immemorial, beyond remembering because it has always already exceeded the grasp of that consciousness which would seek to retain it in discourse; the instant that both silences and demands language, cannot be present and is not simply absent. It has always already slipped away; it is always returning. Just as watching eyes and empathic muscles grasp the position of the dancer's body, it has moved on.

The eternal return, the Nietzschean doctrine the complex possibilities of which are still unfolding for us, is central to this understanding. In the language rendered fragmentary by the force of intensity we see the effect of "the ceaselessness of the return, effect of disastrous instability."[19] The instant is violent, silent, irreplaceably singular. But, as Gilles Deleuze remarks in *Difference and Repetition,* "repetition is a necessary and justified conduct only in relation to that which cannot be replaced. Repetition as a conduct and as a point of view concerns non-exchangeable and non-substitutable singularities."[20] The eternal return can never be the recurrence of the identical, nor even of a series of instants that are copies of an original same that would be for each cycle the same again.

That is, for words and bodies alike in motion, it is the love of the moment that demands the moment in all its irreplaceable, indeed its unplaceable, singularity. It is the impossible recognition of every moment as infinitely lost already, the infinite longing for the moment that as lost is always yet to come. This longing and love for the moment (as an irreplaceable singularity caught up in repetition) are as essential to dance, the art of mobile bodies, as to literature, the art of ordered words.

Not all writing is, at least self-evidently, of this nature. Much writing minimizes fragmentation as best it can, attempts with reasonable success to repress the immemorial. But this success is because we minimize intensity, suppress excess; because we never look to the outside for fear (like many fears, this one is oddly complacent) of recognizing our own insecurity. We read as if the text were simply present, not as if we shared Blanchot's destabilizing belief that "if a book could for a first time really begin, it would for one last time, long since have ended."[21] The eternal return is an utterly rupturing thought, as Nietzsche's formulation in *The Gay Science* makes clear:

> What if some day or night a demon were to steal after you into your loneliest loneliness and say to you: "This life as you now live it and have lived it, you will have to live once more and innumerable times more; and there will be nothing new in it, but . . . everything unutterably small or great in your life will have to return to you, all in the same succession and sequence. . . ."
>
> Would you not throw yourself down and gnash your teeth and curse the demon who spoke thus? Or have you once experienced a tremendous moment when you would have answered him: "you are a god and never have I heard anything more divine." If this thought gained possession of you, it would change you as you are or perhaps crush you.[22]

This is not a cosmological doctrine to be intellectually accepted (or disregarded) and neatly set aside. Only from this shattered and disrupted perspective can we "write in order not simply to destroy, not simply to conserve, in order not to transmit; write in the thrall of the impossible real, that share of disaster wherein every reality, safe and sound, sinks."[23] Our efforts to keep language bounded deny the fullness of meaning, experience, time—which is to say, their transgressive, excessive intensification into non-knowledge, the inexperienceable, infinite and irreplaceable return. The memory of the muscles, the forthcoming performance, the still point around which the dance circles and returns.

*L'ecriture du désastre:* the constant possibility, the delightedly self-destructive temptation, of writing, the dazzling outburst of the return. Any meaning can be intensified, pushed until it breaks—

## Dance, Time and Stillness

> *We must be still and still moving*
> *Into another intensity.*
> —T. S. Eliot, "East Coker"

And any movement can be danced, pushed beyond its meanings. We do not have to look so far beyond ourselves as we might think for the intensification and curious temporality manifest by the literature of excess. As I have noted already, beyond the literature, we find it as well at the surface of the mobile body, in the movement of the dance. Dance intensifies ordinary movement as literature intensifies ordinary language, thus, paradoxically, bringing into it that which opposes it. Some elaboration as to how it does so might be of value here.

To understand dance as the intensification of movement, we ought first to see what "ordinary" movement entails, and represses, just as "ordinary" language forgets the fragmenting silence always pushing against its efforts at order and remembering, past forgetting to the repetition of the immemorial.

Difficult as movement-intensity will be to define, it is not at all difficult to see (from the audience) or feel (as a dancer, and sometimes as a viewer as well). It is the difference between dancing and marking steps, between taking up ordinary movement into dance and presenting it as if acting. Dancing fragments ordinary movements into precise steps; it links and blurs them into *enchaînements;* it exaggerates them into dancing. The number of intensified elements, if we try to analyze this difference, is large, but I shall focus on the two that link dance most nearly to literature: the kinesthetic, or embodied, senses of space and time.[24]

The dance's sense of space and time, when it takes up the dancer until, just for these moments, she is indistinguishable from it; when it takes up the audience so that, just for those moments, it forgets its objective distance, is profoundly seductive. We know how readily seduction cuts across boundaries[25]—how it undermines orders of meaning from within—but we have to see how this might work spatiotemporally, on and across dancing bodies. It is here that Bataille's insight into the transgressivity of intensification, its destructive generosity, becomes important.

Like language, space is ordered: objects array themselves in it like words in a sentence—and just about as deceptively in their seeming passivity. This order, like language, presents itself as both coherent (we can take in at once, or quickly, the array of corporeal things in a visible space) and transversal (corresponding to the diachronic element of linguistic coherence: we must cross space over a distance as we must read to the end of a sentence). And as we seldom read in reverse, we find also a teleological element to the crossing of space; we pass through it not for the sake of so doing but to get to another part of it. Both placement and distance thus make sense to us.

Dance, in which no object or body occupies its place except rightly— that is, by design or by the designed incorporation of chance—intensifies place. It does so first by this element of design, which is choreography or the embodied intensity of improvisation. It does so by the dancer's sense of air and ground, the upward stretch and the downward rootedness. But this stretch and rootedness also show us the seductiveness of space, in which the dancer-as-dance draws and is drawn (outward as well as vertically). That is, this very intensity of place brings into play the mobility of spatiality, in the pull between and across places.

Watch a dancer reach upward—if she is doing it well, you cannot help watching. Thus a critic of early modern dance was mesmerized by a thematic gesture in the dancing of Ruth St. Denis: "At one moment, she stands utterly still except that the hand . . . moves slowly upward, almost hugging the body and head, until the dancer herself seems to have become a holy stele, a column of truth, or, perhaps a stilled human receptacle for divine illumination."[26]

Space opens ineluctably before that hand (or foot: for example, the arabesque, especially with the balletic winged foot, has precisely this effect). But it is also drawn toward and around the reaching hand, the stretched foot, the tilted head or arched back: *this place* becomes the place where everything is, and if *this* is multiple and our attention is drawn beyond choice to the places where many bodies move, the seductiveness of the emplacement is no less. The place where the dance is is at once *everywhere*—as the joy of it opens out to the audience, as the energy of it washes over the spectators and engulfs them—and just precisely *here,* as it wraps all of the world's space into this exact point. Body and space in their mutual seduction acquire that remarkable elasticity which is dancing.

But dancers do not, and dance does not, often occupy *a* place, remain in place. It is almost definitionally mobile, and so we must consider not just array in places but movement across distances. Dance delights by treating distance non-teleologically; it does not present itself as to-be-crossed so as to have done with it, but in the manner of that which (stealing yet another, this time Derridean, literary insight) seductively draws us precisely by refusing closure. Our sense of distance as the openness of space is intensified by the very movement that slices across distance to no purpose but joy, refusing the meaning of distance by refusing a teleological spatiality.

What draws the dancer into and across the stage or any other space of performance is not the possibility of having done with that space (nor the lure of what's on the other side of it) but the possibilities its openings present—and delight finds possibilities, whether in the choreographer's advance-work or the performer's improvisation. Again we find both an inward draw and an outward reach; we see too that place and distance cross each other here, both of the utterly precise and impossibly expansive, both of the inexhaustible in their joy.

Inexhaustibility is a trait of artistic transgressivity the importance of which is inestimable. It means that we can never come to the finality of art; of dance, here, but this trait carries across art forms (as evidenced not just by theories of exploded meaning in literature but by, for example, Jean-Luc Nancy's remarks on visual spaces opened by painting).[27] Literature forces us to confront what we cannot understand in language, the inexhaustibility, the impossible nonsensical excess, of "meaning," which turns out to be everywhere and absent; dance forces us to confront what our bodies alone can "understand," the inexhaustible joy and desire of spaces. Inexhaustibility means that we are always exceeded by the work, that it is always in excess of our comprehension, and this is this joy and its terror. To move toward a proper sense of that toward which we gesture (to try to see what exceeds us, if only to see that it exceeds us), it is essential that we make the turn to time.

Time, too, seems to have its version of place (the moment, the now) and of distance (its passage or duration). Dance's effect on time, or its sense of time, is as seductive and inexhaustible as its spatiality. Here the structure of placement and crossing is that of rhythm, multiplied by attention, desire, love of time that bursts its boundaries to bring us to the immemorial without original, repetition's simulacrum, the eternal return of the event. Time flows and is fragmented, as we have noted already, giving to each position the value of what cannot be held.

In some sense dance is the body's devotion to the moment that cannot be kept; attentiveness to each moment is essential if the dance is to seduce and delight us. Reflective consciousness or intentional thought (what we usually call "paying attention") is far exceeded here. Consciousness, that relatively late and weak development,[28] cannot be adequate to the saturated time of the dance. Dancers are taught not to lose attention, a loss that the audience will feel immediately in the loss of the dance's seductiveness.[29] The dancers' attention to time, the utter valuation of each instant and the impossible generosity of giving all to each instant, is essential: only thus is the dance time saturated, full (and overfull, so that as we shall see, it bursts) of the dance. There is no time not to pay attention. This completeness of the dancer's attention is the only way to keep the attention of the audience and draw the spectators out of their easy, passive distance: attention, devoted desire, calls to desire, demands attention.

One might argue that attention all the time, even the all-absorbing, postintentional attention of the body, is not attention *to* time, but it is not so evident that there is a difference, at least here, where we already know that the moment must be in movement. It is the movement as passing moment, bursting with possibilities yet guaranteeing loss (we cannot remain in this place), to which the dance attends, attention to which it demands. One must be fully alert at once to the infinity of possibility and the ineluctability of loss. It is thus that dance stillness remains so seductively vital: the dancer is not just waiting around but is utterly awake to the movement in the moment, the passage of stillness, too. She is fully "present," fully attentive to this coming absence. And because she knows, and delights in, movement—because, in other words, she turns her full devotion to the loss of the moment that nonetheless absorbs her entirely—the dancer-dancing intensifies, by her generosity, the pinpoint instant *and* the passage across time. She loves each in their opposition.

Dance, then, attends to the moment as to the place, devotedly attentive to its presence-as-vanishing, and attends to movement as to distance. An element more immediately evident than attentiveness is the rhythmicity of dance time, at least if we remember that "rhythmic" need not mean "predictable." As Deleuze notes, rhythm is not simply cadence ("an isochronic recurrence of identical elements")[30] in which we might see the (eternal) return of the same-as-identical. Rather, "a bare, material repetition (repetition of the Same) appears only in the sense that another repetition is disguised within it constituting it and constituting itself in disguising itself."[31] Within the repetition of the Same is the rhythmicity that depends on difference; rhythm as a mode of repetition cannot occur except in difference, and each time a rhythmic phrase recurs it is not the Same phrase but the phrase after, again. The dance doesn't just take up some block of time but intricately structures the movement of time within that "block," thereby altering its temporal boundaries. Introducing repetition into a span of time, dance takes that time beyond its span to a greater repetition.

A recurrence without origin, without a first, is the rhythmic structure of the intense and immemorial. As Martha Graham was fond of noting, all dance begins as a continuation rather than as origin, each class opening on the *and:* "And one . . ."[32] Rhythm permits us the transgressive leap beyond time into a time that is at once pure recurrent passage and impossible sustained instant, a time itself without original, in which

each series exists only by virtue of the return of the others. Everything has become simulacrum, for by simulacrum we should not understand a simple imitation but rather the act by which the very idea of a model or privileged position is challenged and overturned. The simulacrum is the instance which includes a difference within itself.[33]

Rhythm permits this transgression in two important ways. It has a history of intensifying and of drawing attention. Nietzsche writes in *The Gay Science,* "rhythm is a compulsion; it engenders an unconquerable urge to yield and join in."[34] Much earlier, the Greek poet Archilocus advised, "know what rhythm holds men."[35] Rhythm, intensifying the effect of the rhythmic (language or movement or line or sound) draws us in and holds us there—while defying any permanent placement of the *there* at all. It is not a simple repetition-of-the-same but a repetition that emphasizes the always-changing. It carries us forward and yet it recurs. It alternates: up and down, high and low, quick and slow, abrupt and sustained. Yet this alternation, too, is far from simple. Blanchot writes,

> Rhythm does not belong to the order of nature or of language, or even of "art," where it seems to predominate. Rhythm is not the simple alternation of Yes and No, of "giving-withholding," of presence-absence or of living-dying, producing-destroying. Rhythm, while it disengages the multiple from its missing unity, and while it appears regular and seems to govern according to a rule, threatens the rule. For it always exceeds the rule through a reversal whereby, being in play or in operation within measure, it is not measured thereby. The enigma of rhythm—dialectical-nondialectical no more the one than the other is other—is the extreme danger.[36]

Rhythm defines the measure, moves back and forth without simply moving back and forth, carries forward what it sustains. Thus it exceeds simple movement (by its sustaining and its sameness) and it exceeds simple stillness (by its mobility and its forward current). Rhythmicity is the intensifying structure of time.

This decidedly unsimple nature of rhythmic alternation is also what allows its nature as intensification, and its seductiveness as passage. The spatial analogy can be helpful to us here: something that is immediately proximate, taking up all of our space, is unseductive; something that is merely distant, without drawing or beckoning us near, is likewise unseductive. The dancer is away from us, drawing us toward the place where she is, yet by that drawing, and by the elastic expansion of that place over distance, she is not merely far from us. What seduces is what passes *and* draws us after it, without remaining still for us to get there. A place that is one-or-the-other, near or far, is readily comprehended and does not exceed us. A distance that is to-be-crossed and does not shift and change and revert in the crossing is readily traversed and does not exceed us. Unidirectional movement of any sort, whether conceived of spatially or in any moment of time, cannot seduce us. It limits itself. A tempo, for example, cannot increase indefinitely before the beats simply blur to us and our interest in their speed is lost. Rhythm's repetition-in-movement allows for the possibility of continued intensification precisely by its mechanism of return: not always the Same, but always again, always more. We cross neither space nor time definitively when we are, as audience or performers, caught up in the dance; we are drawn across, again and again, always-proximate, never fused. Rhythm is the promise of eternity within time: always again, a passing now that, already lost, is yet still to come. It is the possibility of the sudden stillness within a movement.

But there is more to this, as time's opposite opens within it as silence opens within language, as the still point provides at once an anchor and an open space around which movement is pulled; an opposite that we can conceal only by cheating (and which is no more the lack of time than silence is the lack of language). Time, of course, is opposed to eternity, and tradition links the former to movement (and sometimes to the absence of presence, finding in it only the movement from future to past), the latter to still-presence. "Time," we are told as far back as Augustine, "derives its length only from a great number of moments following one another into the past, because they cannot all continue at once."[37] Time images eternity,[38] rather as Bataille sees language imaging—lyingly—coherence, as a great many words follow each other to spread out a meaning that would truly subsist, if it could, in the instant. But even these instants, as Augustine also noted, cannot really be present: "We cannot rightly say that time *is,* except by its impending state of *not being.*"[39] Dance, as we can already see, sets before us time at its most intense; the dance is precisely by its movement toward not-being.

Eternity is "time" without the attributes of time: duration and passage. It takes up no temporal "space"; it is not even localizable as the instant, the temporal equivalent of the point. It does not, despite occasional confusion with sempiternity,[40] endure. It *is.* It cannot be tensed. It is all at once and forever. Thus it seems the least likely element of dance, long considered the most transient of arts.

And yet this paradoxical all-of-time is what is given us by the attention to each instant, each instant that has no temporal extension at all and is a point only insofar as it is never the same point, always sliding into the past. It is the recurrence within rhythm that promises us the return of the moment, which like the point of the instant is nonetheless never the same. Dance's eternity, the return's opposition to time introduced by the structure of time in dance, is the sense of dance as *suspended* time—that paradoxical combination of stillness and movement at once. The sense of suspension, both felt and willed, both gratified and desired (drawing us in our delight to a possibility of greater pleasure), is the sense of a fermata, a sense of being taken outside of time, *held* there, which nonetheless can only occur in time, and which would lose its vitality and its affirmative quality if it were not part of a passage. (Without the affirmation of the moment that passes, there is no call to suspend time; time does not call to us except as it slips away, calling us after it.) It is the moment in which Nijinsky, sustaining his impossible leaps, forgets to come down. Our desire for the moment to remain forever is fueled in no small part by the fact that no moment goes on forever. Every instant is already slipping away; that perfectly extended foot has already drawn back. Eternity reflects a movement of pleasure and desire so potent that the instant is taken outside the usual sense of moments passing into oblivion and into the time of the immemorial; it is affirmed forever as passing. This is so whether we watch the sweep of a movement (think of a *grande allegro*, the leaps that defy gravity until the very sweep seems to suspend us, as if the movement itself held us still) or of a still pose (especially where the pose itself is captivating: a sustained extension, an arabesque *en pointe*, in which it is the very passage of time that makes the stillness so amazing and enchanting). It is caught up in the time of eternal recurrence.

Because in our devotion to each instant, it is passage we love (and in our devotion to *this* passage, we love each of its instants). Not only is the moment infinitely valuable because it is irreplaceable (because it is never placeable at all, because it must be a loss), it is valuable because its loss makes of it one of a stream of points (this enumeration is of course a lie), a *movement*, a delight in the possibility of movement, in the sense that movement is *not* stillness, not stasis. It is an impatient, joyful push-ahead into time as strong as the desire to hold each instant, to make it perfect, recognizing its infinite value.

The affirmation is our key to the nature of this contradictory eternity, which can only be that of the return, the return the presence/absence of which we have so often marked already. Eternity cannot transgress time except by being caught up in time. The eternal return is in fact nothing other than a movement of affirmation, the intensification of the yes. In the eternal return all time is excessive; it has come already, it will come again, it is unnecessary, and yet the return is its only necessity. Here in this repetition,

We sense something which is contrary to the laws of nature; we think something which is contrary to the principles of thought. Moreover, even if the production of difference is by definition "inexplicable," how can we avoid *implicating* the inexplicable at the heart of thought itself? How can the unthinkable not lie at the heart of thought? Or delirium at the heart of good sense? How can we be content to relegate the improbable to the beginning of a partial evolution, without also grasping it as the highest power of the past, or as the immemorial in memory? (In this sense the partial synthesis of the present already leads us into another synthesis of time, that of the immemorial memory, at the risk of leading us further still . . .).[41]

This suggests the inherence of the immemorial in the recurrent (thus bringing non-knowledge into conjunction with rhythm). Charles Scott sees the Nietzschean recurrence as "repeating without totality or an originary foundation."[42] Thus it is, importantly, a "repetition without origin."[43] It repeats what never began (or always begins on the "and"); it does not continue to move only forward, yet it moves ever forward. It is, like time, ever moving; like eternity, ever present. But this is an ever presence that contains in motion its own absence; a time that contains in stillness its own overcoming.

The eternal return is a double demand: for the passage of the moment, for stillness in time. Held forever, it would stop the passage it loves; sweeping unceasingly forward in the motion it so desires, it would seek its own end. Played between, it does neither. This is the infinite generosity of the dancer's attention, her gift of herself to the time of the dance, knowing that "to give is not to give something—even lavishly, asking naught in return. It is neither to dispense something nor to expend oneself. It is rather to give what is always taken, which is perhaps to say time . . . without present and always returning."[44] The dance, which gives us eternity, does so only by taking, eternally, in a greed indistinguishable from generosity, our time.

The time of dance, like its space, is both intensely ordered and, as excess, transgressive of order: it always exceeds us and our attempts to grasp it. Dance remains a fascination, a seduction, and a delight precisely in this excess; we have never exhausted it, we cannot become one with it any more than we can keep our distance from it; it takes us beyond ourselves. I would like to close by pointing to a trait of this inexhaustibility that gives us as well a last, important point of communication between theories of literature and those of dance, based upon the poststructural sense of meaning, a point that will help us to understand how this emptying out of the point and the moment is also their intensification.

A grossly oversimplified but not wildly inaccurate sketch of structural linguistics tells us that words acquire their meanings not by correspondence or ostention but by their place within the structure of an entire language—positionally, we might say. So (to use the always used example), "cat" is meaningful not because it points out or designates a small, furry carnivore with the capacity to purr but because it is not "rat" or "mat" or "bat"—because it has its place defined by all those other language elements in *their* places, and the whole structure works together. Change in the structure is, except in dead languages, both possible and actual, but the structure of the whole is still what means. Words are meaningful together, in sentences and paragraphs and whole languages, not in isolation.

To continue the oversimplification, one of the central insights of poststructuralism is the infinitude of exclusion. There are an infinite number of language positions not occupied by any given word: other sounds, other "meanings," other possibilities. And so "meaning" is at once *inexhaustible* (because it is defined by exclusion, by the infinite number of positions that the word does not occupy, an always multipliable set); and *absent* (because it is always elsewhere than within the word, and we cannot even totalize these "elsewheres" to sum up its position). So silence, and nonsense, and the "impossible truth" of the wordless scream[45] appear at the center of language, in the attempt at presence, as the very possibility of that attempt.

And so, too, the place of the dance is always invaded by distance, emptied out of itself to be everywhere, impossibly drawing everywhere into that place from which it has already moved, retaining its distance precisely to draw us to that place from which it must move, and must have moved, because the instant in which the body takes the perfect position, the instant so desperately right that we would retain it forever, has always emptied itself into the before-and-after of repetition, the lack of presence that is all we finally have of presence, the dance that in a brief bit of the span of our lives has always already exceeded us, and always will.

# Notes

André Lepecki: Introduction

1. I cannot begin this introduction without acknowledging the extraordinary dedication, patience, and support I received from contributors, friends, and the people at Wesleyan University Press throughout the quite long process of preparing this anthology. I share my sincerest thanks with Suzanna Taminnen, editor-in-chief at Wesleyan University Press (her belief in this project since its prehistory was at times my only driving force), and with all the contributors as well (whose writing demonstrated an enormous trust and dedication to the project).

2. Susan Leigh Foster, ed., *Choreographing History* (Bloomington: Indiana University Press, 1995); Ellen W Goellner and Jacqueline Shea Murphy, eds., *Bodies of the Text: Dance as Theory, Literature as Dance* (New Brunswick: Rutgers University Press, 1995); Susan Leigh Foster, ed., *Corporealities* (New York: Routledge, 1996); Mark Franko and Annette Richards, eds., *Acting on the Past : Historical Performance Across the Disciplines* (Hanover: Wesleyan University Press, published by University Press of New England, 2000).

3. Lincoln Kirstein, *Dance: A Short History of Classic Theatrical Dancing* (Princeton, N.J.: Princeton Book, 1987), 19. Sondra Fraleigh discusses Kirstein's notion extensively in her *Dance and the Lived Body* (Pittsburgh: University of Pittsburgh Press, 1987), 77–93.

4. Mark Franko, *The Dancing Body in Renaissance Choreography (c. 1416– 1589)* (Birmingham, Ala.: Summa Publications, 1986).

5. A struggle for autonomy that only stops with dance's entrance into modernism at the beginning of the twentieth century, when John Martin announces modern dance as "completely self-contained." John Martin, *The Modern Dance* (Brooklyn, N.Y.: Dance Horizons, 1972), 6.

6. Susan Leigh Foster, *Choreography & Narrative: Ballet's Staging of Story and Desire* (Bloomington: Indiana University Press, 1996), xv.

7. Randy Martin, *Critical Moves: Dance Studies in Theory and Politics* (Durham: Duke University Press, 1998), 185.

8. Ibid., 13.

9. Ibid., 14.

10. Mark Franko and Annette Richards, *Acting on the Past*, 1.

11. Philip Auslander, *Presence and Resistance: Postmodernism and Cultural Politics in Contemporary American Performance* (Ann Arbor: University of Michigan Press, 1992); Peggy Phelan, *Unmarked: The Politics of Performance* (New York: Routledge, 1993); Peggy Phelan, "Thirteen Ways of Looking at Choreographing Writing," in *Choreographing History*, ed. Susan Leigh Foster (Bloomington: Indiana University Press, 1995), 200–210; Peggy Phelan, "Immobile Legs, Stalled Words: Psychoanalysis and Moving Deaths," in her *Mourning Sex: Performing Public Memories* (New York: Routledge, 1997), 44–72.

12. Mark Franko, "Mimique," in *Bodies of the Text: Dance as Theory, Literature as Dance*, ed. Ellen W. Goellner and Jacqueline Shea Murphy (New Brunswick: Rutgers University Press, 1995), 205–216.

13. Mark Franko, *Dancing Modernism / Performing Politics* (Bloomington: Indiana University Press, 1995).

14. Heidi Gilpin, "Tracing Displacement and Disappearance," in *Corporealities*, ed. Susan Leigh Foster (New York: Routledge, 1996), 106–128.

15. Peggy Phelan, "Thirteen Ways of Looking at Choreographing Writing."

16. Peggy Phelan, *Unmarked*, 148.

## 1. Peggy Phelan: Trisha Brown's *Orfeo*

1. Sally Banes, *Democracy's Body: Judson Dance Theater, 1962–64* (Durham: Duke University Press, 1983), 21. I am grateful to Janice Ross for her extremely helpful comments on an earlier draft of this paper, especially in relation to Brown's early work. Sally Banes's documentation and analysis of the work of the Judson dancers has informed all of what I say about it here. I am also grateful to Elizabeth Grainger and André Lepecki for their helpful comments and patient editing.

2. Trisha Brown quoted in Lise Bruenel, ed., *Trisha Brown* (Paris: Editions Bourge), 56.

3. Brown's 1994 solo, *If You Couldn't See Me*, a performance in which she keeps her back to the audience throughout also indicates her sustained interest in prohibitions against the reciprocal gaze. In this piece, of course, the conditional "if" must be meant ironically because the audience can certainly see Brown dancing (and her back's snaking motion is worthy of serious looking). The dance actually prevents Brown from seeing the audience, which on some level must be something of a relief. But the overall structure of the dance preserves the drama of voyeurism so central to feminist film theory. In this sense, the title announces something that the dance circumvents.

4. Trisha Brown quoted in Lise Bruenel, *Trisha Brown*, 39–42.

5. Ian Fenlon, "The Mantuan Orfeo," in *Claudio Monteverdi: Orfeo*, ed. John Whenham (Cambridge: Cambridge University Press, 1986), 1–19.

6. Ibid., 1.

7. The part of Orfeo alternated between Simon Keenlyside and Carlo Vincento Allemano. Gracelia Oddone sang The Messenger; Paul Gerimone performed the role of Charon. Apollo was sung by Mauro Utzeri. Prosperina was sung by Martina Dika, and Tomas Tomasson sang Pluto.

8. The translation is Anne Ridler's, in Nicholas John, ed., *The Operas of Monteverdi* (London: Calder Publications, 1992), p. 46. It is useful to compare this refrain with Eurydice's earlier celebration of love in act 1:

I cannot tell Orfeo
the joy that fills my heart at your rejoicing,
since my heart's mine no longer—
for you it left me, and both by Love were stolen. (p. 37)

Thus, for Striggio, both love and death are potentially fatal experiences. For the woman, however, love tends to come a little slower, and death a little faster.

9. Jacques Lacan, "The Essence of Tragedy: A Commentary on Sophocles' *Antigone*," in *The Seminar of Jacques Lacan, Book VII: The Ethics of Psychoanalysis, 1959–60*, ed. Jacques-Alain Miller, trans. Dennis Porter (New York: Norton, 1992), 243–290.

10. For a full account of these interweaving histories, see Sally Banes, *Democracy's Body*.

11. Joseph Kerman, "Orpheus: The Neoclassic Vision," in *Claudio Monteverdi: Orfeo*, 129.

12. Roland Aeschlimann was responsible for the costumes. Quotation is from *Claudio Monteverdi: Orfeo*, ed. John Whenham (Cambridge: Cambridge University Press, 1986), 56.

13. I am grateful to Trisha Brown for sharing excerpts of her notated score.

## 2. Ramsay Burt: Genealogy and Dance History

1. Yvonne Rainer, *Work, 1961–73* (Halifax: The Press of the Nova Scotia College of Art, 1974), 71.
2. Michel Foucault, "Nietzsche, Genealogy, History," in *Language, Counter-memory, Practice: Selected Essays and Interviews by Michel Foucault,* ed. Donald F. Bouchard (Ithaca: Cornell University Press, 1977), 139–164.
3. Ibid., 148.
4. Foucault's earlier books on madness and the clinic are often called archaeological while his later work on the prison, and on sexuality constitutes a pessimistic genealogy that uncovers a scene of destruction.
5. Foucault, "Nietzsche, Genealogy, History," 152.
6. Ibid., 164.
7. Michel Foucault, "What is an Author," in *Language, Countermemory, Practice,* 138.
8. Jacques Derrida, "The Theater of Cruelty and the Closure of Representation," in his *Writing and Difference* (London: Routledge, 1978), 232–250.
9. Ibid., 240.
10. Ibid., 247.
11. Ibid., 237.
12. Judith Butler, "Performative Acts and Gender Constitution: An Essay in Phenomenology and Feminist Theory," in *Performing Feminisms: Feminist Critical Theory and Theatre,* ed. Sue-Ellen Case (Baltimore: Johns Hopkins University Press, 1990), 277.
13. Ibid.
14. Ibid., 276.
15. Judith Butler, *Gender Trouble* (London: Routledge, 1990), 130.
16. Ibid.
17. Ibid., 131.
18. Yvonne Rainer, *Works, 1961–73,* 68.
19. Yvonne Rainer, *A Woman Who . . . Essays, Interviews, Scripts* (Baltimore: Johns Hopkins University Press, 1999), 64.
20. I am grateful to Douglas Dunn, who came to my class at New York University in November 1999 to teach us the opening moves of *Trio A,* and to Yvonne Rainer for giving him permission to do so.
21. Yvonne Rainer, *Works, 1961–73,* 67.
22. Ibid.
23. Ibid.
24. Ibid.,75.
25. Yvonne Rainer, *A Woman Who . . . ,* 63.
26. Yvonne Rainer, *Works, 1961–73,* 69.
27. Ibid., 67.
28. Ibid., 238.
29. Ibid., 71.
30. All quotes in this paragraph from Yvonne Rainer, *Works, 1961–73* 71 (emphasis mine).
31. Zygmunt Bauman, *Modernity and Ambivalence* (Cambridge: Polity Press, 1991), 9.
32. Judith Butler, *Antigone's Claim: Kinship Between Life and Death* (New York: Columbia University Press, 2000), 2.
33. Michel Foucault, *Language, Countermemory, Practice,* 164.
34. There is a story of one spectator mounting the stage in Wuppertal with a bucket of water to throw at the dancers; they ducked out of the way, however, so that people in the front row of the stalls were soaked instead.

35. Jochem Schmidt, Anna Kisselgoff, Ann Daly, et al., "Tanztheater: The Thrill of the Lynch Mob or the Rage of a Woman," *Drama Review* 30, no. 2 (Summer 1986): 46–56; see also Johannes H. Birringer, "Pina Bausch : Dancing Across Borders," *Drama Review* 30, no. 2 (Summer 1986) 85–97.

36. Louis Althusser, *Lenin and Philosophy and Other Essays* (New York: Monthly Review Press, 1971), 170–177.

37. Judith Butler, *Bodies that Matter: On the Discursive Limits of Sex* (New York: Routledge, 1995), 121–124.

38. Jacques Derrida, "Signature Event Context," in *Glyph,* ed. Samuel Weber and Henry Sussman (Baltimore: Johns Hopkins University Press, 1977), 172–197. See also Judith Butler, "Performative Acts," *Gender Trouble,* and *Bodies That Matter;* as well as Andrew Parker and Eve Kosofsky Sedgwick, eds., *Performativity and Performance* (New York: Routledge, 1995). For a critique of the application of these ideas to dance studies see Susan Leigh Foster, "Choreographies of Gender," *Signs* 24, no. 1 (1998): 1–24.

39. Yvonne Rainer, *Works, 1961–73,* 71.

40. I saw this piece at the first F.I.N.D in Montreal in 1985, but my memory of it has been helped by viewing the recent video version of the piece. My description, however, refers to the live version.

41. My memory of the performance in Montreal is that these emotions were much less pronounced than they are in De Mey's video.

42. Steve Paxton, "Trance Script: Judson Project Interview," *Contact Quarterly* (Winter 1989): 14–21; David Gordon, "It's About Time," *Drama Review* 19 (1975): 43–52; Yvonne Rainer, *A Woman Who . . . ,* 65.

## 3. Randy Martin: Dance and Its Others

1. The content of the crisis and its conceptual entailments are variously described in a range of books to appear in the past twenty years: some representative perspectives are Samir Amin, Giovanni Arrighi, Andre Gunder Frank, and Immanuel Wallerstein, *Dynamics of Global Crisis* (New York: Monthly Review, 1982); Robin Blackburn, ed., *After the Fall: The Failure of Communism and the Future of Socialism* (London: Verso, 1991); and Charles Lemert, *Sociology After the Crisis* (Boulder, Colo.: Westview, 1995).

2. Jean-François Lyotard, *The Postmodern Condition: A Report on Knowledge* (Minneapolis: University of Minnesota Press, 1984).

3. An early view of the collapse in dance can be found in Roger Copeland, "A Curmudgeonly View of the American Dance Boom," *Dance Theater Journal* 4, no. 1 (1986): 10–13. See also Leila Sussman, "Anatomy of the Dance Company Boom, 1958–1980," *Dance Research Journal* 16, no. 2 (1984): 23–38.

4. Augusto Boal, *Theater of the Oppressed* (New York: Urizen Books, 1979).

5. Jean Baudrillard, *Simulations* (New York: Semiotexte, 1983).

6. Susan Leigh Foster, *Choreography and Narrative: Ballet's Staging of Story and Desire* (Bloomington: Indiana University Press, 1996), 262.

7. Nicos Poulantzas, *State, Power, Socialism* (London: New Left Books, 1978).

8. Cynthia Novack, *Sharing the Dance: Contact Improvisation and American Culture* (Madison: University of Wisconsin Press, 1990).

9. For discussion of the spatial entailments of globalization, see Kevin Cox, ed., *Spaces of Globalization* (New York: Guilford, 1997), and Andrew Leyshon and Nigel Thrift, *MoneySpace: Geographies of Monetary Transformation* (New York: Routledge, 1997).

10. For a contextualization of these occurrences, see George Yudice, "The Privatization of Culture," *Social Text* 59 (Summer 1999): 17–34.

11. Karl Marx and Frederick Engels, *The Communist Manifesto* (London: Verso, 1998).

12. Arlene Croce, "Discussing the Undiscussable," *New Yorker* (December 26, 1994–January 2, 1995): 54–60. For a fuller discussion, see Carol Martin, "High Critics / Low Arts," in *Moving Words: Re-Writing Dance*, ed. Gay Morris (London: Routledge, 1996), 320–333.

13. National Endowment for the Arts, Research Division Notes no. 73, "Artist Employment in 1998," April 1999.

## 4. Thomas F. DeFrantz: The Black Beat Made Visible

1. I use the term *black social dance* to describe dances of the African diaspora not transferred to the concert stage, that is, diasporic dances performed and watched by other participating dancers. Here, I intend for the term *black* to imply a shared cultural and political heritage of Africans in diaspora, in particular those whose ancestors survived the Middle Passage.

2. W. E. Burghardt Du Bois, *The Souls of Black Folks* (New York: Dodd, Mead, 1961), 3.

3. Roger D. Abrahams, *Singing the Master: The Emergence of African-American Culture in the Plantation South* (New York: Penguin Books, 1992), 155.

4. Robert Hinton, "Black Dance in American History," in *The Black Tradition in American Modern Dance*, ed. Gerald Myers (n.p.: American Dance Festival Program, 1988), 4.

5. Ibid., 4.

6. Pearl Primus, "Primitive African Dance (and Its Influence on the Churches of the South)," in *The Dance Encyclopedia*, ed. Anatole Chujoy (New York: A. S. Barnes, 1949), 387.

7. Ibid., 389.

8. Eve Kosofsky Sedgwick, *Tendencies* (Durham: Duke University Press, 1993), 11.

9. I borrow the word "actionable" from legal parlance, where it conveys the sense of giving cause for [legal] action.

10. I draw the notion of efficacious performative gestures from Judith Butler, *Bodies That Matter: On the Discursive Limits of "Sex"* (New York: Routledge: 1993).

11. Cornel West, "On Afro-American Popular Music: From Bebop to Rap," in *Sacred Music of the Secular City: From Blues to Rap*, ed. Jon Michael Spencer (Durham: Duke University Press, 1992), 288.

12. Hinton's argument cited above also suggests that black social dance emerged as an inevitability of the Middle Passage.

13. Robert Farris Thompson, "Hip Hop 101," in *Droppin' Science: Critical Essays on Rap Music and Hip Hop Culture*, ed. William Eric Perkins (Philadelphia: Temple University Press, 1996), 213.

14. Walter Hughes, "In the Empire of the Beat: Discipline and Disco" in *Microphone Fiends: Youth Music & Youth Culture*, ed. Andrew Ross and Tricia Rose (New York: Routledge, 1994), 149.

15. Hughes seems to imply that these two categories—black expressive culture, represented by the black singing disco diva, and [white] gay culture, represented by the homosocial dancing bodies in gay clubs—assume a binary of irreconcilable difference: "the evolution of disco is one of appropriation and integration, both exploitation and empathy; the negotiation between usually straight black women and usually white gay men seemed to open up and make visible all the various subject positions between these previously polarized identities. Since the actual author and audience of any disco song are both indeterminate, disco's racial, sex-

ual and gender identity cannot be finally fixed as 'black music,' 'women's music' or 'gay music.'" Ibid., 153. Of course, the intention of disco music as it evolved as dance music by and for black dancers, must be explored.

16. Ibid., 149.

17. Robert Farris Thompson, *African Art in Motion: Icon and Act* (Berkeley and Los Angeles: University of California Press, 1963); Marshall Stearns and Jean Stearns, *Jazz Dance: The Story of American Vernacular Dance* (New York: Schirmer Books [1964]1979); Dolores Kirton Cayou, *Modern Jazz Dance* (Palo Alto, Calif.: Mayfield, 1971); Katrina Hazzard-Donald, "Dance in Hip Hop Culture" in *Droppin' Science: Critical Essays on Rap Music and Hip Hop Culture*, ed. William Eric Perkins (Philadelphia, Temple University Press, 1996), 220–223; Jacqui Malone, *Steppin' On The Blues: The Visible Rhythms of African American Dance* (Urbana: University of Illinois Press, 1996); Brenda Dixon Gottschild, *Digging the Africanist Presence in American Performance: Dance and Other Contexts* (Westport, Conn.: Greenwood, 1996).

18. Robert Farris Thompson, "Dance and Culture, an Aesthetic of the Cool: West African Dance," *African Forum* 2, no. 2 (Fall 1966): 88.

19. Robert Farris Thompson, *Flash of the Spirit: African & Afro-American Art & Philosophy* (New York: 1st Vintage Books ed., 1983), xiii. Nowhere does Thompson employ the mistaken concept of "polyrhythm"—an impossibility to a dancer. The rhythms of African diaspora music and dance may become exceedingly complex, but they are also inextricably linked; it is unnecessary to separate one meter out from the next. Inside the dance, the separation of competing meters rarely occurs.

20. Brenda Dixon Gottschild, *Digging the Africanist Presence in American Performance*, 12.

21. Ibid., 13–16.

22. Dolores Kirton Cayou, *Modern Jazz Dance*, 6.

23. Charles Dickens, *American Notes* (Gloucester, Mass.: Peter Smith [1842] 1968), 110.

24. Ibid., 112.

25. Ibid., 112.

26. Jan Michael Spencer, ed., *The Emergence of Black and the Emergence of Rap*. In *Black Sacred Music: A Journal of Theomusicology* 5, no. 1 (Spring 1991): 9.

27. Robert Farris Thompson, "Dance and Culture," 85–102. This synthesis corresponds to Cayou's articulation of "functionalism."

28. Katrina Hazzard-Donald, "Dance in Hip Hop Culture," 229.

29. Tricia Rose, *Black Noise: Rap Music and Black Culture in Contemporary America* (Hanover: Wesleyan University Press, 1994), 99.

30. Jon Michael Spencer, *The Rhythms of Black Folk: Race, Religion, and Pan-Africanisms* (Trenton, N.J.: Africa World Press, 1995), 10.

31. Philip Royster, "The Rapper as Shaman for a Band of Dancers of the Spirit: 'U Can't Touch This,'" in *The Emergence of Black and the Emergence of Rap*, ed. Jon Michael Spencer, 61.

32. Jacqui Malone, *Steppin' On The Blues*, 29.

33. This collaboration is not possible for the frozen audience of competition judges, or the still bodies glued silently into the seats of a proscenium theater.

34. Tricia Rose, *Black Noise*, 36.

35. Cornel West, "On Afro-American Popular Music: From Bebop to Rap," 292.

36. Katrina Hazzard-Donald, "Dance in Hip Hop Culture," 227.

37. Tricia Rose, *Black Noise*, 83.

38. I do not intend to amplify Paul Gilroy's assertion that break dancing "disappeared" after a short heyday as a commodity in the mid-1980s. Certainly break dancing became the most conspicuously consumed black social dance product of the late twentieth century. Although the form's expressive potentials became diluted during its commercial overexposure, the dance retained elements of its genesis as a social dance form and surfaced in nightclubs throughout the 1990s. See Paul Gilroy, "Exer(or)cising Power: Black Bodies in the Black Public Sphere," in *Dance in the City*, ed. Helen Thomas (New York: St. Martin's, 1997).

39. Jacqui Malone, *Steppin' On The Blues*, 35.

40. Brenda Dixon Gottschild, *Digging the Africanist Presence in American Performance*, 144.

41. Katrina Hazzard-Donald, "Dance in Hip Hop Culture," 227.

42. Ibid., 226.

43. Michael Eric Dyson, "Rap Culture, the Church, and American Society," in *Sacred Music of the Secular City: From Blues to Rap*, ed. Jon Michael Spencer (Durham: Duke University Press, 1992), 269.

44. Houston Baker, *Black Studies, Rap, and the Academy* (Chicago: University of Chicago Press, 1993), 85.

45. Ibid., 89.

46. Ibid., 92.

47. Spencer, ed. *The Emergence of Black and the Emergence of Rap*.

48. Ibid., v.

49. Ibid., v.

50. Ibid., vii.

51. Jon Michael Spencer, *The Rhythms of Black Folk*, 145.

52. Jacqui Malone, *Steppin' On The Blues*, 36.

## 5. Susan Manning: Danced Spirituals

1. This essay originated as a talk delivered at Performance Studies International and the CORD conference "African-American Dance: Researching a Complex History" in 1996 and at the Unnatural Acts conference at the University of California, Riverside and at the Centre for Dance Research at the Roehampton Institute (London) in 1997. My thanks to the organizers and audiences at all four events. I have decided to publish this essay as it was commissioned in 1996–97, because subsequent elaborations of my argument do not reiterate the comparative stage history presented here. For later revisions of my argument, see "Black Voices, White Bodies: The Performance of Race and Gender in *How Long Brethren*," *American Quarterly* 50, no. 1 (March 1998): 24–46; "Modern Dance, Negro Dance and Katherine Dunham," *Textual Practice* 15, no. 3 (Winter 2001): 487–505; and my *Modern Dance, Negro Dance*, forthcoming from the University of Minnesota Press.

2. The figures for Tamiris and Shawn come from Christena L. Schlundt, *Tamiris: A Chronicle of Her Dance Career, 1927–1955* (New York: New York Public Library, 1972), and *The Professional Apperances of Ted Shawn & His Men Dancers* (New York: New York Public Library, 1967 [©1966]). Nicholson documents performances by Guy and Wilson Williams, while Perpener documents performances by Charles Williams's Hampton Institute Create Dance Group, featuring the choreography of Moton Kennedy. Josephine Monica Nicholson, "Three Black Pioneers in American Modern Dance 1931–1945: The Dance Careers of Hemsley Winfield, Edna Guy and Wilson Williams" (M.A. Thesis, George Washington University, 1984); and John Perpener, "The Seminal Years of Black Concert Dance" (Ph.D. dissertation, New York University, 1992). Lloyd

mentions danced spirituals performed by Bales (187–188) and Bettis (256), while Terry's *The Dance* notes performances by La Meri (189). Margaret Lloyd, *The Borzoi Book of Modern Dance* (New York: Alfred Knopf, 1949), and Walter Terry, *The Dance in America* (New York: Harper & Row, 1956). My own research in primary sources at the Dance Collection, New York Public Library for the Performing Arts and at the Midwest Dance Archive, Newberry Library, has yielded documentation on danced spirituals by Dunham, Littlefield, Mumaw, Segal, and Winfield.

3. Emery mentions the danced spirituals choreographed by Johnson. See Lynne Fauley Emery, *Black Dance from 1619 to Today* (Princeton: Princeton Book, 1988), 291. All other documentation comes from my own research at the Dance Collection.

4. *Continuing Revelations*, videotape of symposium held at the Dance Collection, New York Public Library for the Performing Arts, May 11, 1992. Housed at Dance Collection.

5. My research at the Dance Collection has turned up versions by Ronald K. Brown, Bebe Miller, and Kevin Wynn.

6. When I wrote this essay, I did not realize that other historians were asking this question too. See Mary L. Dudziak, *Cold War Civil Rights: Race and the Image of American Democracy* (Princeton: Princeton University Press, 2000). See David Savran. *Communists, Cowboys, and Queers: The Politics of Masculinity in the Work of Arthur Miller and Tennessee Williams* (Minneapolis: University of Minnesota Press, 1992).

7. Film available for viewing at the Dance Collection or for rental through the Dance Films Association. Interestingly, the sequence of solos Tamiris chose to record for posterity she never performed in exactly that order onstage. The film recorded five spirituals choreographed between 1928 and 1932, omitting "Nobody Knows de Trouble I Seen," which typically had opened Tamiris's performances of spirituals during those years. The film more closely resembles programs from 1939 to 1942, which usually opened with "Go Down, Moses." Here and elsewhere my stage history of *Negro Spirituals* synthesizes evidence gleaned from programs and reviews (many found in Tamiris's *Scrapbooks* at the Dance Collection) as well as from the choreochronicle published in Schlundt, *Tamiris*.

8. Subsequent revivals—including a revival of all nine spirituals that Tamiris herself directed in 1965—have featured both black and white dancers. These revivals raise the question of how to read Tamiris's choreographic intention in retrospect. Did Tamiris's casting of the solos for black and white dancers in 1965 render her earlier embodiment of the solos incidental to their choreographic design? In other words, does the casting of the solos since 1965 reflect intentions implicit, though not realized, in their performances from 1928 to 1944? Yes, argues reconstructor Holly Lau, who believes that Tamiris's works created "a bridge for the acceptance of the black dance." Holly Lau, "*The Negro Spirituals*: Memphis 1992," in *Dance ReConstructed* (New Brunswick, N.J.: Mason Gross School of the Arts, 1993), 238. Here I take a different position: that revivals since 1965 reflect casting conventions that did not emerge until the postwar period. Thus the embodiment of the solos by their creator—a white female dancer—was not incidental to their meaning as long as they were performed onstage. Differently stated, contemporary productions of *Negro Spirituals* constitute a fundamentally different text from Tamiris's own performances.

9. John Martin, "Art of Tamiris Wins Plaudits at Stadium," *New York Times*, August 19, 1933, 14.

10. Frederick Orme, "The Negro in the Dance as Katherine Dunham Sees Him," *American Dancer* 11 (March 1938): 46.

11. John Martin, "Dance Recital Given By Negro Artists," *New York Times,* April 30, 1931, 27.

12. John Perpener, "The Seminal Years of Black Concert Dance," 165.

13. Walter Terry, "To the Negro Dance," *New York Herald Tribune,* January 28, 1940, F10.

14. Ted Shawn quoted in Schlundt, *Professional Appearances of Ted Shawn,* 63.

15. Jane Sherman and Barton Mumaw, *Barton Mumaw, Dancer* (New York: Dance Horizons, 1986), 144.

16. Ibid., 129.

17. Silent film of *Negro Spirituals* available for viewing at the Dance Collection. The solo, "Nobody Knows de Trouble I've Seen," also was performed as part of Shawn's solo cycle *Four Dances Based on American Folk Music.* A restored film version of *Four Dances,* with a soundtrack added by Jess Meeker as part of Jacob's Pillow project to document Shawn's choreography, is also available for viewing at the Dance Collection or for rental through the Jacob's Pillow Archive.

18. In his memoir, contemporary dancer and choreographer Bill T. Jones writes, "Two generations ago the code word 'Greek' was used by men to speak of anal sex." Bill T. Jones, *Last Night on Earth* (New York: Pantheon, 1995), 228.

19. Ted Shawn, *Scrapbooks,* Dance Collection, New York Public Library for the Performing Arts.

20. Schlundt, *Professional Appearances of Ted Shawn,* 63.

21. Ellen Graff, *Stepping Left: Dance and Politics in New York City, 1928–1942* (Durham: Duke University Press, 1997).

22. My analysis of *Revelations* is based on a survey of programs and reviews, Ailey's posthumously published *Revelations: The Autobiography of Alvin Ailey* (with Peter Bailey) (New York: Birch Lane, 1995), film versions from different periods housed at the Dance Collection, and regular viewing of the work in performance since 1972. As noted above, my information on other danced spirituals from the postwar period comes from primary research at the Dance Collection.

23. Arthur Todd, "Roots of the Blues," *Dance and Dancers* (November 1961), 24.

24. From the film *An Evening with Alvin Ailey* (Chicago: Home Vision, 1986).

25. Ailey, *Revelations,* 101.

26. Edward Thorpe, *Black Dance* (Woodstock, N.Y.: Overlook, 1989), 113.

27. Zita Allen, "Memorabaileya," *Dance Magazine* (August 1974): 26.

28. Ailey, *Revelations,* 128.

29. Ramsay Burt, *The Male Dancer: Bodies, Spectacle, Sexualities* (London: Routledge, 1995).

## 6. Barbara Browning: Breast Milk Is Sweet and Salty

1. There were, of course, several layers of complexity in this performance: the stylized staging of "nontheatrical" religious dances, the confluent performances of Africanness and Brazilianness in this event, the presentation of cultural forms within a museum of "natural" history, and my own participation as the only white (although not the only North American) dancer in an Afro-Brazilian company. I signal but shall not unpack these layers of complexity. The larger point of the essay is that for all of the ways in which this performance may seem obviously denaturalized, there is no "natural" choreography of maternity.

2. Barbara Browning, *Samba: Resistance in Motion* (Bloomington: Indiana University Press, 1995).

3. Barbara Browning, *Infectious Rhythm: Metaphors of Contagion and the Spread of African Culture* (New York: Routledge, 1998).

4. Gilberto Freyre, *The Masters and the Slaves: A Study in the Development of Brazilian Civilization*, trans. David H. P. Maybury-Lewis (Berkeley and Los Angeles: University of California Press, 1986), 312.

5. Hermano Vianna, *The Mystery of Samba: Popular Music and National Identity in Brazil*, trans. John Charles Chasteen (Chapel Hill: University of North Carolina Press, 1999), 9.

6. In *Samba,* I discussed some of the figures used in popular histories of the form, notably that of "café com leite," (coffee with milk). In some of the elaborations of this figure, milk, or whiteness, is clearly associated with European men as they infused African women's "coffee" bodies with their cultural influence (17–18). The confluence of narratives of cultural admixture and racial miscegenation through the figure of milk speaks, of course, to this essay. And I noted in *Samba* the irony of one bodily fluid (semen) being replaced by another (milk), which would seem to erase the realities of gender politics in Brazil's racial history. This very figural replacement is taken up below in reference to the work of Nancy Scheper-Hughes on artificial milk and gender relations in Brazil.

7. Freyre, *The Masters and the Slaves*, 312.

8. Ibid., 321.

9. Ibid., 323.

10. Ibid., 325.

11. Barbara Browning, *Infectious Rhythm,* chap. 1 et passim.

12. Michael Specter, "Breast-Feeding and HIV: Weighing Health Risks and Treatment Costs," *New York Times,* August 19, 1998, sec. A, p. 14.

13. This, despite the surprising and heartening progress in recent years in parts of the developing world in making HIV medications available. Brazil has been at the vanguard of the movement for universal drug access, but distressing gaps in infrastructural support continue to make prevention and treatment a challenge for the poor.

14. Nancy Scheper-Hughes, *Death Without Weeping: The Violence of Everyday Life in Brazil* (Berkeley and Los Angeles: University of California Press, 1992). The book is not only poignant, but also controversial. Scheper-Hughes treads the difficult fault line between cultural relativism and ethically and politically articulated claims of child abuse. While the driving force of the book is a desire to demonstrate the catastrophic effects of poverty on the lives of women and children, Scheper-Hughes implicates poor women in the high rates of infant mortality through what she calls their "mortal neglect." While this essay will make it clear that I appreciate her attempt not merely to make visible the impossible "choices" such women are forced to make, but also to "culture" maternity itself, it is my sense that the inference of blame might be more broadly—and rightly— cast if the role of the potential nurturer were understood as proper to men as well as women. This is not to deny the caretaking realities of most women and mothers; it is, however, to imply that "deconstructionist" critiques of restrictive gender identity might offer more to Scheper-Hughes's practical political argument than she admits. See below.

15. Ibid., 322.

16. Ibid., 322.

17. Donna Haraway, *Modest_Witness@Second_Millenium. FemaleMan©_ Meets_OncoMouse™.* (New York: Routledge, 1997), 208.

18. Donna Haraway, *Simians, Cyborgs and Women: The Reinvention of Nature* (New York: Routledge, 1991), 166.

19. Nancy Scheper-Hughes, *Death Without Weeping,* 323–324.

20. Nancy Scheper-Hughes and Carolyn Sargent, eds., *Small Wars: The Cultural Politics of Childhood* (Berkeley and Los Angeles: University of California Press, 1998), 6.

21. This is true not merely of this song, of course, but of many performances of diasporic identity, including the performance of Yemanjá's choreography at the American Museum of Natural History. Audiences and listeners may have various degrees of attunement to the artificiality of the naturalizing of Africanness, but it can retain or recuperate political significance nonetheless.

22. Nancy Scheper-Hughes, *Death Without Weeping*, 326.

23. Marcel Mauss, "Body Techniques," in *Sociology and Psychology: Essays*, trans. Ben Brewster (London: Routledge and Kegan Paul, 1979), 118.

24. Ibid., 116.

25. Paul Farmer, "Bad Blood, Spoiled Milk: Bodily Fluids as Moral Barometers In Rural Haiti," *American Ethnologist* 15, no. 1 (1988): 62.

26. Ibid., 77.

27. Ibid., 79–80.

28. Leonard B. Lerer, "Who Is the Rogue? Hunger, Death, and Circumstance in John Mampe Square," in *Small Wars: The Cultural Politics of Childhood*, ed. Nancy Scheper-Hughes and Carolyn Sargent (Berkeley and Los Angeles: University of California Press, 1998), 239.

29. Nancy Scheper-Hughes, *Death Without Weeping*, 326.

30. Paul Farmer, "Bad Blood, Spoiled Milk," 791.

31. Ibid., 791.

32. Nancy Scheper-Hughes, *Death Without Weeping*, 355.

33. Barbara Browning, *Infectious Rhythm*, chap. 10.

34. I have made this suggestion in specific reference to Angie Extravaganza's performance of maternity in the film *Paris Is Burning*. See Barbara Browning, *Infectious Rhythm*, chap. 9.

35. I write here of the *apparent* distinction of the project of Scheper-Hughes, for whom the gender and maternity of her informants are painfully literal, and that of Haraway, who points to their constructed "nature." Pai Laércio's dance is thoroughly invested in the naturalization—in fact, the divine manifestation—of woman and mother, even as he demonstrates that these are choreographies that can be embodied by a man. His role as caretaker and nurturer to HIV-positive children, of course, is an extension of this choreography.

36. I use, for simplicity's sake, Deren's spelling, although contemporary Kryól orthography would render his name "Gede."

37. Maya Deren, *Divine Horsemen* (New York: Thames and Hudson, 1953), 111.

38. Ibid., 113.

39. Ibid., 114.

40. Barbara Browning, *Infectious Rhythm*, 88–101 et passim.

41. Nancy Scheper-Hughes and Margaret M. Lock, eds., "The Mindful Body: A Prolegomenon to Future Work in Medical Anthropology," *Medical Anthropology Quarterly* 1, no. 1 (1987): 6–7. This is, of course, the central argument in Mary Douglas.

42. Ibid., 6–7. Here, the principal theoretical reference is to Michel Foucault.

## 7. Mark Franko: Given Movement

1. "La vie rendue à la mort, c'est l'opération même du symbolique . . . ," Jean Baudrillard, *L'Echange symbolique et la mort* (Paris: Gallimard, 1976), 201. This essay was read at the conference "Post-Ritual: Events/Performance/Art" at the University of California, Santa Cruz, January 5, 2003. I wish to thank Giovanni

Careri, André Lepecki, Richard Schechner, and Catherine M. Soussloff for their helpful comments.

2. Arnold Van Gennep, *The Rites of Passage*, trans. Monika B. Vizedom and Gabrielle L. Caffee (Chicago: University of Chicago Press, 1960), 91 n. 4.

3. Stephen C. Foster, "Event Structures and Art Situations," in *"Event" Arts and Art Events*, ed. Stephen C. Foster (Ann Arbor: UMI Research Press, 1988), 3.

4. Ibid.

5. Coco Fusco, "Performative Interventions and the Politics of Witnessing," paper read at the panel "Responses to 9/11 and its Aftermaths," New York University, April 11, 2002.

6. Anne Cubilie, "Grounded Ethics: A Center/Field Discussion of Testimonial Witnessing from Rural Afghanistan to the United States," paper read at the panel "Responses to 9/11 and its Aftermaths," New York University, April 11, 2002.

7. Barbara Kirshenblatt-Gimblett, "Kodak Moments, Flashbulb Memories: Reflections on 9/11," paper read at the panel "Theatres of Place and Space," New York University, April 12, 2002.

8. For one of many such calls, see Anne Midgette, "Responding to Crisis, Art Must Look Beyond Itself," in *New York Times* (March 3, 2002), sect. 2, pp. 1 and 8. See also Bill T. Jones, "The Aftermath: A Louder Public Voice," at the following web address: http://palmbeachica.org/Louder%20Voice.htm.

9. The subject of Derrida's talk, published as *L'Université sans conditions* (Paris: Galilée, 2001), was the future of the university, and the event referred to is, What can supersede the performativity of the Humanities? For a further development of performance and performativity with respect to the arts disciplines in the academy, see Catherine M. Soussloff and Mark Franko, "Visual and Performance Studies: A New History of Interdisciplinarity," *Social Text*, 20, no. 14 (Winter 2003): 29–46.

10. J. L. Austin, *How To Do Things With Words* (Cambridge, Mass.: Harvard University Press, 1975), 67. As Derrida recently paraphrased Austin's position: "Pure performativity implies the presence of a living being, and of a living being speaking one time only, in its own name, in the first person. And speaking in a manner that is at once spontaneous, intentional, free, and irreplaceable." "Typewriter Ribbon: Limited Ink (2) ("within such limits")," in *Material Events: Paul de Man and the Afterlife of Theory*, ed. Tom Cohen, Barbara Cohen, J. Hillis Miller, and Andrzej Warminski (Minneapolis: University of Minnesota Press, 2001), 279.

11. "Signature événement contexte," a talk given in 1971, was first published in French in his *Marges de la philosophie* (Paris: Minuit, 1972), 365–393. The English translation appeared in *Glyph* 1 (1977): 172–197. John Searle published a reply to Derrida in the same issue, and further debate ensued in *Glyph* 2 (1977). Also in 1971, Jean-François Lyotard undertook his influential theorization of the figure as event in *Discours, Figure* (Paris: Klincksieck, 1971).

12. Jacques Derrida, "Signature Event Context," 192.

13. "We must notice that the illocutionary act is a conventional act: an act done as conforming to a convention." Austin, *How To Do Things With Words*, 105.

14. I shall return shortly to the important way that iterability becomes associated with expressive action in Derrida's second intervention on speech act theory, "Limited Inc," translated by Samuel Weber in *Glyph* 2 (1977): 162–251. The French text was published in a supplement to *Glyph* 2 (1977).

15. Maurice Blanchot, *The Writing of the Disaster*, translated by Ann Smock (Lincoln: University of Nebraska Press, 1986), 36. Derrida's references to Blanchot in the first seminar were limited to *La Folie du jour* (1975). In *The Writing*

*of the Disaster*, Blanchot discusses the disaster as gift (49–50) and the event (109). *L'Ecriture du désastre* first appeared in France in 1980.

16. Martin Heidegger, *On Time and Being*, trans. Joan Stambaugh (New York: Harper Colophon Books, 1972), 6. With Heidegger, the concept of the gift moves toward the inclusion of time and being in the event (*Ereignis*).

17. Ibid., 16.

18. Indeed, 9/11 has all the earmarks of a "meaningless event, which seems all the more present for its defying comprehension." Agata Bielik-robson, "Bad Timing: The Subject as a Work of Time," in *Angelaki* 5/3 (December 2000), 74. Bielik-robson discusses the event in terms of the classical concept of fate. I thank Karen Bassi for calling my attention to this article.

19. Jacques Derrida, *Given Time: I. Counterfeit Money*, trans. Peggy Kamuf (Chicago: University of Chicago Press, 1991), 7.

20. Ibid., 13.

21. Marcel Mauss, "Essai sur le don. Forme et Raison de l'Echange dans le Sociétés Archaïques," in *Sociologie et Anthropologie* (Paris: PUF, 1950), 143–279 (originally published in 1923–24). *The Gift: The Form and Reason for Exchange in Archaic Societies*, trans. W. D. Halls (New York: Norton, 1990). In 1933 Georges Bataille replaced Mauss's gift (*don*) with expenditure (*dépense*), thus connecting sumptuary destruction with class and religious warfare. From Bataille's perspective one can conceive of homicide bombing as a kind of potlatch. See Georges Bataille, "La Notion de dépense," in *La Part maudite* (Paris: Minuit, 1967), 23–45 (*The Accursed Share*, trans. Robert Hurley [New York: Zone Books, 1991]); "The Notion of Expenditure," in *Visions of Excess: Selected Writings, 1927–1939*, ed. Allan Stoekl (Minneapolis: University of Minnesota Press, 1993), 116–129.

22. Jean-François Lyotard, "March 23," in *Political Writings,* trans. Bill Readings and Kevin Paul Geiman (Minneapolis: University of Minnesota Press, 1993), 64.

23. Ibid.

24. "Signature Event Context," 172.

25. "Signature Event Context," 175. I would note in passing that the value of absence in the instrumentality of writing does not necessarily "risk introducing a certain break in the homogeneity of the system" (176) of communication. The volume *Acting on the Past* is designed to demonstrate this important point.

26. "Signature Event Context," 173 (emphasis mine).

27. See Philip Auslander, *Liveness: Performance in a Mediatized Culture* (London: Routledge, 1999).

28. "Signature Event Context," 183.

29. "Mario of Tabanan," notes Mead elsewhere, "is the dancer chiefly responsible for the evolutions of *kebiar* dance which has become very popular in Bali in the last twenty years. The dance is performed sitting in a square space surrounded by instruments of the orchestra, but though the principal emphasis is upon the head and hands, the dance involves the whole body, and Mario has introduced a great deal of virtuosity into the difficult feat of rapid locomotion without rising from the sitting position." Margaret Mead and Gregory Bateson, *Balinese Character: A Photographic Analysis* (New York: New York Academy of Sciences, 1942), 87.

30. Sally Ann Ness, "Dancing in the Field: Notes from Memory," in *Corporealities: Dancing Knowledge, Culture and Power*, ed. Susan L. Foster (New York: Routledge, 1996), 131.

31. Ibid.

32. Beryl de Zoete and William Spies, *Dance and Drama in Bali* (London: Faber and Faber, 1938), 32.

33. "Hence it follows that to make a gift of something to someone is to make a present of some part of one self. Next, in this way we can better account for the very nature of exchange through gifts, of everything we call 'total services' ('prestations totales'), and among these, potlatch." Mauss, *The Gift*, 12; "Essai sur le don," 161.

34. Mauss, *The Gift*, 46; "Essai sur le don," 227.

35. "Learning to walk, learning the first appropriate gestures of playing musical instruments, learning to eat, and to dance are all accomplished with the teacher behind the pupil, conveying directly by pressure, and almost always with a minimum of words, the gesture to be performed. Under such a system of learning, one can only learn if one is completely relaxed and if will and consciousness, as we understand those terms, are almost in abeyance. The flexible body of the dancing pupil is twisted and turned in the teacher's hands; teacher and pupil go through the proper gesture, then suddenly the teacher springs aside, leaving the pupil to continue the pattern to which he has surrendered himself" (ibid., 15). This commentary accompanies a set of photographic plates of Mario teaching entitled "Visual and Kinaesthetic Learning."

36. It is through Derrida's reading of de Man in "Typewriter Ribbon" that he intercepts the language of Heinrich von Kleist's essay "On the Marionette Theatre," a locus classicus of dance theory. Derrida asks: "How is one to think together the machine *and* the event, a machine-like repetition *and* what happens?" (307). Dance traditions can furnish one answer to that question.

37. It is in line with these considerations that an important and easily overlooked point emerging from Derrida's reading of Heidegger and Mauss deserves emphasis: what we mean by gift must be linked to intention and intentionality. "There must be chance, encounter, the involuntary, even unconsciousness or disorder, and there must be intentional freedom, and these two conditions must— miraculously, graciously—agree with each other" (Derrida, *Given Time*). Intention and intentionality must operate as extraneous from subjectivity, but they still must operate. It is to this double condition of irruption and intentionality that the events of 9/11 seem uncannily to correspond. Though hardly through "gracious" agreement, this double condition is realized in the name of a secret, or of the inexplicable, as well as of the unrepresentable.

38. Tatsumi Hijikata, "Speech," Tokyo, February 9, 1985; repr. Mark Holborn et al., *Butoh: Dance of the Dark Soul* (New York: Aperture, 1987), 127.

39. I thank Patrick de Vos for introducing me to this film.

40. Derrida, "Typewriter Ribbon," 314.

41. Jean Baudrillard, *L'Echange symbolique et la mort* (Paris: Gallimard, 1976), 203. The term *symbolic* for Baudrillard regains its anthropological dimension at the expense of its linguistic connotation. The term *symbolization* resists the meanings attributed to the symbolic register by poststructural psychoanalysis.

42. Indeed, it is perhaps this very idea of transmission and inscription that defines what we mean by form in the case of dances. When I presented this paper at a recent conference, some exception was taken to my use of the word "form" in the phrase "dance form." The word was taken to signal the return to an idealism. One could of course recur to the alternative formulation: dance type. Whatever term one uses, however, the point is that dances tend to be identifiable and transferable by their marks. Certainly, the whole issue of training and transmission implies there is something of a formal or typical profile that requires mastery. Even butoh has marks without which it may no longer be butoh despite its

evolutions: white face paint, dilated reddened eyes, uplifted chin, and the particularly "drained" approach to experience that is visible at each moment.

## 8. André Lepecki: Inscribing Dance

1. For the threat of femininity in the making of modern dance see Ramsay Burt, *The Male Dancer: Bodies, Spectacle, Sexualities* (New York: Routledge, 1995).

2. Gaston Bachelard, "The Dialectics of Outside and Inside," in *The Poetics of Space*, trans. Maria Jolas. (Boston: Beacon, 1969), 212.

3. Barbara Browning objects to this proposition when she writes that "dance negates writing" in Brazilian candomblé and Haitian vodun. Barbara Browning, *Samba: Resistance in Motion* (Bloomington: Indiana University Press, 1995), 40. With the caution any transcultural remark always demands, I would suggest that this culturally specific negation of writing as described by Browning still proposes an interesting pairing between inscription and dancing. According to Browning, in candomblé and vodun, the ground where dance takes its place is previously defined, and literally demarcated, as an explicit space for writing. Dance occupies the space of writing and erases it over (ibid., 39–40). As Heidegger and Derrida remind us, to put writing under erasure is not yet to negate writing.

4. By modern choreography I mean here dance forms that emerged within and along modernity, and not the style of dance developed in the early decades of the twentieth century known as modern dance. Mark Franko also notes how "Western systems of kinetic theatricality," even contemporary ones, are grounded on Renaissance choreography. Mark Franko, *The Dancing Body in Renaissance Choreography* (Birmingham, Ala.: Summa Publications, 1986), 2. The radical consequence of such insight is that choreography participates fully in, and is unthinkable without, the project of modernity. For a discussion of the project of choreographing as intrinsic to the constitution of the practice of modernity see Susan Foster, *Choreography and Narrative* (Bloomington: Indiana University Press, 1996).

5. Jean-Georges Noverre, "Letters on Dancing and Ballets," in *What is Dancing?* ed. Roger Copeland and Marshall Cohen (Oxford: Oxford University Press, 1983), 10.

6. Thoinot Arbeau, *Orchesography: A Treatise in the Form of a Dialogue Whereby All Manner of Persons May Easily Acquire and Practise the Honourable Exercise of Dancing*, trans. Cyril W. Beaumont (New York: Dance Horizons, [1589] 1968), 15.

7. Jacques Derrida, *Archive Fever: A Freudian Impression*, trans. Eric Prenowitz (Chicago: University of Chicago Press, 1996), 1.

8. Arbeau, *Orchesography*, 15.

9. Jean-Noël Laurenti, "Feuillet's Thinking," in *Traces of Dance: Drawings and Notations of Choreographers*, ed. Laurence Louppe, trans. Brian Holmes (Paris: Editions Dis Voir, 1994), 86.

10. For a discussion of Descartes's views of the body as machine, see Dennis de Chene, *Spirits and Clocks: Machine and Organism in Descartes* (Ithaca: Cornell University Press, 2001).

11. Laurenti, "Feuillet's Thinking," 82.

12. On the book as extension of the academy as structure of command, see Denis Hollier, *Against Architecture: The Writings of Georges Bataille*, trans. Betsy Wing (Cambridge, Mass.: MIT Press, 1989).

13. Laurenti, "Feuillet's Thinking," 86.

14. Mark Franko notes how in late sixteenth-century France, "choreography

was frequently likened to, and indeed contrived to suggest, a written text," and how "the body—within its very presentations as a spectacular entity—was also identified as a textual entity." Mark Franko, *Dance as Text: Ideologies of the Baroque Body* (Cambridge: Cambridge University Press, 1993), 15. This symmetry between text and body will sustain gradual transformation. Susan Leigh Foster writes that in mid-eighteenth-century France, "Enlightenment humanism encumbers the body with a new and distinctive expressive function, and it also specifies a new relation between writing and dancing." If, by the mid-seventeenth century dance and writing are both articulated as "forms of inscription . . . equally capable of articulateness" by the time of Noverre, "words and movements, while each forming the vocabulary of a kind of language, are apprehended as unique in their expressive abilities. . . . movement's message appeals to heart and soul in a way words cannot." Susan Leigh Foster, "Textual Evidances," in *Bodies of the Text: Dance as Theory, Literature as Dance,* ed. Ellen W. Goellner and Jacqueline Shea Murphy (New Brunswick: Rutgers University Press, 1995), 234.

15. Ibid., 234.

16. Siegfried Giedion writes of the seventeenth century as founding the beginning of "a new idea of the world based on movement." Siegfried Giedion, *Mechanization Takes Command* (New York: Norton, 1975), 16. Recently Jonathan Crary has analyzed the role of attention in the excavation of this world absolutely inscribed in motion. Jonathan Crary, *Suspensions of Perception: Attention, Spectacle, and Modern Culture* (Cambridge, Mass.: MIT Press, 1999).

17. Francis Barker, *The Tremulous Private Body: Essays in Subjection* (New York: Methuen, 1984).

18. Pierre Rameau, *The Dancing Master,* trans. Cyril W. Beaumont (Brooklyn: Dance Horizons, 1970), 9.

19. Ibid., 116.

20. Peggy Pelan, *Unmarked: The Politics of Performance* (New York: Routledge, 1993), 6.

21. Sigmund Freud, "Mourning and Melancholia," in *The Standard Edition of the Complete Psychological Works of Sigmund Freud,* ed. James Strachey, trans. Anna Freud, Alix Strachey, and Alan Tyson (London: Hogarth, 1966), 14:255.

22. Jacques Derrida identifies the entire project of Western metaphysics as a photology, or science of light. Jacques Derrida, "Force and Signification," in *Writing and Difference,* trans. Alan Bass (Chicago: University of Chicago Press, 1978), 27. See below on how dance studies sides with photology.

23. Marcia Siegel, *The Shapes of Change* (Berkeley and Los Angeles, London: University of California Press, 1985), xv.

24. Ibid., xv.

25. Mark Franko, *Dancing Modernism / Performing Politics* (Bloomington: Indiana University Press, 1995). Peggy Phelan makes a parallel argument regarding performance in general: "Performance theory and criticism have tended to respond to the loss of the object by adapting a primarily conservative and conserving method." Peggy Phelan, *Mourning Sex: Performing Public Memories* (New York: Routledge, 1997), 3.

26. Mark Franko, "Mimique," in *Bodies of the Text: Dance as Theory, Literature as Dance,* ed. E. W. Goellner and J. S. Murphy (New Brunswick: Rutgers University Press, 1995), 206.

27. Ibid., 206.

28. Both "concept" and "trace" must remain under erasure here. Derrida explains how the "trace" is not a concept, but more a "thought," as trace is that which escapes binarism but also allows binarism to become operational "on the

basis of nothing." However, for the sake of intelligibility, I shall follow Spivak's strategic and provisional use of the word "concept" when applied to the Derridean trace. See Jacques Derrida, "Freud and the Scene of Writing," in *Writing and Difference;* and Gayatri Spivak, "Translator's Preface," in *Of Grammatology,* trans. Gayatri Spivak (Baltimore: The Johns Hopkins University Press, 1976).

29. Spivak, "Translator's Preface," xxi.

30. Derrida, *Writing and Difference,* 279.

31. Ibid., 279.

32. Jacques Derrida, "Structure, Sign and Play in the Discourse of the Human Sciences," in *Writing and Difference,* 280.

33. Spivak "Translator's Preface," xxix.

34. Derrida, *Writing and Difference,* passim.

35. A term that, in French, already denotes the disappearance and the remnants of movement; it also means "footprint" as well as "track."

36. Derrida, "Freud and the Scene of Writing," 230.

37. Franko, "Mimique," 206.

38. Phelan, *Unmarked.*

39. Spivak, "Translators Preface," xxxix.

40. Franko, *Dancing Modernism / Performing Politics,* xiii.

41. Derrida, "Force and Signification," in *Writing and Difference,* 27.

42. Siegel, *The Shapes of Change,* xv.

43. For a discussion of Derrida's critique of description see Spivak, "Translator's Preface," lvii–lviii.

44. This introduces the question of parallax in both spectatorship and critical theory as "the angle of displacement of an object caused by the movement of its observer), by which I mean that our framings of the two depend on our position in the present *and* that this poisition is defined in such framings." Hal Foster, *The Return of the Real: The Avant-Garde at the End of the Century* (Cambridge, Mass.: MIT Press, 1996), 207.

45. Henry Sayre, *The Object of Performance* (Chicago: University of Chicago Press, 1989), 116.

46. Ibid., 116.

47. Jacques Derrida, *Spurs: Nietzsche's Styles,* trans. Barbara Harlow (Chicago: University of Chicago Press, 1979), 45–51.

48. Ibid., 51.

49. Ibid., 145.

50. Ann Cooper Albright, "Incalculable Choreographies," in *Bodies of the Text: Dance as Theory, Literature as Dance,* ed. Ellen W. Goellner and Jacqueline Shea Murphy (New Brunswick: Rutgers University Press, 1995), 159.

51. Franko, "Mimique," 206.

52. Peggy Phelan, "Thirteen Ways of Looking at Choreographing History," in *Choreographing History,* ed. Susan Leigh Foster (Bloomington: Indiana University Press, 1995), passim.

53. Ibid., 200.

54. Mark Franko and Annette Richards, "Actualizing Absence: The Pastness of Performance," in *Acting on the Past: Historical Performance Across the Disciplines,* ed. Mark Franko and Annette Richards (Hanover: Wesleyan University Press, 2000), 1.

55. Giorgio Agambem, while writing on Derrida's grammatology, notes how "placing writing and the trace in an initial position means putting the emphasis on this original presence [at the core of Western metaphysics], but not transcending it." Giorgio Agambem, *Stanzas: Word and Phantasm in Western Culture,* trans. Ronald L. Martinez (Minneapolis: University of Minnesota Press, 1993), 156.

56. Jacques Riviere, "Le Sacre du Printemps, 1913," in *Nijinsky Dancing*, ed. Lincoln Kirstein (New York: Knopf, 1975),164.

57. Phelan, *Unmarked*, 70.

## 9. Karmen MacKendrick: Embodying Transgression

1. Maurice Blanchot, *The Step Not Beyond*, trans. Lycette Nelson (Albany: State University of New York Press, 1992), 101.

2. Michel Foucault, "Preface to Transgression," in *Language, Countermemory, Practice*, ed. Donald F. Bouchard, trans. Donald F. Bouchard and Sherry Simon (Ithaca: Cornell University Press, 1977), 37.

3. Plato makes this point primarily in the *Timaeus*; in Aristotle, see *Metaphysics*, passim.

4. I take this statement from notes made at an informal seminar with Gallop at the State University of New York–Stony Brook in 1993; while I doubt I have misrepresented her meaning, there is some danger that I may have paraphrased. I have attempted to explore this relation more thoroughly in my own recent work; in brief, I would note that this calling takes place as part of a limit-relation between body and language, each at the boundary of the other.

5. Though I write what I can never, properly, read. On this disjunction between writing and reading, see Maurice Blanchot, "The Essential Solitude," in *The Sirens' Song*, ed. Gabriel Jospovici, trans. Sacha Rabinovitch (Bloomington: Indiana University Press, 1982), 99f. See also Maurice Blanchot, *The Step Not Beyond*: "what was written in the past will be read in the future, without any relation of presence being able to establish itself *between* writing and reading" (30). I have developed this idea at greater length in chapters 1 and 2 of *Immemorial Silence* (Albany: State University of New York Press, 2001).

6. "Let us think of the obscure combat between language and presence, always lost by one and by the other." Blanchot, *The Step not Beyond*, 31.

7. Maurice Blanchot, *The Writing of the Disaster*, trans. Ann Smock (Lincoln: University of Nebraska Press, 1986), 93.

8. Blanchot, *The Writing of the Disaster*, 51.

9. Georges Bataille, *Erotism: Death and Sensuality*, trans. Mary Dalwood (San Francisco: City Lights Press, 1986), 275.

10. It is Foucault who most clearly attributes this from-the-outside character to Blanchot's writing. See Michel Foucault, "Maurice Blanchot: The Thought from Outside," in *Foucault/Blanchot* (New York: Zone Books, 1987), and Michel Foucault, "Language to Infinity" in *Language, Countermemory, Practice*.

11. Bataille, *Erotism: Death and Sensuality*, 186.

12. Ibid., 46.

13. Foucault, *Language, Countermemory, Practice*, 43.

14. Blanchot, *The Writing of the Disaster*, 11.

15. Ibid., 29.

16. Bataille, *Erotism: Death and Sensuality*, 187.

17. Ibid., 274.

18. Blanchot, *The Writing of the Disaster*, 60.

19. Ibid., 89.

20. Gilles Deleuze, *Difference and Repetition*, trans. Paul Patton (New York: Columbia University Press, 1994), 1.

21. Blanchot, *The Writing of the Disaster*, 36.

22. Friedrich Nietzsche, *The Gay Science*, trans. Walter Kaufmann (New York: Vintage Books, 1974), sec. 341.

23. Blanchot, *The Writing of the Disaster*, 38.

24. Among the interesting elements that I am *not* analyzing are those more clearly unique to the body: the stretch and strength of the dancing form, a muscular and physiological intensification.

25. See, for instance, Jean Baudrillard, *Seduction*, trans. Brian Singer (New York: St. Martin's, 1990).

26. Dance critic Walter Terry, quoted in Joseph Mazo, *Prime Movers: The Makers of Modern Dance in America* (Princeton: Princeton Book Publishers, 1977), 74.

27. Jean-Luc Nancy, "Of Divine Places," in *The Inoperative Community*, ed. Peter Connor, trans. Michael Holland (Minneapolis: University of Minnesota Press, 1991), sec. 19f.

28. Nietzsche, *The Gay Science*, sec. 354.

29. Choreographer Deborah Hay writes: "A performer's inattention is glaringly visible. Questions rush in to fill the space where attention has been—whereas a performer's attention, without question, elicits audience attention." See Deborah Hay, *Lamb at the Altar / the story of a dance* (Durham: Duke University Press, 1994), 11.

30. Deleuze, *Difference and Repetition*, 21.

31. Ibid., 21.

32. Martha Graham, *Blood Memory* (New York: Doubleday, 1991), 276.

33. Baudrillard, *Seduction*, 69.

34. Nietzsche, *The Gay Science*, sec. 84.

35. Cited in Blanchot, *The Writing of the Disaster*, 5.

36. Ibid., 112–113.

37. Augustine of Hippo, *Confessions*, trans. Henry Chadwick (Oxford: Oxford University Press, 1991), book XI, sec. 2. Lest a church father seem terribly out of place in this "postmodern" discussion, we should remind ourselves that Bataille, for all his Sadean and Nietzschean heritage, was a Jesuit seminarian briefly and a medievalist librarian throughout his life, and that he saw in the works of such religious figures as Saint Teresa and Angele de Foligno a parallel to the excesses of his own "inner experience."

38. "Wherefore [the creator] resolved to have a moving image of eternity, and . . . he made this image eternal but moving according to number, while eternity itself rests in unity, and this image we call time." Plato, "Timaeus," in *The Collected Dialogues of Plato*, ed. E. Hamilton and H. Cairns, trans. Benjamin Jowett (Princeton: Princeton University Press, 1989), 37d.

39. Augustine of Hippo, *Confessions*, book XI, sec. 14.

40. Just to avoid this confusion, *sempiternity* is existence throughout all of time, from beginning to end; *eternity* is outside of time.

41. Deleuze, *Difference and Repetition*, 227.

42. Charles Scott, *The Language of Difference*, (Atlantic Highlands, N.J.: Humanities Press, 1987), 104.

43. Ibid., 169.

44. Blanchot, *The Writing of the Disaster*, 89.

45. Georges Bataille, *Theory of Religion*, trans. Robert Hurley (New York: Zone Books, 1989), 13.

# Contributors

**Barbara Browning** currently serves as chair of the Department of Performance Studies at New York University. She is the author of *Samba: Resistance in Motion* (Indiana University Press, 1995), and *Infectious Rhythm: Metaphors of Contagion and the Spread of African Culture* (Routledge, 1998).

**Ramsay Burt** is senior research fellow in dance at De Montfort University, Leicester, in the United Kingdom. His publications include *The Male Dancer: Bodies, Spectacle, Sexualities* (Routledge, 1995) and *Alien Bodies: Representations of Modernity, "Race," and Nation in Early Modern Dance* (Routledge, 1998), and he is currently working on the relationship between Judson Dance Theatre and more recent European dance. In 1999 he was a visiting professor at the Department of Performance Studies, New York University. With Susan Foster, he is the founder and editor of *Discourses in Dance.*

**Thomas DeFrantz** is associate professor at the Massachusetts Institute of Technology, where he holds the Class of 1948 Career Development Professorship. He organizes the dance history program at the Alvin Ailey School, and edited *Dancing Many Drums: Excavations in African American Dance*, (University of Wisconsin Press, 2002). His creative work includes *Monk's Mood: A Performance Meditation on Thelonius Monk* and *Queer Theory: A Musical Travesty.*

**Mark Franko** is the author of *The Work of Dance: Labor, Movement, and Identity in the 1930s* (Wesleyan University Press, 2002), *Dancing Modernism/Performing Politics* (Indiana University Press, 1995), *Dance as Text: Ideologies of the Baroque Body* (Cambridge University Press, 1993), *The Dancing Body in Renaissance Choreography* (Summa), and coeditor, with Annette Richards, of *Acting on the Past: Historical Performance Across the Disciplines* (Wesleyan University Press, 2000). He has published numerous articles in anthologies and journals such as *Res, Drama Review, Theatre Journal, Annals of Scholarship, Discourse, Social Text,* and *Performance Research.* His research has been supported by the Getty Research Center, the American Philosophical Society, the American Council of Learned Societies, and the France/Berkeley Fund. Dancer and choreographer, Franko has presented his work internationally since 1985, and is professor of dance and performance studies at the University of California, Santa Cruz.

**André Lepecki** is Assistant Professor in the department of Performance Studies at New York University. He is editor of *Intensification: Contemporary Portuguese Performance* (Theaterschrift Extra / Cotovia, 1998); and coeditor with Sally Banes of *The Senses in Performance* (Routledge, forthcoming). He has contributed to the journals *Performance Research, Drama Review, Ballet International, Art Forum, Nouvelles de Danse,* and the anthologies *Re/membering the Body* (Cantz

Verlag, 2000), *The Salt of the Earth* (Vlaams Theater Instituut, 2001), *Lusosex* (University of Minnesota Press, 2002), among others. In 2000, he codirected with Bruce Mau the installation *STRESS* presented at MAK (Museum for Applied and Contemporary Arts in Vienna). In 2002, he codirected with Rachel Swain the installation *proXy* (presented by Performance Space, Sydney). He is currently working on a book titled *Exhausting Dance*, a critical approach to the intersections of visual and performance art in contemporary European dance.

**Karmen Mackendrick** is associate professor of philosophy at Le Moyne College in Syracuse, New York. Her work includes *Counterpleasures* and *Immemorial Silence* (State University of New York Press, 1999 and 2001), and essays in aesthetics, cultural studies and theology. After many years of ballet training, she is currently studying Middle Eastern dance.

**Susan Manning** is associate professor of English, theater, and performance studies at Northwestern University. Her book on the dances of Mary Wigman, *Ecstasy and the Demon* (University of California Press, 1993), won the 1994 de la Torre Bueno Prize; a second edition is in preparation. Her forthcoming book *Modern Dance, Negro Dance* explores interrelations between American modern dance and black concert dance at midcentury.

**Randy Martin** is professor of art and public policy and associate dean of faculty and interdisciplinary programs at Tisch School of the Arts, New York University. His most recent books are *Financialization of Daily Life* (Temple University Press, 2002), *On Your Marx: Relinking Socialism and the Left* (University of Minnesota Press, 2001), and *Critical Moves: Dance Studies in Theory and Politics* (Duke University Press, 1998). He is also coeditor of the journal *Social Text*.

**Peggy Phelan** is the Ann O'Day Chair in the Arts, Stanford University. She is the author of *Unmarked: The Politics of Performance* (Routledge, 1993), and *Mourning Sex: Performing Public Memories* (Routledge, 1997). She is also the author of the "Survey" essays in *Art and Feminism* (Phaidon, 2001), and *Pipilotti Rist* (Phaidon, 2001).

# Index

Abrahams, Roger, 64, 73
*Accumulation with Talking* (Brown), 17–18
Aeschilmann, Roland, 20
Ahearn, Charlie, 76
AIDS/HIV, 100–101, 104–107, 166n13, 167n35
Ailey, Alvin, 7, 82, 83, 86, 93–96
Airaudo, Malou, 38–41
Albright, Ann Cooper, 136
Allen, Zita, 94
Althusser, Louis, 30, 38, 40
*Americana Suite* (Dunham), 93
*American Notes* (Dickens), 70
Anderson Theater, 36
Arbeau, Thoinot, 125–126, 127
Archilocus, 151
Aristotle, 141; Aristotelian tragedy, 51, 59
Artaud, Antonin, 32
audience, 47, 53; complicitous relationship with, 44; pandering to, 36; and race, 69–70, 72, 78–79, 93–94, 96, 159n34, 162n33
Augustine, 153
Austin, J. L., 8, 115–116, 123, 168n10

Bach, Johann Sebastian, 13, 24
Bachelard, Gaston, 2, 124
Bahamian folk dances, 87
Baker, Houston, 78
Bales, William, 82
*Balinese Character: A Photographer's Analysis* (Mead), 169n29
Banes, Sally, 13
Barker, Francis, 128
Bataille, Georges, 115, 142–142, 144, 145, 148, 153, 169n21
Bateson, Gregory, 113
Baudrillard, Jean, 51, 53, 115, 123, 170n41
Bauman, Zygmunt, 37–38
Bausch, Pina, 6, 29, 32, 34, 38–41, 44
*Beat Street* (Belafonte), 76

Beatty, Colin, 43–44
Beatty, Talley, 82, 93
Beethoven, Ludwig van, 24
Bel, Jérôme, 43
Belafonte, Harry, 76
Bettis, Valerie, 82
Bizet, 13
black choreographers, 82, 83
black social dance, 7, 64, 65–70, 73, 76, 79, 161nn1, 12
*Black Studies, Rap, and The Academy* (Baker), 78
Blanchot, Maurice, 8, 9, 115, 142–143, 145–147, 168–169n15, 174n10
Boal, Augusto, 51
body, 1–6, 30; black, 94; dancing black body, 64–66, 71, 72; dancing body, 29, 32, 37, 44, 48, 132; destruction of, 31; and hip hop, 7; identification with, 60; inscription of, 33; physicality of, 34, 36; and rap, 79; reality of, 41; in Renaissance dance manuals, 2; of resistance, 7. *See also* presence
"Body Techniques" (Mauss), 104
Borzick, Rolf, 38
Bourdieu, Pierre, 115
break dancing, 74–75, 163n38
*Breakin'*, 76
Brooklyn Academy of Music, 14, 50
Brown, Lawrence, 86
Brown, Trisha, 6, 13–15, 17–28, 134, 158n3
Browning, Barbara, 7, 166n6, 171n3
Burt, Ramsay, 6, 96
Butler, Judith, 33–34, 38, 40
butoh, 113, 122, 170–171n42

*Café Müller* (Bausch), 6, 29, 30, 38–42
Cage, John, 23
*candomblé*, 8
capoeira, 58, 75
*Carmen* (Bizet), Lina Wertmuller's production of, 13, 14
Cayou, Delores K., 69

*Central Station*, 103
César, Chico, 103
*Chorégraphie ou l'Art de Décrire la Danse, par Caractères, Figures et Signes Démonstratifs* (Choreography, or the art of describing dance with demonstrative characters, figures and signs; Feuillet), 3, 126
"Choreographies" (Derrida), 135–136
*Choreography and Narrative* (Foster), 4
Collegium Vocale Gent, 20
Collins, Janet, 82, 93
contact improvisation, 54
*Continuous Process Altered Daily* (Rainer), 43
*Convalescent Dance* (Rainer), 42–43
*Critical Moves* (Martin), 4
Croce, Arlene, 57
"Crucifixion" (Tamiris), 86
Cubilie, Anne, 114
Cunningham, Merce, 92
Cypriano, Tânia, 107

dance: documentation, 130, 133, 135; and femininity, 8, 124–125, 131, 135, 138–139; as transgression, 140–142; transmission of, 118–121, 123, 170n35; and writing, 8, 124–125, 134
*Dance as Text: Ideologies of the Baroque Body* (Franko), 171–172n14
*Dance Encyclopedia*, 66
*Dancing Body in Renaissance Choreography, The* (Franko), 171n4
*Dancing Master* (Rameau), 128–129
"Day is Past and Gone, The" (Ailey), 95
*Death Without Weeping: The Violence of Everyday Life in Brazil* (Scheper-Hughes), 101–102, 166n14
deconstruction, 125, 131, 136. *See also* Derrida, Jacques
deferment, 137–138. *See also* Derrida, Jaques
DeFrantz, Thomas F., 7
de Goés e Siqueira, Dr. José, 99
de Keersmaeker, Anne Teresa, 6, 29, 32, 34, 38, 41–42, 44
Deleuze, Gilles, 30, 146, 154
de Mey, Thierry, 42
Denishawn, 88

Deren, Maya, 108
Derrida, Jacques, 5, 8, 30, 32, 115–118, 120–121, 122, 131–138, 168nn9, 10, 170nn36, 37, 172n22, 172–173n28. *See also* deconstruction; deferment; différance; trace
Dickens, Charles, 70, 72
"Didn't My Lord Deliver Daniel" (Ailey), 95
Dies Committee, 92
différance, 131, 134, 135, 137. *See also* Derrida, Jaques
*Difference and Repetition* (Deleuze), 146
*Discipline and Punish* (Foucault), 40
*Divine Horsemen* (Deren), 108
Doo, Shabba (Adolfo Quinones), 76
Dubois, W. E. B., 64
Duncan, Randy, 83
Dunham, Katherine, 82, 87–88, 93
Dunn, Judith, 13
Dunn, Robert, 13, 26
Dylan, Bob, 13–14
Dyson, Michael Eric, 77

*Emergency of Black and the Emergence of Rap, The* (Spencer), 78

Farmer, Paul, 105, 106
Federal Dance and Theatre Projects, 92
Ferrari, Cherubino, 20
Feuillet, Raoul-Auger, 3–4, 5, 126–127
*Figure from Angkor Vat, A* (Denishawn) (Guy), 88
"First Negro Dance Recital in America" (Winfield) (Guy), 88
"Fix Me, Jesus" (Ailey), 95
*Flashdance*, 76, 77
*Flash of the Spirit: African & Afro-American Art & Philosophy* (Thompson), 162n19
Fokine, Michel 138
Foster, Stephen C., 113–114
Foster, Susan Leigh, 4, 52, 127, 171–172n14
Foucault, Michel, 6, 29, 30–34, 38, 39, 40, 42, 141, 144, 159n4, 174n10. *See also* poststructuralism
*Foucault/Blanchot* (Foucault), 174n10
Franko, Mark, 2, 4–5, 8, 130–131, 132, 136, 171n4, 171–172n14

Freud, Sigmund, 131–132
Freyre, Gilberto, 98–100
funk, 67
Fusco, Coco, 114

Gallop, Jane, 141
Gautie, Théophile, 52
Gay Science, The (Nietzsche), 147, 151
gender, 55, 83, 84; and genealogy, 33
"Get on Board, Little Chillun" (Guy), 88
Giese, Al, 35–36
Gilpin, Heidi, 5
Giselle, ou les Wilis (Gautie), 52
"Git on Board, Li'l Chillun" (Tamiris), 86
Glacial Decoy (Brown), 14, 134
"Go Down, Moses" (Shawn), 90
"Go Down, Moses" (Tamiris), 86
Gordon, David, 43
Gottschild, Brenda Dixon, 69
Graham, Martha, 83, 92, 94, 151. See also Martha Graham Company
Group Primary Accumulation (Brown), 25
Guy, Edna, 82, 88

Halprin, Anna, 134
Hampton Institute Creative Dance Group, 89
Hammer, M.C., 73
Haraway, Donna, 102, 106–107, 167n35
Hawkins, Erick, 92
Hazzard-Donald, Katrina, 72, 75, 77
Hazzard-Gordon, Katrina, 69
Hegel, Gerog Wilhelm Friedrich, 30
Heidegger, Martin, 116–117, 131–132, 169n16, 170n37
Hijikata, Tatsumi, 113, 121–123
hip hop, 7, 71–74, 76–78; and race, 78
HIV. See AIDS/HIV
Holder, Geoffrey, 82
Holm, Hanya, 92
Hosoe, Eikoh, 121
House Un-American Activities Committee, 92. See also McCarthyism
How To Do Things With Words (Austin), 168n10
Hughes, Walter, 68, 161–162n15
Humphrey, Doris, 92

"I Been 'Buked" (Ailey), 95
If You Couldn't See Me (Brown), 158n3
"I Want to be Ready" (Ailey), 95
Irigaray, Luce, 138

Jacobs, Rene, 20
Jamison, Judith, 82
Johnson, Hall, 93
Johnson, J. Rosamon, 86
Johnson, Louis, 82
Jones, Bill T., 57–58, 165n18
"Joshua Fit de Battle ob Jericho" (Tamiris), 86
Juba, Master, 70
Judson Dance Theater, 6–7, 13, 29, 31, 43
Judson Memorial Church, 31, 35–36, 43

Kennedy, Charlotte Moton, 82, 89
Kerman, Joseph, 24
King, Martin Luther, Jr., 37
Kirshenblatt-Gimblett, Barbara, 114
Kirstein, Lincoln, 2
Kissinger, Henry, 38
Kleist, Heinrich von, 170n36

Laban movement analysis, 120
Lacan, Jacques, 23
Laércio, Pai, 107, 167n35
Lascarro, Juanita, 22
Last Supper at Uncle Tom's Cabin/ The Promised Land (Jones), 58
La Sylphide (Taglioni), 52
Laurenti, Jean-Noël, 126–127
Learning to Dance in Bali (Bateson, Mead), 113, 119–121
Lerer, Leonard B., 105–106
Lester Horton Dancers, 93
Letters on Dancing and Ballets (Noverre), 125, 128
Levine, Dick, 13
Lewisohn Stadium, 86, 87
Lightfoot, Gordon, 14
Littlefield, Catherine, 82
Lock, Margaret, 109
Lockers, The, 77
Lyotard, Jean-François, 49–50, 115, 118

MacDougall, Christie, 135
MacKendrick, Karmen, 8
Male Dancer: Bodies, Spectacle, Sexuality, The (Burt), 96

Malone, Jacqui, 69, 73, 79
"Mama África" (César), 103
Mangolte, Babbete, 14–15
Manning, Susan, 7
Man Who Envied Women, The (Rainer),
    14–15
martial arts, 58
Martha Graham Company, 50. See also
    Graham, Martha
Martin, John, 87, 88, 89
Martin, Randy, 4, 7
masculinity, 125
Masters and the Slaves, The (Freyre),
    99
Mauss, Marcel, 104, 113, 115, 117,
    169n21, 170n37
McCarthyism, 85. See also House Un-
    American Activities Committee
Mead, Margaret, 113, 119, 169n29
Meeker, Jess, 90
Mercy, Dominic, 38–41
Meri, La (Russell Meriwether Hughes),
    82
mimesis, 7, 51–54, 57, 58, 61. See also
    simulacra
Minarik, Jan, 38–41
Mind is a Muscle, The (Rainer), 29,
    36–37
M.O. (Brown), 13
modernity, 38
Monteverdi, Claudio, 6, 13, 15, 19–24,
    26–28
Mourning Sex: Performing Public Mem-
    ories (Phelan), 172n25
movement, 141, 147–149, 154
Mumaw, Barton, 82, 89–90
MURDER and murder (Rainer), 44
Musical Offering (Bach), 13

Nancy, Jean-Luc, 150
Naval and A-Bomb (Hosoe), 113,
    121–123
Negro Dance Group, 87
Negro Spirituals (Shawn), 82, 83,
    89–91, 94
Negro Spirituals (Tamiris), 82, 83,
    86–87, 89
Ness, Sally Ann, 119
New York City Breakers, 76
New Yorker, The, 57

New York Times, 87, 88, 100
Next Wave Festival, 50
Nietzsche, Friedrich, 6, 9, 131–132,
    135, 138, 146, 147, 151, 154
"Nietzsche, Genealogy, History"
    (Foucault), 30
Nijinsky, Vaslav, 89, 153
9/11, 8, 113, 114, 115, 117, 123,
    169n18, 170n37
92nd Street YMHA, 93
Nixon, Richard, 38
"Nobody Knows de Trouble I've Seen"
    (Shawn), 90
Noverre, Jean-Georges, 125–128, 130,
    133, 139

Oddone, Graciela, 24
Odo Ya! (Life with AIDS) (Cypriano),
    107
On My Mother's Side (Weidman), 84
"On the Valorization of Things Black"
    (Freyre), 99
opp. 5 and 28 (Webern), 13
Orchesography (Arbeau), 126
Orfeo (Monteverdi) (Brown), 6, 13–17,
    19–28
Ovid, 26

Paxton, Steve, 36, 43
Perpener, John, 88
Phaedrus (Plato), 32
Phelan, Peggy, 5–6, 129, 132, 136, 138,
    172n25
Pitot, Genevieve, 86
Planes (Brown), 25
Plato, 32, 141
Postmodern Condition, The (Lyotard),
    49–50
poststructuralism, 29, 38. See also
    Foucault, Michel
presence, 1–6, 30, 32, 79, 131–133,
    134, 137, 138; and absence of
    women, 15; and repetition, 156.
    See also body; trace
Primitive Mysteries, (Graham), 83
Primus, Pearl, 66, 82, 93
"Processional" (Ailey), 95

"A Quasi Survey of Some 'Minimalist'
    Tendencies on the Quantitatively

Minimal Dance Activity amidst the Plethora, or an Analysis of *Trio A*," 34
Quattuor Albrecht Knust, 43

race, 55, 83, 84; mixing, 98–99
Rainbow Room, 86
Rainer, Yvonne, 6, 14–15, 29, 32, 34–38, 40–44, 134
Rameau, Pierre, 128–129
Rauschenberg, Robert, 14
"Religious Dances" (Shawn), 91
*Revelations* (Ailey), 7, 82, 83, 86, 93–96
Richards, Annette, 4
*Rites of Passage, The* (Van Gennep), 113
Rivière, Jacques, 132, 138
Roberts, Howard, 93
"Rocka My Soul in the Bosom of Abraham" (Ailey), 96
Roosevelt, Teddy, 91
Rosas Danst Rosas (de Keersmaeker), 29, 30, 38, 41–42
Rose, Tricia, 72, 75
Royster, Philip, 73

*Samba: Resistance in Motion* (Browning), 166n6, 171n3
*Satisfyin' Lover* (Paxton), 43
Saussurean sign, 132
Sayre, Henry, 134, 136
Scheper-Hughes, Nancy, 101–102, 104, 107, 109, 166n14, 167n35
Scott, Charles, 154
Sedgewick, Eve, 66
Segal, Edith, 82
September 11, 2001. *See* 9/11
*Set and Reset* (Brown), 134
sexuality: and depravity, 99; gay male 90–91, 165n18
Shakespeare, William, 23
Shawn, Ted, 82, 83, 89–91, 94, 96; and his Men Dancers, 89–91
Siegel, Marcia, 130
"Signature Event Context" (Derrida), 118
simulacra, 7, 51, 53–55, 57, 58, 61. *See also* mimesis
"Sinner Man" (Ailey), 95
socialism, 47–51, 56, 57, 60–63

*Southern Landscape* (Beatty), 93
*Spanish Dance* (Brown), 13–14
speech act theory, 40, 113, 115–116
Spencer, Jon Michael, 73, 78–79
Spivak, Gayatri, 131–132
*Spurs: Nietzsche's Styles* (Derrida), 135
St. Denis, Ruth, 88, 149
Stearns, Marshall and Jean, 69
*Step Not Beyond, The* (Blanchot), 140
*Still/Here* (Jones), 57–58
Striggio the Younger, Alessandro, 19–20, 26, 27
"Swing Low, Sweet Chariot" (Shawn), 91
"Swing Low, Sweet Chariot" (Tamiris), 86

Taglioni, Filippo, 52
Tamiris, Helen, 82, 83, 86–87, 89, 92, 164nn7, 8
Tanztheatre Wuppertal, 39
Temple Offerings (Denishawn) (Guy), 88
Terry, Walter, 89
*Theater of the Oppressed* (Boal), 51
Théâtre de la Monnaie, 14
Thompson, Robert Farris, 67, 69, 71–72, 162n19
Thorpe, Edward, 94
trace, 4–5, 8, 32, 125, 131–132, 133, 136, 138, 172–173n28. *See also* Derrida
*Trio A* (Rainer), 6, 29, 30, 34–37, 39, 42–44
*Trio A Pressured* (Rainer), 29, 43
Truitte, James, 82, 93
*Twelve-Ton Rose* (Brown), 13

*Unmarked: The Politics of Performance* (Phelan), 138

Van Gennep, Arnold, 113
Verdi, Giuseppe, 24
*Village Voice*, 37
Virgil, 26
Viviana, Hermano, 98–99

"Wade in the Water" (Ailey), 95
*Water Motor* (Brown), 14
Wavelet, Christopher, 43

Webern, Anton, 13
*Weeping Mary* (Guy), 88
Weidman, Charles, 84, 92
Wertmuller, Lina, 13,14
West, Cornel, 67, 74, 79
*Wild Style* (Ahearn), 76
Williams, Wilson, 82
Winfield, Hemsley, 82, 88

*Writing of the Disaster, The* (Blanchot), 168–169n15

*Xavier LeRoy* (Bel), 43

"You May Run On" (Ailey), 95

Zane, Arnie, 58